Central Glass Company
The First Thirty Years
1863-1893

Marilyn R. Hallock

4880 Lower Valley Road, Atglen, PA 19310 USA

Dedication

This book is dedicated in the memory of my mother,
Betty Jane *Cassell* Markell Hallock

Library of Congress Cataloging-in-Publication Data

Hallock, Marilyn.
    Central Glass Company : the first thirty years, 1863-1893
/ by Marilyn Hallock.
        p. cm.
    ISBN 0-7643-1762-8
    1. Central Glass Co. (Wheeling, W. Va.)--History. 2. Pressed
    glass--West Virginia--Wheeling--History--19th century. 3.
    Tableware--West Virginia--Wheeling--History--19th
century. I. Title.
NK5205.C45 H35 2002
748.29154'14--dc21
                                2002153433

Copyright © 2002 by Marilyn R. Hallock

Designed by Mark David Bowyer
Type set in Korinna BT

ISBN: 0-7643-1762-8
Printed in China
1 2 3 4

Published by Schiffer Publishing Ltd.
4880 Lower Valley Road
Atglen, PA 19310
Phone: (610) 593-1777; Fax: (610) 593-2002
E-mail: info@schifferbooks.com
Please visit our web site catalog at **www.schifferbooks.com**
We are always looking for people to write books on new and
related subjects. If you have an idea for a book please contact
us at the above address.

This book may be purchased from the publisher.
Include $3.95 for shipping.
Please try your bookstore first.
You may write for a free catalog.

In Europe, Schiffer books are distributed by
Bushwood Books
6 Marksbury Ave.
Kew Gardens
Surrey TW9 4JF England
Phone: 44 (0) 20 8392-8585; Fax: 44 (0) 20 8392-9876
E-mail: Bushwd@aol.com
Free postage in the U.K., Europe; air mail at cost.

On the front cover (top to bottom, left to right):
U.S. Coin (Silver Age) Compote
Pattern 876 Star toy mug, Pattern 748 Lutted's Log Cabin
Pattern 796 Rope and Thumbprint High Foot Bowl
Pattern 700 Horse Ink Stand, Pattern 311 Mountain Laurel Stand Lamp

On the back cover (top to bottom, left to right):
Pattern 725 Barrel Stand Lamp, Pattern 650 Dot & Dash Butter
Pattern 829 Oesterling Cream Pitcher, Pattern 439 Scalloped Diamond Point HF Bowl,
    Pattern 153 Oak Wreath LF Bowl
Pattern 876 Star Molasses Can, Pattern 810 Tudor Ice Cream Bowl and Cover
Pattern 831 Slipper Skate, Pattern 870 Brick Window Spooner
Pattern 140 Rose Bitter Bottle

Acknowledgments

Special thanks to the many individuals, museums, and pattern glass dealers, who assisted me with finding glass patterns for this book or in my research. Most important was my family which supported me, including my husband, Jerry Chaplain, and my Wheeling connection and cousin, Anne Lamb. Without their assistance and support this book probably would not have been made.

I am grateful for the computer assistance from my son, Gregory Zipperer, early assistance from a former colleague, Rod McCausland, later assistance from Ray Nicoud, and to Peggy Williams for the pattern layout.

Thanks goes to those mentioned below and others too numerous to mention especially my friends from the Early American Pattern Glass Society who were always looking for Central patterns for me.

Holly McCluskey, The Museums of Oblebay Institute, Wheeling, WV

Gerald Reilly formerly of Oglebay Institute, Wheeling, WV

The Ohio County Library, Wheeling, WV

John and Tom Weishar, Island Mould & Machine Co., Wheeling, WV

The Rakow Library, Corning, NY

Henry Ford Museum & Greenfield Village Research Center, Dearborn, MI

Eason Eige

The Huntington Museum of Art, Huntington, WV

Carnegie Library of Pittsburgh, PA

Dean Six

Fenton Glass Company, Williamstown, WV

Betty June Wymer, Wymer's General Store, Wheeling, WV

Bob Sanford, Research Glass Facts, DeLeon Springs, FL

Tim Timmerman, *U.S. Coin Glass A Century of Mystery*, Beaverton, OR

Bethany College, Bethany, WV

The Metropolitan Museum of Art, New York City, NY

David Richardson, The Glass Press, Inc, Marietta, OH

Contents

Foreword

The city of Wheeling, West Virginia, was one of the greatest manufacturing centers of its size in the Victorian era. In 1888, Wheeling made over 1,100,000 tons of iron and steel, 30,000 tons of glass, 10,000 tons of pottery, and millions of cigars. It boasted lumber yards, breweries, woolen mills, and had seventy-eight wholesale houses selling dry goods. With steamboats traveling the Ohio with passengers, hundreds of people pouring through the city on the National Road each day, and thousands of people on the railroad, Wheeling was a gateway to the west.

Easy access to America's major transportation routes, combined with an abundant supply of coal and, later, natural gas for fuel made Wheeling an ideal location for manufacturing glass. Over 50% of America's pressed glass tableware came from the Ohio River Valley corridor, including Pittsburgh and Wheeling.

The city of Wheeling boasted three glass houses that were among the largest and most prolific in America: the J.H. Hobbs, Brockunier and Company, the Central Glass Company, and H. Northwood and Company. Of these, Central was the largest and its products among the least known. In the early 1880s, it employed over 400 people, boasted three furnaces with a total of 32 pots, had its own coal mine, and, in one day, shipped over 20 tons of glass to Europe.

Although the firm is known for its pressed tableware it also produced some of America's most collectible glass, including Log Cabin and the Silver Age (US Coin) patterns. Yet few catalogues exist to show us what this company actually made, and Central Glass Company's pieces were rarely, if ever, marked. While some patterns are well-known to collectors and researchers, many of Central's products remained unattributed and unknown until this publication.

This is the first definitive work on the history and products of this giant glass house. Marilyn Hallock has spent a decade meticulously researching through catalogues, trade journals, newspapers, and city directories as well as traveling to shows and working with her own collection to develop the material for this book.

All of us who are interested in American pattern glass owe Marilyn our gratitude in making her research available. It is a long-awaited and much needed chapter in the history of our American glass industry.

Holly McCluskey, Director of the Museum
The Museums of Oblebay Institute
Wheeling, West Virginia

Preface

The history of the Central Glass Company, Wheeling, West Virginia is an important example of the many successes that collectively made up the greater 19th century American business story. Typically, a group of eight talented investors came together in 1863, pooling their resources to purchase an abandoned building for the purpose of opening a new glass manufacturing company. Wheeling in the pre-Civil War years was already a noted center for glass production. The Central Glass Company would quickly become a giant in the industry. It would rival any glass producer in the world in volume and technology.

The Central Glass Company demonstrated that attention to consumer demands would lead to diverse and innovative products. Its design ranged from common bar wares to humorous original and complex patterns that appealed to the late Victorian homemaker. Their glass added much coveted color to the American dining table or parlor. Tableware patterns were offered in a seemingly endless variety of forms. Geometric patterns with historical reference were illustrated in their wholesale catalogs along with fashionable novelties depicting floral designs, log cabins, barrels, fish, horses, ducks, human hands, and even United States coins. Central utilized the considerable skills of local mold-makers in the Wheeling and Pittsburgh area to give highly detailed form to their imaginative glasswares. It also drew upon the knowledge of Ohio Valley craftsmen skilled in the art of pressing the soda-lime formula for glass, which had only recently been invented in Wheeling at the rival Hobbs, Brockunier and Company. The Central Glass Company would make its fortune on this new, less expensive glass, which all but replaced lead glass in America. Central offered a wide variety of lower priced glassware's without sacrificing design or quality.

This book adds to the expanding literature on American glass. In 1980 I was asked to produce an exhibition and catalogue on the glass made in West Virginia. It became *A Century of Glassmaking in West Virginia* at the Huntington Museum of Art (then Huntington Galleries). I found few books in the library in 1980. Since that time, however, many books have been published on individual Midwestern glass manufacturing companies that were so important during the late 19th and early 20th centuries. Some recent research has brought us multiple volume accounts of the history and production of these great glass houses.

In this book, *Central Glass Company 1863-1893*, Marilyn Hallock, driven by her desire to chronicle her Central Glass family connection, has brought together many of the actual pieces made by Central. To document them, she includes carefully gathered contemporary accounts published in trade papers and newspapers of the time. Perhaps most useful to the researcher, she includes previously unpublished Central Glass Company catalog illustrations which have been difficult to access in museums and private collections. Combined, these resources give a clear and concise picture of the wonderful pressed glass made by one of our most interesting and important American glass manufacturers.

Eason Eige, Albuquerque, NM 2002

Author's Note

This book project was because of my maternal connection with the Central Glass Company. John Henderson was my great-great-great-grandfather, and Peter Cassell was my great-great-grandfather. They were two of the original founders of the Central Glass Company. John Henderson was listed in early city directories under the firm "Oesterling, Henderson and Company", glass manufacturers. This was the name before the company became Central Glass Company. Very little is known about John.

Peter Cassell married John Henderson's daughter, Elizabeth Jane and they had three children, two sons, William and Levi, and a daughter, Virginia. William worked with the company in many areas including secretary and sales manager. Levi also worked with the company, but very little was written mentioning him. However, an article from the "Crockery and Glass Journal" of February 09, 1882 said "Levi Cassell, an excellent citizen of Bellaire, left yesterday for Hamilton, Ontario to assume management of a glass house there." Neither William or Levi had any offspring.

Virginia married Frank Stamm and had a daughter, Elizabeth, who is my grandmother. Her father, Frank Stamm, not only married into a Central Glass family, but was part owner of the McClure Hotel where Central displayed glass in the 1890s (see "Research" for July 21, 1887 and 1890s).

Both Peter and William Cassell were involved with Central until the time of their deaths in the early 1900s which was after the Company reformed and became Central Glass Works. Peter was one of Central's largest stockholders at the time of his death. Another family tie with Central was a great uncle, George Stamm (Frank Stamm's brother), who was Vice President in the 1930s and also on the Board of Directors. He was active with Central until his death in 1934 just five years before it closed its doors for good in 1939.

Introduction

When the early pattern glass catalogs were designed, their illustrations were drawn so accurately that it made identifying and authenticating the patterns quite easy. Sadly, most of the earliest Central Glass Company catalogs, from its beginning until it joined U.S. Glass Company in 1891, were destroyed many years ago, making it quite a challenge to find the original pattern names and descriptions. The few that have survived in museum collections are usually incomplete. Fortunately, with the help of The Oglebay Museum in Wheeling, West Virginia, Bethany College in Bethany, West Virginia, the Henry Ford Museum in Dearborn, Michigan, and the Corning Glass Museum in Corning New York, it has been possible to compile the patterns from number 1 to over 1000 from the catalogs in their collections.

Augmenting these museum resources was a very early 1860s catalog with "Photographic Illustrations of Flint Glassware," in the private collection of John and Tom Weisher of Island Mould and Machine Company in Wheeling, West Virginia. This catalog gives the names of some of Central's earliest patterns and those pattern names will be used in this book. This catalog is extremely rare as it was one of Central's first catalogs showing the first 200 patterns made. The catalog is even more rare because the patterns were photographed while all the other catalogs were illustrated with drawings.

Below is the cover page of the Central Glass catalog with "Photographic Illustrations of Flint Glassware".

Photographic Illustrations

— OF —

FLINT GLASSWARE,

MANUFACTURED BY THE

CENTRAL GLASS COMPANY,

Wheeling, W. Va.

Cover page of Island Mould Central Catalog, "Flint Glassware"

There are, unfortunately, still quite a few of the early patterns that Central made in their first 30 years that remain unidentified at this time due to lack of catalogs.

Not only are there very few surviving catalogs on Central Glass, but very little has been written about the company. When I first started collecting Central, it was very difficult to find patterns due to lack of information. Only a few books had any Central patterns in them at all. My first reference was *American Pressed Glass and Figure Bottles*, by Albert Christian Revi. It gave me my start in searching for Central patterns. The next best source was Minnie Watson Kamm's *Glass Pitcher* series of eight books. She did a wonderful job identifying glass, but there were a couple of attributions she made to Central that I was not able to verify, and recently they have been attributed to other glass companies. The best reference for oil lamps was found in the oil lamp books written by Catherine M.V. Thuro. Other reference books may be found in the bibliography. Some current pattern identification guides have had only a couple of Central patterns in them, missing some very important pressed glass patterns.

The goal of this book is to address this lack of information about one of the era's largest glass companies. It is meant to be used as a pattern identification guide for Central Glass patterns up to 1891 when the company joined the U.S. Glass Company. At that time the U.S. Glass Company acquired Central's molds and many of the patterns have been attributed to them instead of Central. Hopefully, this book will clear up some of those incorrect pattern attributions, and Central will get the credit they deserve.

As the years pass and early American pattern glass becomes scarcer and scarcer, proper pattern identification becomes more of a challenge. Several patterns made by Central are well known and documented, but through this book, the reader will discover many previously unknown Central patterns and be able to clear up some discrepancies about the Central Glass Company.

Authors note: A late 1890s or early 1900s Central Glass Works catalog contains illustrations of some of the earlier Central Glass Company patterns, especially barware, which were again being produced using the same exact pattern numbers. This is a very large catalog and the patterns were drawn to scale, in other words, in exact sizes unless otherwise noted. This catalog also had numerous patterns with numbers in the 900s through 1000 which helped to fill in some of the blank pattern numbers before they joined the U.S. Glass Company. The pattern number cutoff is unknown and is also mentioned in the "Pattern" section of this book. Central Glass Works made more than just barware which the company was so famous for as they made eloquent glassware with beautiful etchings up until they closed in 1939. The period from 1896 to 1939 will have to be covered in another book.

Historical Maps, Catalog Covers, and Factory Photographs

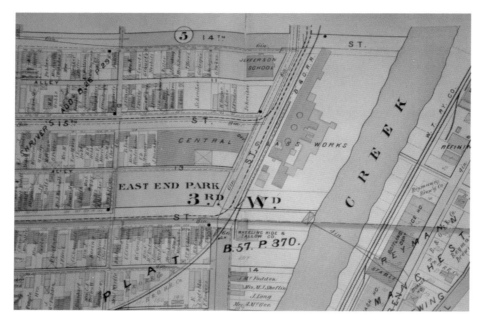

City of Wheeling, West Virginia. Plat Map, Plate 6, showing Central Glass location on Wheeling Creek. *Courtesy of Betty June Wymer, Wymer's General Store, Wheeling, WV*

Below:
Central Glass Company Illustrated Catalogue cover. *Courtesy Bethany College, Bethany, WV.*

Central Glass Company Illustrated Catalogue cover. *Courtesy Bethany College, Bethany, WV.*

Central Glass Company Etching on the back page of a catalog. *Courtesy Bethany College, Bethany, WV*

"Works of Central Glass Company," 1867 broadside. Courtesy Bethany College, Bethany, WV

View of Wheeling from Chapline's Hill showing the Central Glass factory. *Photo courtesy of The Point Overlook Museum and Creative Designs, Wheeling, WV.*

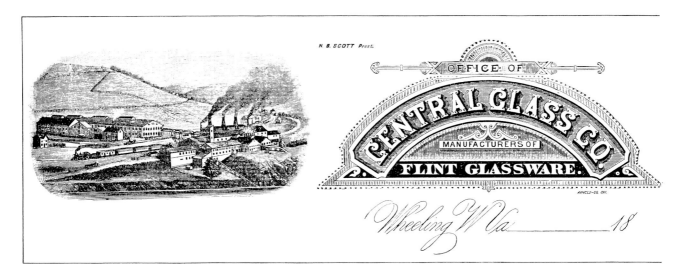

Letterhead of Central Glass Company

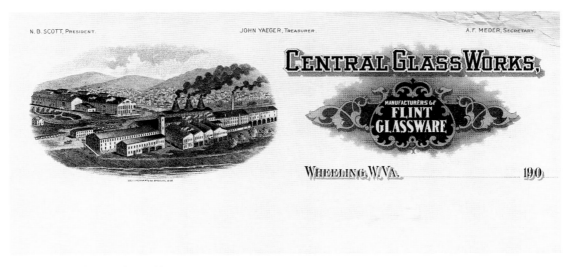

Letterhead of Central Glass Works

Central Glass Company:
Its History
Research

In her history of the glass industry in Wheeling, West Virginia, *Wheeling Glass* (1947), Josephine Jefferson wrote:

"At the foot of Fifteenth Street on McColloch a new glasshouse made its appearance in 1863. The company was composed of dissatisfied workers who had left the Hobbs-Barnes Factory in order to start a new business of their own. With a capital of only $5,000.00, the new enterprise known as Oesterling and Co. had a difficult time. But in 1866 the men bought additional ground, and in 1867 obtained a new charter and a capital of $80,000.00. The firm became the Central Glass Co., manufacturers of tableware, bar goods, and lamps.

"As the years passed, the business grew, and Central Glass was sold all over the United States. Elaborate catalogs, comprising bar goods and tableware soon made their appearance...."

The group of eight dissatisfied workers were, John Oesterling, John Henderson, Roy Combs, James Leasure, Peter Cassell, William Elson, Theodore Schultz, and Andrew Baggs. Please note that in the city directory above Andrew Baggs was not listed, but Daniel McAfee and Westcomb Attwell were.

An early listing for the company, before it became the Central Glass Company, was "Oesterling, Henderson & Co." In the *Wheeling Williams Directory* page 143 in 1864 the plant was listed as:

"Oesterling, Henderson & Co., (John O., John H., Daniel McAfee, Roy Combs, Westcomb Attwell, James Leasure, Peter Cassell, Wm. Elson & Theodore Schultz,) Manufactures of Flint Glass n e c German and 1st." [Author's note: the n e c stands for Northeast corner of German and First Streets]

John Oesterling and John Henderson were the principal members.

In the 1860s, some city directories listed the name of the plant as "Central Glass Works, Oesterling, Hall and Co., Proprietors, head of John." Research suggests that the Hall was a typographical error that should have read Henderson, and without correction it remained on the directories as late as 1867 and 1868.

An advertisement dated July 17, 1863, was published, probably the first advertisement for the company, to inform glass merchants that Central was then in business. The advertisement was as follows:

"Oesterling, Henderson & Co., Manufacturers of Flint Glass, Corner German and First Streets, Wheeling, West Virginia Respectfully inform the Glass Merchants that they manufacture Blown and Pressed Glassware of all descriptions, at lowest market prices. Particular attention is called to their assortment of Jars, Lamps and Chimneys."

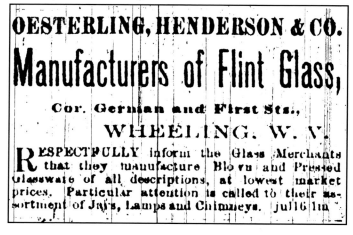

Advertisement from the *Wheeling Intelligencer* newspaper July 17, 1863 for Oesterling, Henderson & Co. Manufacturers of Flint Glass

OESTERLING, HENDERSON & CO., (John O., John H., Daniel McAfee, Roy Combs, Westcomb Attwell, James Leasure, Peter Cassell, Wm. Elson & Theodore Schultz,) Manufacturers of Flint Glass, n e c German and 1st. Oesterling John, (O., Henderson & Co.) h n s 4th b Vine and Walnut

Oesterling, Henderson & Co. 1864 company listing from *Williams Wheeling Directory*

On July 27, 1863, the plant was incorporated as Central Glass Company.

Advertisement in the *Wheeling Business Directory* for 1862-1863 for Bar Goods, Lamps and Table Glassware

On the following pages, the history of the company from these earliest days through the death of Peter Cassell is traced through contemporaneous historical articles and materials. Unless otherwise noted, they were found in *The American Pottery and Glassware Reporter (AP&GR)*; *Crockery and Glass Journal (C&GJ)*, or *China, Glass and Lamps (CG&L)*. Some of the articles are purposely repeated in the Pattern Identification pages when they refer to a specific pattern.

The dates are shown for the majority of the research herein, however, when doing research and copying data for the book sometimes a date was not legible. The wording and spelling are exactly as copied from these periodicals and have not been changed, thus there are many discrepancies and misspellings. The employees' names are quite often misspelled. For example, Peter Cassell is often spelled Cassel, and molds may appear this way one time and as "moulds" another.

• From *History of The Pan-Handle; being Historical Collections of the Counties of Ohio, Brooke, Marshall and Hancock, West Virginia*. Compiled and Written by J.H. Newton, G.G. Nichols, and A.G. Sprankle – Published by J.A. Caldwell, 1879, pages 239 and 240.

Central Glass House – A Brief Sketch Of One Of West Virginia's Most Extensive and Prosperous Manufactories with a National Reputation.

The business of the Central Glass Company was started on the co-operative plan in the spring of 1863, with a capital of $5,000. After the expiration of three years, the company bought the ground and buildings of the East Wheeling distillery and pork packing house, for the purpose of converting it into a glass manufacturing establishment that in point of magnitude

and completeness should stand on a par with anything of the kind in the United States. And successful, indeed have they been, as is demonstrated by their present extensive works, which the public, and even the trade generally, will admit is an honor and a compliment to American enterprise. In 1867, they obtained a charter to conduct the business on the joint stock plan, under the firm name of the Central Glass Company, with a capital of $80,000, which also represented the original capital of $5,000. The new company, however, reserved the right of buying in and cancelling all the shares which might be offered for sale by its individual members, and the result has been that the original four hundred and thirty-four shares have thus been reduced to less than one-half of the original number.

The capital of the company for several years past, has been $260,000—the average sales per month $25,000, and they employ 330 hands, (including boys,) whose united weekly earnings average $3,300. They operate their own coal field, comprising fifty acres, in the vicinity of the works. Their manufactures, which are of the finest in the market, find a ready sale throughout the United States, and are extensively shipped to the Canadas, West Indies, South America, and Europe. With Europe, especially, they have done a large business for the last four years, which, however, will be somewhat reduced by the effects of the new tariff of the German Empire that goes in effect January 1st, 1880. The productions of these works are confined to table ware, bar and lamp goods, the variety, quality and beauty of which cannot be excelled. Up to the year 1872, they operated only two furnaces, but during that year was added a third, with the necessary out-buildings. They also erected on the south side of McCulloch Street, their new two story warehouse, with excellent offices and selecting and packing room attached. The main packing room is 65x84 feet, and the warehouse 287x70 feet. Both are acknowledged to be the most extensive as well as the most practically arranged buildings in this country. Both buildings are connected with the manufactory by means of an elevated bridge with narrow gauge track. A steam elevator hoists the glass in open hand boxes from the factory floor to the floor of the bridge, which is on a level with the selecting and packing rooms. Nor should we fail to mention there are added to the main factory, on the east side of the following departments: The mould and mechanic's shop, cutting shop, pot-making rooms, blacksmith's shop, engine houses, carpenter's shop, coke ovens, mixing room and two buildings with six annealing ovens therein.

Mr. John Oesterling, the present manager, who is a gentleman of wide practical experience and shrewd executive ability, has been at the head of the enterprise from its inception, in 1863, to which is mainly attributable the great success it has achieved, and which, from present gratifying indications, is more than likely will be unmeasurably excelled in the future.

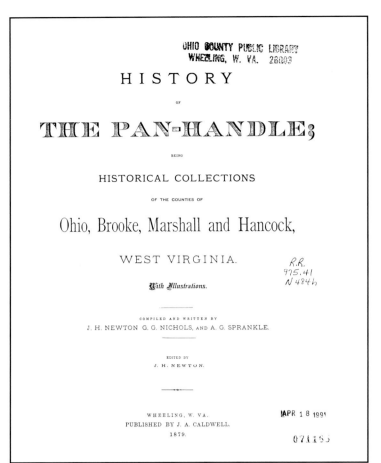

HISTORY

OF

THE PAN-HANDLE;

BEING

HISTORICAL COLLECTIONS

OF THE COUNTIES OF

Ohio, Brooke, Marshall and Hancock,

WEST VIRGINIA.

With Illustrations.

R.R.
975.41
N 484h

COMPILED AND WRITTEN BY

J. H. NEWTON G. G. NICHOLS, AND A. G. SPRANKLE.

EDITED BY

J. H. NEWTON.

WHEELING, W. VA.
PUBLISHED BY J. A. CALDWELL.
1879.

Cover of *History of The Pan-Handle, Being Historical Collections of the Counties of Ohio, Brooke, Marshall and Hancock, West Virginia*

• From *History of the Upper Ohio Valley, Vol. 1, 1890. Greater Wheeling and Vicinity*, page 794. Author's note: this article covers Central Glass Company through Central Glass Works.

The Central Glass Company, of Wheeling, originated in the firm of Osterling, Henderson & Company, established in July 1863. Mr. John Osterling and Mr. John Henderson were the principal members, the latter being the grandfather of W.H. Cassell, now manager of the sales department. The first factory was built at the corner of Twenty-fifth and Jacob streets on the south side. On July 27, 1860, the business was incorporated as the Central Glass Company, and the factory was moved to the site in East Wheeling where it has been in continuous operation ever since with the exception of the years 1894-96. During this period it was known as Factory O of the United States Glass Company of Pittsburgh, the combine consisting of eighteen widely scattered plants. Owing to labor troubles this company never operated the plant and in December, 1895, it was bought back by Wheeling capitalists. In January, 1896, it was incorporated as the Central Glass Works.

The Central Glass Works is one of the largest manufacturers of fine flint glassware in the world. Originally it manufactured pressed tableware and lamps, having a large trade all over the world. The present company manufactures a much higher grade of lead blown and pressed ware, decorated and cut, supplying the finest hotels, clubs and leading railroads in the United States. Shipments from the factory are also frequently made to distant parts of the world, the wares from the "House of Quality," as the Central Works are known, have a high reputation among dealers everywhere.

The factory of the Central Glass Works covers two and a half acres, and there are three furnaces of twelve pots each. About seven hundred persons are employed, so that this industry is one of the principal resources that support the population of the city. The company operates its own cooperage and packing plant.

The principal officers of the Central Glass Works are: N.B. Scott, president; Jos. Speidel, vice-president; John Yaeger, secretary and treasurer; and W.H. Cassell, manager of the sales department.

Oesterling, Henderson & Co., estab. In July, 1863 by John Oesterling, John Henderson, W.K. Elson, et. al., with a capital stock of $5,000.00.

Incorporated July 25, 1867, and name changed to the Central Glass Company. The East Wheeling Distillery and Pork Packing Plant purchased, and converted into a Flint Glass Factory. Capitalization, $80,000.00.

Authors note: There is not a lot of recorded or written information available regarding the Central Glass Company before the 1880s, so research material is limited in the first ten or so years.

1870s

• **1878**

From "Report of Glass and Glassware" by Mr. Charles Colne, Ass't. Sec. to the U.S. Commissioners, Universal Exposition, Paris, 1878, page 244.

Central Glass Exhibited at Paris Universal Exposition.

The United States, as we have already mentioned, had but a very scant exhibit—a few cut flint-glass articles from the Meriden Glass Company of Connecticut. It is much to be regretted that more of our works did not exhibit some of their celebrated pressed wares. Feeling that America should not remain unrepresented at a World's Fair, the writer of this report had some glass-ware sent to him and exhibited, but unfortunately too late to receive any premium which it certainly would have received. These goods were exhibited in the United States annex. Although, through delays and slowness of management of the French line of steamers, these goods were only on exhibition about a month, they nevertheless attracted a great deal of attention from the European manufacturers. Many were the inquiries to know how such thin and large pieces could be pressed without mold marks and with such clearness of metal… These samples were furnished by the Central Glass Company of Wheeling, W. Va., a company which well deserves the praise bestowed on it in the French report of our Centennial Exhibition. Nothing was found to equal or even approach this American pressed ware in any of the other departments. The beauty and brilliancy of the metal, lime glass excited the admiration of the foreign manufacturers.

From *CG&L:*

The goods of the Central Glass Co., Wheeling, have been so long and favorably known to the trade, that little need here be said of quality and finish of their pressed and blown ware. That was all ready an established fact, when, at the Paris Exposition of 1878, their fine thin pressed tumblers and stemware astonished European manufacturers and was especially named as entitled to honorable mention in the special report of Mr. Chas. Colne. The Central is now making a specialty of blown and pressed bar goods, cut and etched lead tumblers and stemware, bar bottles, decanters, water bottles, finger bowls, and all kinds of the finer grades of blown ware for the home, hotel, restaurant and bar use. Jobbers having a trade in the fine lines of blown ware will be casting an anchor to the windward by writing for the literature and illustrations of the Central Glass Co., Wheeling, W. Va.

• 1879

August 14, 1879, Thursday, from *AP&GR:*

Trade is excellent with the Central glass works, Wheeling. They are running full time on bar goods, beer mugs, lamps and their other specialties.

November 20, 1879, Thursday, from *AP&GR:*

In one day recently, the Central Glass works, Wheeling, shipped twenty tons of glassware, made up into 115 packages.

1880s

• 1880

January 22, 1880, Thursday, from *AP&GR:*

Mr. Leasure, foreman of the Central, Wheeling spent two or three days knocking about among Pittsburgh factories this week.

The Central Glass Company, of Wheeling, and the Rochester Tumbler Company get the credit of doing a larger export trade than any other glass concerns in the country. They ship whole train loads at a time to New York for foreign customers.

The Central Glass Works, Wheeling, had a very narrow escape from destruction by fire on Monday night last. An old stable standing near it was burned, and it required considerable exertion to save the factory. Wheeling seems to be having a boom of incendiarism just now.

March 25, 1880, Thursday, from *AP&GR:*

It is stated that the Central Glass Works, Wheeling, will soon have a Gill gas furnace.

April 8, 1880, Thursday, from *AP&GR:*

John Oesterling, of the Central Glass Works, Wheeling, will in about three weeks leave for Germany, where he will spend some time. During his absence the works will be in charge of N.B. Scott, the secretary of the company.

April 8, 1880 from *C&GJ,* "Wheeling Trade Notes:"

Since my last letter I have made the tour of several glass houses, both in this city and those in the immediate vicinity. Nails and glass are our two staples, but there is a wide difference in their respective standings just now. For the past two weeks, the nail factories have been closed down, and at a recent meeting of the powers that be, it was determined to close down for two weeks longer to allow the stock of nails on the market to become absorbed, and thus necessitate the maintenance of the present card rates. In this branch we say, then, the outlook is rather gloomy, while on the other hand among all of our glass manufacturers the most cheerful condition of things possible prevails, and the fact that nearly all the traveling salesmen are at home and have been for months, and the further fact that most of our glass manufactories are erecting new and larger furnaces or other essential improvements, are the best commentaries we can offer on the situation here just now. This is not written of one glass house, but of all we have visited, and there is no possibility of an abatement in demands for glassware until late in the summer, if then.

Among our city factories we first called at the Central Glasshouse, and found the employees there all as busy as they could be, as it was pay-day, and, consequently, a busier one than usual. Adjoining the factory, we noticed a small but rather important-looking new building which upon inquiry, we learned had been erected for acid rooms, etching-rooms, etc., and fitted up with steam-pipes and all the conveniences possible to facilitate etching. Four new machines are now being built for this purpose, and in a short time very complete appliances will be ready here for carrying out the designs peculiar to this company in etching. We also noticed a large number of molds of new design in beer-mugs, etc., which, we were informed, would be brought out as soon as the present rush of business would admit, for the demand for their present manufactures was so great just now, that is was impossible to give attention to anything novel.

Active preparations are going on for the erection of a new thirteen-pot Gill furnace, and if the foundation can be so arranged, they will make it a fifteen-pot furnace, which will be the largest one known of, or the largest ever attempted. When this is completed this company will have 5 furnaces aggregating 35 pots, or if one of the furnaces contains only 13 pots, have 33 pots, they will makeing them the largest in the Union. In anticipation of the demands of this new furnace, two new lehrs are being put up, which will be ready for use as soon as or before the furnace is ready. Several new coke ovens are also being built in addition to those already on hand, the better to supply their demands for this kind of fuel. This company probably does a larger export business than any other glass-house in this county, and it is steadily increasing; for while we were in the factory, a large order from Bremen was being put up and weekly shipments are being made to the German States. Mr. N.B. Scott has been elected secretary of this company, and in the absence of Mr. John Oesterling in Europe, will have charge of the works. Mr. Oesterling goes to Europe to visit his native province, and will be gone some months. Rhody Robinson and James A. Leasure are in charge of the mechanical part of the factory as managers, and are among the most efficient men in this business.

April 08, 1880 from *C&GJ*:
The Central Glass Company pays out $6,000 every two weeks to its employees.

May 06, 1880 from *C&GJ*, "Wheeling Glass–Houses:"
The Central Glass-works are very busy on orders at present. They are as yet undecided as to the size of the new furnace. They have a present three old style furnaces, and one of these they will take down to make room for their new and improved one and until it is taken down the diameter of the base of the new Gill furnace cannot be ascertained. If the proper diameter can be readily obtained the furnace will be a 15 pot one, if not only a 13 pot furnace will be erected. This will give a capacity of either 33 or 35 pots as the case may be. They are also building an additional slower-house, which the recent completion of 2 new lehrs made necessary. A new steam pump is a recent improvement at these works. This pump is used in pumping oil or benzine from railroad gondolas to an oil-house near by, in which is an iron tank with a capacity of 150 barrels, and a car can easily be emptied in an hour and a half. The material for the erection of their new furnace is all on the grounds and awaiting until a lull in the "boom" will allow it to be utilized. John Oesterling, Esq., president of these works, will leave New York for Germany in a few days, on a visit to the land of his nativity. He goes for two reasons, the first one for the benefit of his health, which has become somewhat impaired by close attention to his business and close confinement to his office, and second, to take an inventory of European glass-works for the benefit of his own. Mr. Oesterling is one of the shrewdest and most practical of our glass-men, and the result of his observations among European industries will be looked forward to with much interest by our glass-men in this country, and the works in this city will doubtless profit by his trip. The traveling agent of these works has been on the road but one trip of three weeks this season.

July 15, 1880 from *AP&GR*:
The Central Glass Company, Wheeling, had so many orders on land that they could not afford to stop and will continue in operation right along.

August 12, 1880, Thursday, from *AP&GR*:
The Wheeling "News Letter" of the 8th inst, says: The gas furnace at the Central Glass Works was finished Wednesday morning…The new gas furnace at the Central Glass Works will be fired up this week.

From 1880s *C&GJ*:
The Central Glass-works will have finished their gas furnace in a day or two, and will be making glass the week after next. To their great disappointment, this furnace will be only a 12 pot instead of a 15 or 16 pot one as they originally intended; but as their factory was not large enough for the larger one they were compelled to content themselves with the smaller one. However, their capacity, even with this one will be three furnaces of 32 pots. Mr. N.B. Scott, the secretary, says that

they are making heavy shipments almost daily to all parts of the country and to Europe, with which last-named place their trade is daily becoming more important. He also says there is no trouble to maintain prices, and that the coming year will be a booming one in the glass business. New coke sheds have been built, a tramway for the easy hauling of their goods, and other improvements are going on.

August 26, 1880 from *AP&GR*:
From Wheeling "News Letter for the 22nd….The work of making ware from the new twelve-pot furnace at the Central Glass Works was commenced Thursday, but owing to the breaking of four of the pots, operations have been somewhat delayed. The broken pots were reset yesterday, and the furnace will be running full blast tomorrow morning.

August 29, 1880 from *C&GJ*, "Wheeling Reports:"
For a campaign year, and a very hot one at that, business is exceptionally good. "Whenever there is a President of these United States to elect, there is not much business done or to be done," is a saying of national application, and its application and extent verifies it, or rather has until this year, and this year it really does seem to be at fault for once. We have heretofore given you a partial idea of what is going on in our glass factories, and from what we have written will readily be seen that business has been most satisfactory in all of them. In other departments of trade there is the same healthy state of affairs, or nearly so. Our iron and nail mills are running full now, except in instances where the heat has been so intense as to compel only a partial run in some of them. Large quantities of nails are being made and shipped daily to all parts of the South and West. The blast furnaces that have been idle for months are being prepared for work again as rapidly as possible, and all the mill owners say that indications point to a brisk and satisfactory fall trade. Other branches of industry are also going on satisfactorily, our paper mills are rushed, furniture factories are working to their fullest capacity, and the wholesale business generally all through this section is booming.

In the glass trade, manufactures are very much encouraged, and are vigorously at work preparing a stock against the fall trade, which all of them confidently predict will be an exceptionally large one. Several of the manufacturers have told your corespondent that never at so early a date in the season did prospects look so encouraging.

At the Central Glass-works, in this city, some inconvenience has resulted on account of the destruction of pots in their new furnace, caused by some defect in it, but this has been discovered and repaired, and they are now working to their fullest capacity. Mr. John Osterling, the president of the Central Glass Company, who has been in Europe for some months, partially on account of his health, and also in the interest of his corporation, is expected home early in September. Mr. Osterling is a thorough glass man, and his visit will be productive of much good to his company.

September 02, 1880 from *AP&GR*:
From Wheeling "News Letter" for the 29th…The Central Glass Company made a large shipment of glassware to southern points on the steamer Sydney yesterday afternoon…

The Central Glass Works has been running full blast during the past week. The new twelve pot furnace does splendidly, and there has been no trouble from broken pots, as mentioned by another city paper.

September 16, 1880, Thursday, from *AP&GR:*
From the Wheeling "News Letter" of the 12th ....The Central Glass Works have thirty pots in full blast, and are shipping ware as fast as they make it.

October 28, 1880, Thursday, from *AP&GR:*
The Wheeling "News Letter" of the 23rd day: The Central Glass Works recently made two large shipments of glassware to the heart of the European glass manufacturing region.

Mr. John Oesterling, of the Central Glass Company, Wheeling, has just returned from an extended tour through Europe, including a stay of some length in the glass manufacturing districts of Germany. He comes back more than ever impressed with the absolute necessity of maintaining our Protective Tariff. He states that they are making some kinds of glass there very much cheaper than it can be done in the United States, and the manufacturers are not slow in making known their anxiety that our Tariff should be broken down, in order that they may come in and control the American market. Mr. Oesterling gathered some interesting statistics as to wages of labor in the glass industry in the various countries he visited, which show a striking contrast to the pay received by our glass workers.

November 25, 1880, Thursday, from *AP&GR:*
Twenty tons of glassware were shipped to Europe from the Central Glass Works, Wheeling, one day recently.

November 25, 1880 from *C&GJ*, "Wheeling Reports:"
As we have already said, there is a good business doing in every branch of trade in this city – every mill, furniture factory, and glass-house is in full swing—and their operatives say, confidently, "we think there will be no let-up for a long time." The glass-houses in this city are two large ones, viz., the Central, and Hobbs, Brockunier & Co., and both are doing an immense business. The Central has made large and essential improvements, enlarging their facilities and bettering the quality of their manufactures. The etching, heretofore very good, has been materially bettered, and the proprietors of these works claim that they are unsurpassed in this line of business in the country. The shipments made by the Central during the last three months have been simply immense, and there is no abatement in orders. Twenty tons of ware were shipped to Europe yesterday. This branch of their trade is assuming large proportions, and is attracting much attention.

December 16, 1880 from *AP&GR:*
The Central Glass Works, Wheeling, recently made two large shipments of glassware to the heart of the European glass manufacturing region.

December 26, 1880 from *AP&GR*—"Wheeling Reports:"
At the Central Glass-works materials are on the ground for the erection of another twelve-pot Gill gas furnace.

• **1881**

January 27, 1881, Thursday, from *AP&GR:*
The Central have under way a new Gill gas furnace of twelve pots, which points to the fact that they are satisfied with the workings of their other furnace of Mr. Gill's patent.

February 24, 1881, Thursday, from *AP&GR:*
The stack of the new Gill gas furnace at the Central glass works has reached 50 feet in height and will be finished the coming week. The brick work is being done by Messrs. John R. Butts and John Britt. The stack will be 75 feet high when completed. —Wheeling News Letter

March 31, 1881, Thursday, from *AP&GR:*
The Central Glass Company, notwithstanding the New York "Crockery Journal's" statement that they would not put fire in their new furnace, lighted the furnace last Friday, and it works to their entire satisfaction.

May 19, 1881, Thursday, from *AP&GR:*
The employees of the cutting department at the Central Glass Works, Wheeling, are compelled to work extra time about four days each week, on account of the large number of orders pouring in upon them.

June 30, 1881, Thursday, from *AP&GR:*
The Central glass company, Wheeling, are running on full time in all departments.

July 14, 1881, Thursday, from *AP&GR:*
The Central Glass Works, at Wheeling, are building a new boiler stack 75 feet high.

July 28, 1881, Thursday, from *AP&GR:*
The Central Glass Company, of Wheeling, are changing their third furnace from its present form to be operated by the Gill gas process. This will make the third one of the latter kind they have now in operation. They have also considerably enlarged their cutting shop, and made other necessary improvements.

August 11, 1881, Thursday, from *AP&GR:*
At the Central Glass Company's factory, Wheeling, work is progressing on the alterations in the furnace. They expect to have it completed in about two weeks.

September 15, 1881, Thursday, from *AP&GR:*
The Central Glass Co., Wheeling, are running all their furnaces now and report trade moderately fair. Last week they made a large foreign shipment, part of it to Germany and the balance to Denmark.

November 03, 1881, Thursday, from *AP&GR:*
The Central Glass Co., Wheeling, W. Va., have been delayed by a strike among their boys. The matter has been adjusted however, and work was resumed on the 27th ult. Trade with this house is very fair.

December 08, 1881 from *C&GJ:*
Wheeling – At the Central Glass Co., things move along in the old steady way. They are still working on odds and ends of orders left with them in the early part of the season. They expect to keep all three of their furnaces running until the close of the year. From what we can learn, this company has made this fall more lamps than was ever turned out at their works before in any one season. They will have some very attractive

goods to offer to the trade this spring. Especially will this be so of their new table-ware. And, of course, no one doubts but that they will have their usual variety of bar and beer glasses, as they are certainly the headquarters for such goods. They have now been running a Gill furnace for over fifteen months, and in that time have not spent one cent on repairs; and from the present appearance of the furnace, it can be run six months longer. This certainly speaks well for the Gill furnace and the good success of the Central.

• 1882

February 16, 1882, Thursday, from *AP&GR:*
    W.L. Ewing, formerly of the Central Glass Co., and late of New York City, has accepted a position as general western agent for the Buckeye Glass Co., of Martin's Ferry, Ohio.
    The Central Glass Co., Wheeling, W. Va., have nothing special to report. Everything is going along smoothly and they are having a very fair business, considering that January and February are generally dull months with the trade.

March 23, 1882, Thursday, from *AP&GR:*
    At the Central Glass Co.'s works, Wheeling, they are running their three furnaces, and report trade fair.

March 23, 1882, from *C&GJ:*
    The Central Glass Works, one of the largest in the world, is running full time and its officers report trade very fair. The bad condition of the country roads interferes with the jobbing trade, and thus reduces orders by mail; but enough are coming in to keep everything going. The principal article in demand is the wide-mouthed beer mug.
    The Central Glass Company employs nearly 500 people—men, women and children—and pays out $8,000 every two weeks.
    Four new glass pots will be set at the Central Glass Works to-day.

March 30, 1882 from *C&GJ:*
    Mr. N. B. Scott, of the Central, is taking in the Eastern cities. The Central Glass Co. is preparing a large shipment for Germany. Nappies are in demand in "Faderland."
    The La Belle and Central Glass Works made large shipments by river to St. Louis yesterday….

April 20, 1882, Thursday, from *AP&GR:*
    Rody Robinson, at one time manager of the Central Glass Works, Wheeling, succeeds James Shipman as factory manager at the Buckeye Glass Co.'s works, Martin's Ferry. All three furnaces at this works are in full operation and trade is good.

July 13, 1882, Thursday, from *AP&GR:*
    The Central Glass Works, at Wheeling, have shut down for repairs, and will re-open about the 15th. inst.

August 17, 1882 from *C&GJ:*
    In making our weekly tour among the factories at Wheeling, Bellaire and Martin's Ferry, we found all prospering.
    The Central Glass Co., established in 1863, at present employ 400 hands, who receive annually as wages upwards of $180,000, while the value of the articles manufactured amounts to over $340,000 per year. Their trade extends not only over the entire Union, but reaches Canada, West Indies, South America and Europe.

• 1883

March 01, 1883 from *C&GJ*, "The Glass Factories:"
    The funeral of Mr. John Osterling, Jr., son of Mr. John Osterling, proprietor of the East End Glass House took place yesterday.
    The East End Glass House is running to its full capacity. A workman was approached on Saturday and asked how it was that this establishment was running full force when there is not a glass factory in the United States rushed with work. He, of course, could not give any definite information on the subject, but stated that it was principally owing to this firm not dealing exclusively in fancy ware.

April 19, 1883 from *C&GJ:*
    The addition to the Central Works is quite an imposing building. With the completion of this structure the Central will be one of the largest concerns in the country. Their exports to South America and Europe are very large.

May 10, 1883 from *C&GJ:*
    The East End Glass Works have been doing a fair trade all winter despite the untoward circumstances that have operated against all other factories in this vicinity. A very large addition to the already immense factory building has been erected, and in the course of a few weeks will be ready for operations. A novelty in the shape of a beer glass has lately been turned out there which is attracting general attention. The glass is made of very light and firm ware and strongly resembles an old-fashioned hour glass. The new style of bar goods is rapidly supplanting the old and cumbersome beer mug. The East End is also preparing to turn out a number of new sets and some small pieces, which will be described in a succeeding letter.

May 24, 1883 from *C&GJ:*
    The East End Works are running full, with plenty of orders. Quite a number of new articles have been turned out recently. Workmen began yesterday to drill a gas well within a few yards of the factory and within the next thirty days it is likely that a new kind of fuel will be in use at this works.

May 24, 1883, Thursday, from *AP&GR:*
    John Oesterling, of Wheeling, sailed last Wednesday week for Europe in steamer Elbe.

May 31, 1883, Thursday, from *AP&GR:*
    The Central Glass Company, of Wheeling, will close for six weeks on July 1.
    The Central Glass Works are also rushing their hands to their full capacity, showing trade must be very brisk or they wish a stock of ware on hand. —Wheeling *Register*

June 07, 1883, Thursday, from *AP&GR:*
    The Central Glass Works, Wheeling, is just completing a commodious new engraving shop, a large brick building with accommodations for forty engravers' benches.

June 21, 1883 from *C&GJ*:

The East End Works are running night and day in order to fill all the orders that they can before the last of this month. There has been a very large influx of orders from Europe and South America for goods of this concern, and it has been making extra efforts to fill them. A new set bearing a strong resemblance to the Riverside "Jersey Lily" has had an immense run for some weeks, and the orders are much in excess of present ability to fill.

June 28, 1883 from *C&GJ* :

Gas was struck yesterday at the East End Glass Works at a depth of nearly 800 feet. The work of drilling began only a few weeks ago, but it has been interrupted from time to time by the breaking of drills and other accidents. The time occupied in drilling was consequently very short. This is the first gas well that has been developed in this city, the nearest well heretofore struck being nearly twenty miles away. It is the intention of this glass company to make the most thorough and general experiments in all of its departments, with their gas. It has so far been only used in the glory holes, but this company will try it as a glass melting element, and if successful will discard coal altogether. They will now use it to illuminate their factory, an important item of saving.

June 28, 1883, Thursday, from *AP&GR:*

The Central Glass Company of Wheeling have been engaged for some time in sinking a well for natural gas. They struck a vein on Thursday last at a depth of 840 feet, and after being conveyed in pipes to the surface and lighted, it made a blaze thirty feet high. They will utilize it in their factory.

July 12, 1883 from *C&GJ*, "Wheeling:"

The glass houses are all shut down in this locality, and already the work of repairing them has begun. In one or two instances it will require nearly all of the forty-five days to make such alterations as will be necessary or are in contemplation. Some of the factories will make very extended changes in several of their departments.

At the East End Works the trade has not been falling off very materially, notwithstanding the close-down. This concern has had a large number of orders on hand during the last six months and it will require some weeks yet to shape themselves up with the trade. One of their sets had an immense run during April, May, and June, and the enforced stoppage, of course, had a tendency to abridge the run. The secretary says that their designers are at work upon a number of new articles which will be ready for the trade early in the fall. The work upon the sinking of the new gas well is progressing very slowly, on account of the difficulty experienced in forcing the drill through the sand.

July 19, 1883 from *C&GJ*:

At the East End Factory the usual activity about the office was noticeable. The orders for goods, Col. Scott says, has not abated very materially. There is a large demand for lamps, and many varieties of table and bar goods. The demand from the transatlantic customers of this company for goods has been very large of late. I noticed a large consignment of goods at the Baltimore and Ohio Railroad depot, recently, for the North-German States. A vexatious delay has been occasioned in the prosecution of the work of sinking the gas well by the lodgment of the drill in the sand and the trouble experienced in its extrication.

July 26, 1883 from *C&GJ*:

At the Central Works labor upon their gas well has been impeded by various obstacles for several weeks. A very strong vein of gas was struck, but the volume was deemed insufficient for the purposes of the factory, and it was determined to push it still further. A depth of nearly one thousand feet had been reached when the drill became fastened in the sand, and since that time it has required the constant exertions of those in charge to relieve it. When no drawbacks are encountered the drillers make five or six feet an hour. Secretary Scott says that the suspension caught the Central badly because they had no stock on hand, and on that account are at a disadvantage.

August 23, 1883, Thursday, from *AP&GR:*

The Central Glass Company of Wheeling have lighted their fires and will start up in a day or two.

November 22, 1883 from *AP&GR:*

The Central Glass Company, of Wheeling, have given notice of its seccession from the Western Flint and Lime Glass Association, and of its intention to abolish separate charges for packages, speculation is rife as to whether other factories may not follow suit—that is in the matter of packages. Pittsburgh manufacturers seem to be pretty firm in their opposition to any change, but it is said that one or two houses down the Ohio valley may follow the example of the Central. That any such action as that indicated will have any effect on the Western Flint and Lime Glass Association as an organization is not at all probable, but that the defection of even two or three houses, in respect to the recently affirmed rule of charging separately for packages, may compel the rest, in self defense, to take similar action, is not impossible. No decisive steps have yet been taken by the association in the matter.

November 29, 1883 from *AP&GR:*

It is now considered probable that nothing further will be done in regard to the package question, and that the present system will continue indefinitely. It is denied by some that the Central Glass Works of Wheeling have any intention of taking off charges for packages, and that the report was sent out through the misapprehension of a correspondent. Pittsburgh manufacturers expect no change whatever, and it is likely there will be none.

November 29, 1883, Thursday, from *AP&GR:*

This announcement appeared in the Reporter for Thurs., November 22, 1883. It read: "John Oesterling, president of the Central Glass Co., Wheeling, died on last Friday morning of apoplexy, aged 59."

Mr. Oesterling's Death

At a special meeting of the Western Flint and Lime Glass Protective Association, held on the 23rd inst, to make appropriate action on the death of Mr. John Oesterling, of Wheeling, the subjoined paper was presented, ordered to be spread on the minutes of the association, and a copy ordered to be sent to the American Pottery and Glassware Reporter, with the request that it be printed in that paper:

"Again in the providence of God we are called to record the death of one of our members, Mr. John Oesterling, of the Central Glass Company, Wheeling, who was suddenly stricken down on the night of the 15th inst. Mr. Oesterling was born in Germany, on the 4th of January, 1824. He served an apprenticeship in a machine shop in his native country, and soon after his arrival in the land of his adoption entered the establishment of Hobbs, Barnes & Co., at Wheeling, as a mold pattern maker, where he acquired some knowledge of the business in which he spent so many years of his life. In July, 1863, he embarked in the manufacture of flint glass under the firm of Oesterling, Henderson & Co., in which he was the leading spirit. July 25, 1867, the members of that firm were incorporated, and have since done business as the Central Glass Company, Mr. Oesterling being made president, a position he filled with credit to himself and entire satisfaction to his company until his death. He was a man of industrious habits, clear perception, sound judgment and great perseverance, and as a consequence achieved success, that factory being at this time among the largest and most prosperous in this country. His health several years past, impaired by long and absorbing labor, made it necessary to rest for a time on several occasions, on two of which he went to Europe and visited the scenes of his youth, and returned benefited and encouraged. But his time had come and his place among us is vacant."

John Oesterling, a brief account of whose death appeared in our last issue, was born in Hesse Darmstadt, in 1824, and came to this country in 1850. In 1853 he went to Wheeling, and soon after went into the factory of Hobbs, Barnes & Co., as a mold maker. In 1863 he, in company with W.K. Elson, presient of the Elson Glass Works, at Martin's Ferry, Ohio, and several others, organized the Central Glass Co., and erected a factory. Mr. Oesterling was elected president, a position he occupied up to the time of his death, and filled with signal ability. His funeral was attended by most of the glass manufacturers throughout the western district.

December 06, 1883 from *C&GJ:*
Pittsburgh, November 26, 1883. Editor Crockery and Glass Journal:

At a special meeting of this association held on the 23rd inst. to take appropriate action on the death of Mr. John Oesterling, Wheeling, the enclosed paper was present, ordered to be spread on the minutes of this association, and a copy ordered to be sent to you, with the request that you will kindly publish the same in the next issue of the Journal.
Jos. G. Walter, Actuary

Same as above from paragraph starting "Again in the Providence of God we are called to record the death of one of our members—until paragraph ending – and his place among us is vacant."

We recall with pleasure as he sat among us, his calm and judicious counsel, his genial and benignant manner. All who knew him respected and honored as a man of unbending integrity. He was a man of deep feeling and strong convictions, and hence his esteem and friendship were worth something. For meanness and trickery he had a great contempt and was not backward in expressing it. Although his early educational advantages were limited he was a man of enlarged information, his observing faculties being naturally acute, and his mind analytical and tenacious.

We tender our sincere condolence to those that are mourning the death of a kind and loving father, and as one source of consolation point them to the memory of his unblemished life and the esteem and honor in which he was held by all who knew him.

And to the company we extend our sincere sympathy in the loss of its honored head.

December 13, 1883 from *AP&GR:*
Col. N.B. Scott has been elected president of the Central Glass Co., Wheeling, *vice* John Oesterling, deceased. He has been connected with this company for a long time, latterly as secretary.

December 27, 1883 from *C&GJ:*
The Central Works worked every furnace full up to midnight Friday, when the furnaces were banked for a few days. Col. Scot says trade, both domestic and foreign, has been unusually large this season. The shipments to South American and Europe by this company are annually growing larger and have become one of the principal features of the business of the Central Co. Some magnificent goods have been made this fall, and a large number of new designs will be ready for market directly the factory resumes work in January.

• 1884

January 03, 1884 from *C&GJ:*
The Central Works are nearly ready to make glass again. Stock-taking has been going on to the exclusion of all other business for the last ten days, and it will be several days yet before all things are in shape. Col. Scott says his company has nothing to complain of. The season has not been one that has been characterized by any immense sales or anything of a phenomenal nature but it has been a good one generally. The goods that have been sold were all good and reliable, but the prices they brought were not in any sense satisfactory. "Yes, we have a new set ready for the trade, a description of which I will give you later on when we get through taking stock. It will consist of thirty-five or forty pieces and I think it is one of the prettiest things that we have turned out in a long time. We will also have quite a variety of elegant novelties ready for the early spring trade. Now, as it is the first of the new year, I want to say to you that we are not going to take off the charges for packages nor did we intend to do so. We understood that there would be a movement on the part of certain manufacturers to do this, and we merely put ourselves in a position to meet it when it should come. That was all we did, and we said so at the time. Some person or persons spread the report that we intended to abandon the charge for packages and we did not go to the trouble to deny it."

January 17, 1884 from *AP&GR:*

The Central Glass Co. of Wheeling, deny the report that they purpose or ever intended to make any departure from the present rule of charging for packages as established by the tableware manufacturers generally. We believe such a rumor gained currency through the columns of this paper, and we printed it because we had it on what we deemed very good authority. Col. Scott emphatically denies the truth of the report, and his declaration on the matter is, of course, conclusive.

April, 1884 from *C&GJ:*

A cutglass style of goblet and celery stand introduced.

September 25, 1884 from *C&GJ:*

The East End Glass Works are running very full. The demand for goods both in this country and for export purpose, President Scott says, is very encouraging. I noticed while in the factory yesterday some very large and handsome beer mugs being made to fill an immense order for use in the North German Confederation. Their goods are shipped weekly to various European ports. The demand for the fine wares is fully up to the average. The new "log cabin" set is very popular, and they are behind with orders for it.

October 02, 1884 from *C&GJ:*

The East End glass factory is running along smoothly, and reported trade as fair. Col. Scott reports that they will shortly have some new designs in wares for the holiday trade on the market.

The East End Works, of this city are running very full, with a very large demand for all of the goods made by them. Just now the greatest run is being made by the "Log Cabin," a rather unique set that is enjoying a tremendous popularity South and West. The goods are all made in imitation of a very old cabin, and as finished make very attractive table furniture. It came into prominence during the last year and its instantaneous popularity showed that the East End had made a decided hit. Tableware, tumblers, goblets, and staple goods generally are in good demand.

October 23, 1884 from *C&GJ:*

The Central Co. report a splendid domestic and foreign trade, but think prices are very low, "too low to talk about." The "log cabin" set is still in fine demand, and weekly becomes more popular. It is certainly the most unique thing on the market, and deserves all the popularity it has received. Some very attractive new wares are in process of preparation and will be ready for the trade early in December. The Christmas line of goods will be unusually fine. The Central Co. is still impressed with the idea that natural gas abounds in the Wheeling Creek valley, and has made several attempts to develop it, but thus far to no purpose. One or two wells have already been sunk near the factory, and this week another one was started. If it is successful the Central will enlarge its capacity.

October 30, 1884 from *C&GJ:*

The Central Glass Works authorities report a most satisfactory trade in all departments. Their specialty just now is the "log cabin" set, already described in these columns. It is

having a very large run all over the country west and south of the Ohio river. Nothing more unique or attractive has been sold in many years. The new goods for the holiday trade are ready for the road and are very handsome.

Full Page Advertisement December 18, 1884 in *Crockery and Glass Journal* Central Glass Co., Manufacturers of Glass-Ware

• 1885

January 01, 1885 from *C&GJ:*

The Central Glass Works will let out the fires in its furnaces this week, but will be in full blast again in a few weeks. The Central has ready for the market an entire new set of magnificent imitation cut glass which it calls "775". The berry dishes, sugars, creams, and other pieces are cylindrical, the crystals diamond shaped, the diamonds inserted in such an ingenious manner as to give them in certain exposures a fine iridescence. Another novelty is an inkstand of curious design, the leading feature of which is a recumbent horse of exquisite formation. The Central is experimenting with colors, and it is likely that early in the coming year it will place a line of colored goods of all descriptions in its sample rooms.

January 08, 1885 from *C&GJ:*

The Central Glass Co., which has had its three furnaces blocked for the past ten days, will resume work next Monday. Trade has picked up considerably since the first two weeks in December, and promises to be very fair through January. This is no doubt induced by the popularity of the new goods that were lately placed on the market. The colored ware has not yet been placed in the sample room, but will be early in the spring in order to be included in the goods preparing for the spring trade. Stock-taking is still going on, but will be completed next week. President Scott thinks that the demand this spring will be for novelties both in sets and single pieces.

January 08, 1885, Thursday Morning, from *The Wheeling Daily Intelligencer*

The Central Glass Works
President N.B. Scott, of the Central Glass Company, said the mail was never before so light this time of year as this week. The factory has been running two of its three furnaces steadily all along except the week from Christmas to New Year's. About the usual stock is in the warehouses. Usually at the first of the year there is a great influx of buyers. So far this year only one glass dealer from abroad has visited the Central. No change is noted in prices.

Mr. Scott referred to his books, and discovered that the sales now only averaged about one half what they did one year ago.

The stoppage over the river does not affect the trade of the factories here for two reasons. The first is that the Ohio factories now idle nearly all had pretty large stocks on hand when they shut down, and the other that their lines of ware are different from the product of the Wheeling factories.

The Central has lately got out a set in imitation of cut glass which takes. It is also making an attractive new ornamental glass inkstand. It will shortly put on the market a beer and ale glass that is the neatest ever offered the bar trade. It is entirely new in design.

January 10, 1885 from *The Wheeling Daily Intelligencer*
The Gas Problem
As It Affects Wheeling
Discussed at a Small but Respectable Sized Meeting of Citizens Yesterday—The Various Wells That May be Taken up—An Expression of Views—Committee.

The Central's Gas Wells
Mr. Scott said that he was greatly surprised to note the small representation of manufacturers present. For a long time he had been impressed with the necessity of securing gas. He had noticed the articles that had appeared in the press the past few days and had made a few inquiries of the borers at the Central glass house well. It was down 2020 feet. The borers would be willing to go down 1000 further for $2 per foot, and after that an additional 500 feet for $2.5 per foot. Mr. Scott said that the company was now having this well cleaned out for the purpose of securing a better flow for the small vein that had been struck and was now being used in certain portions of the factory, but that it would be willing to surrender it as it now stands, with the understanding that in case it should be taken hold of by a pool for the purpose of going lower to ascertain whether gas in a large quantity could be found, that in case such a supply was struck, the glass

company should have the same on paying back to the members of the pool their contributions with interest, and he further said that in addition to the expense gone to by the company in putting down its two wells, it would contribute to the development of any well in the vicinity.

Mr. Scott gave some very interesting information concerning the developments at the two wells sunk at the Central. In the first, at 800 feet a very good flow was found; that was the one that caused so much excitement here. It was finally cased off and the well sunk lower. At 1025 feet the salt water was struck. That was cased off and the boring continued down to its present depth. The second well, about 45 feet distant, was sunk for the purpose of striking the 800 feet flow, but nothing was found until the salt water flow was encountered and then that well was abandoned. He gave some figures showing the comparison between gas and coal for fuel purposes that were interesting.

January. 15, 1885 from *C&GJ*, "The Glass Factories:"
Two of the three furnaces at the Central Glass Works are in operation, and have run steadily except during the holidays, when the men were given a week's rest. The two houses in this city are the only flint-glass factories in operation in this vicinity with the exception of the Dithridge lead glass works at Martin's Ferry, O. Each of them is making the usual effort to keep ahead of the market and stimulate trade by designing novelties of attractive patterns.

May 28, 1885 from *C&GJ:*
The Central Glass Works of this city, and George Duncan & Sons, of Pittsburgh, have locked horns in a manner. The Pittsburgh firm, some time since, got out a new line of goods, and shortly afterwards a design the exact counterpart of that of Duncan & Sons was introduced by the Central, and the price materially cut. Whether this was by accident or otherwise Duncan & Sons took it up and at once commenced a cut on some of the special lines handled by the Central, and succeeded in bringing about an inquiry and propositions of adjustment.

July 16, 1885 from *AP&GR:*
The Central Glass Works, Wheeling, will suspend operations for a couple of weeks. They are doing fairly well.

September 10, 1885 from *AP&GR:*, "Business Memoranda:"
Central Glass Co. Purchases Brilliant Glass Works:
The Wheeling *Intelligencer* of Friday last says: The Central Glass Company, of this city, has purchased the glass works at Brilliant, Ohio, opposite Wellsburg. It will be remembered that a syndicate composed largely of the principal stockholders of the Central company, attempted a short time ago to secure control of the La Belle works at Bridgeport, but the negotiations were blocked by the refusal of a small portion of the stockholders to entertain the proposal. The Brilliant factory has been idle for several years, and has been offered for sale several times, but withdrawn without a sale being consummated. President Scott has been negotiating for the works for some time, and on Wednesday evening the negotiations

resulted in the sale of the works to the Central company. They will at once start up the works. The furnace is a twelve-pot one, and the factory is one of the most thoroughly and conveniently fitted up in the country, and the premises afford an abundance of room for additions or warehouses. They have secured the services of Mr. August Weyer, late head of the Weyer Art Glass Company, of Long Island, who will have charge of the factory at Brilliant. It is expected that glass can be made inside of a month. Mr. Weyer will bring with him from the east several experienced men in the manufacture of the line of wares it is proposed to make, and the remaining force necessary will be employed in this part of the country. Natural gas from the Spaulding well at Brilliant will be used as fuel for the present, and a well will probably be sunk hereafter to supply the works with gas. Only lead glass will be made, and the company will make a specialty of colored and crystal shades, lead tumblers, fine electric light shades, colored hall gas lamps, signal light globes and all wares in that line. A special dispatch from Steubenville gives the price paid for the Brilliant works as $5,333.34.

September 11, 1885 from *The American Glass Worker*, "Ohio Valley Items:"

The Central Company, of East Wheeling, has purchased the Brilliant, Ohio, factory, and put fire in the furnace on the 7th inst., Mr. Meyers, of Brooklyn, will make glass and super-intend the works. They intend to make fine blown ware.

The Central, Hobbs, Brocurner & Co., and the North Wheeling Bottle Company, of Wheeling, W. Va., are running full time, and report business good.

A advertisement in *(American) Pottery and Glassware Reporter* dated October 29, 1885, shows a shade with a thumbprint design with scalloped edges mentioning: "Central Glass Co., Manufacturers of Tableware, Lamps, Etc., Bar Goods A Specialty. Also Beautiful Designs in Gas and Kerosene Globes and Shades in all colors, Opal and Flint, Wheeling, W. VA." A similar advertisement was in the same periodical on January 07, 1886, see that illustration.

November 05, 1885 from *AP&GR:*

The Brilliant Glass Works, located at Brilliant, Jefferson county, Ohio, are now being worked to their full capacity by the Central Glass Co. of Wheeling. They are making a line of elegant colored shades there of unique designs and there is a large and growing demand for them.

November 26, 1885 from *AP&GR:*

The Central Glass Co., Wheeling, are running full with their three furnaces at that place, as well as the Brilliant Works. They have had a very good season, and trade keeps up well yet. They are getting out an entirely new line of tableware for the spring trade, which will be one of the finest they ever offered to the trade. It will be something altogether new in design and general make up. They are making a large line of colored shades and these are selling well. Their warerooms and packing department are across the street from the factory proper, with which they are connected by a bridge. This building covers an

area of 200x66 feet, with an L 66x80 feet, three stories high. A railroad connects the factory with the warerooms. They have one department specially for open stock, comprising an area of 180x60 feet. Every article is carefully examined before being packed, and nothing with any flaw or defect of any kind is allowed to go out. They pay special attention to the jobbing trade, giving them all the advantage there is in the business. This factory has been in steady operation throughout the year, and their orders are now fully up to the production.

November 27, 1885 from *AP&GR:*

A dispatch dated Wheeling, November 24, says: The striking boys at the Central Glass Works, who number 150 to-day offered to return to work on the old terms, but the proprietors declined to employ them unless they would accept a reduction. The boys took time to consider this. The managers say if they do not accept by Saturday night the fires in both furnaces will be drawn.

December 10, 1885 from *AP&GR* "Business Memoranda:"

The Central Glass Co., Wheeling are running four furnaces, three at Wheeling and one at Brilliant station. Business is very good with them and they have scored a great success in their flint and opal globes and shades, which they make in a large variety of shapes and colors.

• **1886**

The Glass Factory *Directory* for 1886 (Pub. by the *American Glass Worker*) lists under *Flint Glass Factories*
CENTRAL GLASS CO., Wheeling, West Va. 2 furnaces
Fine pressed and blown ware, shades, globes,
Bar ware, etc.

Advertisement January 07, 1886 in *Pottery and Glassware Reporter*

August 17, 1886 from *The Wheeling Daily Intelligencer*

The Central Works.

At the Central Glass Works the force has been somewhat reduced temporarily by the accident to one of the furnaces. Orders are plenty. The Brilliant works of this company are doing a rushing business, their fancy wares being in much demand. The Central recently shipped a large order of table ware, beer glasses, etc. to Copenhagen, Denmark.

August 26, 1886 from AP&GR:

The Central Glass Company, of Wheeling, have three furnaces going at Wheeling as well as one at their works at Brilliant. Trade has opened up well with them. They have quite a number of new articles out this fall and their trade in fancy colored globes and shades is growing rapidly.

CENTRAL GLASS CO.,

MANUFACTURERS OF

Tableware, Lamps, Etc.

BAR GOODS A SPECIALTY.

ALSO BEAUTIFUL **DESIGNS** IN

Gas and Kerosene Globes and Shades in all colors, Opal and Flint.

WHEELING, W. VA.

Advertisement September 09, 1886 in *Crockery and Glass Journal* showing an example of the shades they made

- 1887

February 03, 1887 from *C&GJ*:

The Brilliant factory of the Central Glass Co. is closed indefinitely. These works were purchased two or three years ago with a view of making the finer lines of goods in colors, but more or less trouble has been experienced ever since the first operation of the works, though they turned out some very fine goods there last season. But it has been a source of expense, and since the first of the year a great deal more trouble than ever before accompanied its operation, owing partially to the limited supply of gas that could be obtained there, and Mr. H.F. Webb, the new man who came over from England to take charge of the works, resigned his place, and the factory was shut down for an indefinite period. It will not be started again before April, if then. The Central Works in this city, however, are being operated to their utmost capacity, with a splendid business in hand.

Mr. H.E. Waddell, the wide-awake gentleman who has principal charge of the affairs of the Central Glass Co. during President Scott's temporary absence in the capacity of a senator, was banquetted last week by the employees at the Brilliant Works, which closed down.

March 17, 1887 from *AP&GR*:

The Central Glass Works folks report trade good. The three furnaces are on full and large quantities of ware are being made and shipped. Nos. 829 and 830, plain and engraved, which are both new, are selling rapidly, especially the former, as also are their new novelties such as roller skates, slippers, etc. They are getting ready an elegant line of lamps in three styles for the fall trade. Mr. A.F. Meder returned from a fairly successful Northwestern trip on Friday. The secretary, Mr. H.E. Waddell, is in the East in the interests of the works.

June 09, 1887, Thursday, from *AP&GR*:

The Central Glass Co. has not as yet decided what they will do with their factory at Brilliant, Ohio, which has been idle for some time. Mr. Bacon, formerly of the Windsor Glass Co., of Homestead, Pa., has been negotiating for its purchase, but up to the time of this writing has not purchased it. Several

other glass men have been figuring on it. Three different men visited Brilliant recently in a single day to look at it. When the Central Co. stopped running they had a big stock of ware on hand, especially shades, all of which has been shipped except about 300 hogsheads. They bought the factory for the low price of $6,000 and made extensive improvements and now offer it for $10,000, $6,000 down and the balance in eighteen months. If they don't sell it shortly they will start it on fruit jars for which the demand is unprecedented. The factory is a first class one and has one 12 pot furnace, which would make about 140 gross of jars a day. A number of concerns having the molds are eager to furnish them as they have a good trade already worked up. There is more money in fruit jars now than ever before, and will be for a long time, and the Central Co. thinks if they get into the business at once they can make some money, besides making the chances better for selling the works. Last year was so unusually good a fruit year that the factories engaged in making jars were unable to supply the demand. The common theory is that two good fruit seasons never come in succession, so that this year only a fair trade in jars was expected. Jobbers did not lay in extensive stocks and the factories generally did not make special efforts to more than fill the orders booked. To everybody's' surprise the production of fruit this year, from early strawberries to late quinces, promises to be larger than last year. This has led to an unexpected and sudden stimulus in the trade in fruit jars, which is, under ordinary circumstances, of an extent to surprise any person who has never received an idea of the number of fruit jars sold each year.

June 23, 1887 from *AP&GR*:

At the Central Glass Works trade is reported fair. This enterprise has been running the entire season with their three furnaces on and has turned out an immense quantity of ware, nearly all of which has been sold. The season which is about closing has been a right good one with them. They have suffered from the interstate commerce law especially to points West of the Mississippi. A first class line of lamps is ready for the fall trade which will certainly sell well. The new line consists of five different styles, six sizes each. No. 821, a dew drop in the different colors; No. 556, plain acorn; No. 857, panel groove top and bottom; No. 858, dew drop plain panel, and No. 870, which matches their latest able set. No. 856 is also in colors. All of these lamps have the drip foot on which the company has a patent. They have been making these for nine years and have had a big run on them. Their line of lamps this year is the best they have ever had, which is to say a great deal. All of the lamp shops in the factory are on and they are making extensive preparations for the fall trade. Their new table set, 870, not quite completed, is a handsome thing and will certainly sell well. It is a cutting made to imitate a tower.

July 21, 1887 from *AP&GR*:

Large numbers of handsome orders for lamps and other goods have been received at the Central Glass Works since our last report. Considerable repairing has been done in the factory during the stop. The three furnaces will go in as usual on the 3d prox. The president, Senator N.B. Scott, and Mr. Grant have sold their interests in the McLure House to Messrs Harry B. McLure and Frank Stamm, two enterprising and popular young men of Wheeling.

August 4, 1887 from *AP&GR:*

The Brilliant Glass Works, which was recently purchased from the Central Glass Co. by Mr. Bacon, of Homestead, Pa., will be started about the 1st of September.

Two furnaces started up at the Central Glass Works on Monday and the third one will start today or tomorrow. No. 870, the new line of table ware, is selling well and their new line of lamps are taking like hot cakes. Thus far they have sold more lamps than ever before which is certainly a good indication. Mail orders are coming in every day for goods of different kinds. Mr. H.E. Waddell, who left for the West last week, is already sending in good orders. During the stop the usual summer repairs were made. The charter of this glass factory, which occupies the high rank of being one of the foremost of Wheeling's leading industries, expired last Saturday and was appropriately commemorated by the leading stockholders who tendered the office force and several friends a royal treat, consisting of sparkling champagne and fine cigars, which were highly enjoyed by all present. The Central Glass Works, which is in its twentieth year, never changed presidents until death released Mr. John Oesterling, who was succeeded by Senator N.B. Scott, under whose efficient management the enterprise has continued to prosper.

November 10, 1887 from *AP&GR:*

This week the Central Glass Co. completed the erection of a three-story building, 90x150 feet in dimensions which will add room for the convenience for work. The structure adjoins the old buildings on the north. It is built of brick, with iron girders and tin roof and is fire-proof throughout, the floors being of earth supported by arches of brick. The lower story will be utilized as a lumber room, the second as a mold room and in the third will be located the mold room proper, the heavy machinery in this department of glass manufacturing to be made there. The old mold shop will be utilized for storage. The mold makers are busy on a new line for the spring trade. The Central is running to its fullest capacity and business, while not booming, is fair. Last week a novelty was turned out to order, in the shape of glass duplicates of the electrical nose and ears used by Mr. Evans of Evans & Hoey, in "A Parlor Match." The ears and nose which Mr. Evans has heretofore used were made in London and he was continually afraid they would break and spoil the sensation he creates when as the ghost of the deceased Capt. Kidd, he becomes so excited. His order was filled to his entire satisfaction and hereafter he will be secure in possessing a number of duplicates. Mr. H.E. Waddell got home from a successful trip in the East. Both he and Mr. A.T. Meder will not go out again before the first of the year.

December 8, 1887 from *AP&GR:*

Never has the Central Glass Co. had a better run on lamps and many other goods as during the year which will soon end. Everything has passed off very smoothly during the last year with three furnaces in operation, and January 1st will find about the usual amount of stock on hands at that time. They have had as good luck as usual with their pots and there has been no serious hindrances. Among the improvements made during the year was the erection of a large three story fire proof mold shop, which was recently completed. The President, Hon. N.B. Scott, seems to be the right man in the right place.

• **1888**

June 14, 1888, Thursday, from *AP&GR,* "Wheeling:"

The Central Glass Co. have now ready two new full lines of tableware for the fall trade, of which everyone speaks well who has seen them. The first is the "Star" pattern, No. 876, and is truly a sundowner, and will cut a wide swath among the trade. The other, and greatest of all, is the "Twist" pattern, No. 884, also a perfect honey-color and destined to make inroads in the affections of dealers, as they who have inspected it allow. It is certainly one of the finest lines of crystal ware ever put on the market, and both are bound to prove ready sellers when the regular season opens. They always do get out attractive goods at this factory and have never any trouble in disposing of them even in comparatively dull times.

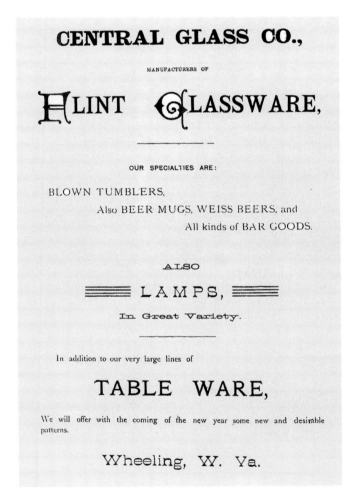

Advertisement December 06, 1888 in *Crockery and Glass Journal*

• **1889**

March 14, 1889 from *AP&GR,* "Wheeling:"

A three story brick building, 60x60 feet, has been built on the site of the one burned at the Central Glass Works some weeks ago for storing straw, etc. The warehouse which was badly damaged has been repaired and the two buildings are better than ever. The three big furnaces are on full and turning out large quantities of ware which is not piled up very fast on account of orders coming in lively. Business is not booming but the Central is doing right well, both in tableware and bar goods. No. 651, the low priced set, Nos. 877 and 895, the plain and engraved lines, are selling as well as expected. The March sales thus far have been satisfactory. The president, Mr. N.B. Scott, is in New York on business. Mr. W.B. Stewartson, is sending in good orders from the Northwest and Mr. Charles B. Ott from the West.

May 24, 1889 from *AP&GR:*

The furnaces in operation at the glass factories in Wheeling and vicinity are as follows: Central, three, North Wheeling, one, Hobbs, one, …

July 4, 1889 from *AP&GR:*

The Central Glass Works closed on Saturday, after operating the three big furnaces nearly every day during the season and had a successful run. The works has had more orders than could be filled for over a month and is still making large shipments. They are having a great run on lamps. Messrs. W.B. Stewartson is in from the West and Northwest and C.W. Ott from the South. Both had good trips. The secretary, Mr. Albert Maeder, sailed on the steamer Suebin last week for Hamburg. He will do Germany, the Paris Exposition and London before returning.

August 29, 1889 from *AP&GR:*

The three furnaces at the Central Glass Works are on full. Owing to the condition of the employes' hands they did not do their best last week, but are down to business now in good style. Business is a good as could be expected. The Central, which has always had a big run on bar goods, is still having a good sale in this line. The last lamps brought out have been selling well. The manufacture of lead tumblers and blown stem goods has been commenced, and the outlook for them is excellent. The Central continues to spring novelties on the trade occasionally. The latest is a lantern novelty and an inkstand, both of which will sell, especially the former. The lantern is made of glass, in the shape of a castle or house top, etched, with plain windows and nickel-plated top and handle. They are made in three different colors, red, white and blue, and after the style of the old-fashioned tin lantern, in which candles were used. It is intended as a night lamp or for the sick room, and is an excellent thing for this purpose, the light being soft and will not hurt the weakest eyes. It is just the thing for illuminating parlors when small parties are given and the gas is turned down, the different colors making a nice effect, or for illuminating lawns, piazzas, etc. Candles guaranteed to last nine hours are used. They are admired by everybody, especially the ladies and are bound to sell. The Central is having a great run on this and may have some difficulty making enough of them. "Oh, give me that, won't you? It's so lovely," said the first lady who saw one. The secretary of the Central, Mr. A.F. Maeder, who has been summering in England, France and Germany, sailed for home last week.

September 12, 1889 from *AP&GR:*

Orders are fairly plentiful at the CENTRAL GLASS WORKS. The new night lamp or lantern is still selling well. The secretary, Mr. Albert Maeder, has returned from his summer vacation in Europe.

1889 from *AP&GR:*

"We have about all we can do," is the way they put it at the Central Glass Works. The demand for the night lamp is enormous. The old fashioned tin lantern carried by "Betsy" in Estella Clayton's play "Along the Hudson," reminded the writer of this one, while at the matinee on Saturday.

October 10, 1889 from *AP&GR:*

No. 950, the new ink stand being made at the Central Glass Works is a very pretty thing and is bound to take. Business is fair. They have a new idea in etching—a process never tried before we believe. It was brought from the Paris Exposition by Mr. Albert Maeder, the secretary. The new line will be made in bar goods principally at first, and will be ready for the trade in a month or so. It is a very attractive novelty and though not new abroad has become more popular there. Recently Senator Scott, the president, received letters patent on a new device for pressing and blowing. The pressed stem is set on a block and then a blow mold is set over it and the bowl blown and put on. After this is done the foot is finished just as in the ordinary process and the stem and foot are made much cheaper and more satisfactorily than by hand. This is a decided improvement. Last week a big lot of the night lamps or lanterns made in red, white, blue and amber, were shipped to Washington, D.C., for Mrs. John A. Logan, to illuminate her residence and grounds while entertaining the Knights of Templars this week. This is certainly a great novelty.

October 24, 1889 from *AP&GR:*

The Central Glass Co. are going into the manufacture of a fine line of lead blown and pressed stem ware and will be ready with it for the spring trade. We will give a more extended notice of the same further on.

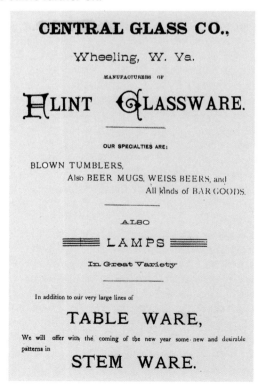

Advertisement December 05, 1889 in *Crockery and Glass Journal*

December 19, 1889 from *AP&GR:*

Have you seen the new spring line of the Central Glass Works? Well, we suppose not. At least not very many of our readers have as the goods have been out only a short time. The number is 365, figured and it is a beauty of the first water. There is a full line of tableware, also a very handsome flower vase made in two styles. These goods are a credit to the Central and are bound to sell. The works, which has been on full, will shut down next Saturday for the holidays. (Note: this pattern is probably No. 965, unless it was a replacement for the earlier stemware pattern No. 365, unfortunately No. 965 is unknown.)

1890s

While most of the glass exhibits were done at the Monongehela House in Pittsburgh, Pennsylvania, in the early 1890s several glass and pottery manufacturers in the Ohio Valley had shows at the McClure House in Wheeling, West Virginia. Frank Stamm (who was married to Peter Cassells daughter) was a partner in this hotel.

1890-1891 from *Callin's Wheeling Directory*, the McLure House:

During the past three years, this hotel, under the efficient management of Messrs. Stamm and McLure, is numbered among the leading hotels in the United States. It is the most centrally located hotel in Wheeling, and is the recognized headquarters for traveling men generally, as well as glass, oil and iron merchants...

April 12, 1890 from *AP&GR:*

The Central Glass Co. has a brand new specialty which is bound to be a great seller. It is a bowl made in the shape of a turkey, in plain, etched, and opal. There are two parts; the bowl and the cover, the latter consisting of the head, back, wings, etc. The bowls will hold about a quart and can be used for various purposes. Three furnaces are being worked for all they are worth and the company reports a big run on their blown stem ware and the usual run on lamps and tableware.

The following patent was filed in November and took over six months to be granted.

November 05, 1891, Glassware Patent 452,722 filed by Louis Schaub, Wheeling, W. Va., Filed November 05, 1890. Granted May 19, 1891. Ser. No. 370,373. A method of forming hollow stems for glass articles.

Claims:
- The method of forming hollow stems for glass articles, which consists in molding the stem with open end with enlargements therearound within the bowl and welding said enlargements to close the end of the stem while the glass is hot, as set forth.
- The herein-described method of forming pressed hollow stems for glass articles, which consists in pressing the stem heavy at the open end of the stem within the bowl and then closing the end of the stem within the bowl by welding the heavy portion while hot and while the stem is in the mold, as set forth.

- A blank for making closed hollow-stemmed glassware, consisting of a bowl, stem and base in one piece, the bowl and stem being hollow and the portions between the bowl and stem being thickened for subsequent closure of the bottom of the bowl and the upper end of the stem, substantially as specified.
- As a new article of manufacture, pressed stemmed glassware having a hollow stem, an integral base, and a jointed bottom to the bowl, as set forth.
- Glassware wherein the bowl, stem, and base are all formed integral with jointless exterior, and a central jointed bottom to the bowl and upper end of the hollow stem, substantially as specified.

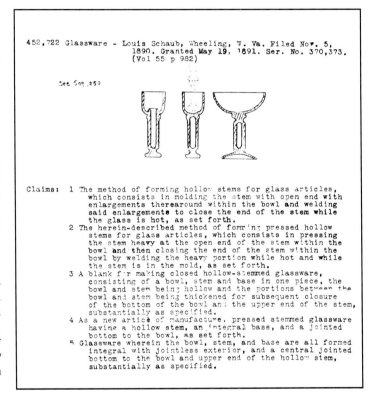

Patent November 05, 1891 for forming hollow stems for glass articles.

December 18, 1890 from *AP&GR:*

President N.B. Scott of the Central Glass Works....reports this the worst year yet. They have run their works full all year, with the exception of the summer stop, and the years business is unsatisfactory. They will have a new line of table ware for the spring trade, which bids fair to be a big seller....

1890 from *C&GJ:*

The Central Glass Co. have not only been doing an immense business all of this season, but have been laying the groundwork for even better business hereafter. They have such a varied line of goods that the average dealer can hardly miss it when he strikes the Central for what he wants. Their lines embrace tableware, stem ware, lamps and novelties beyond number, and they are constantly sending out something new, as will be found by reference to their own announcement. President N.B. Scott is a wide-awake, active man at the head of this immense factory, and he is ably assisted by Mr. Albert Meder, who divides his time between the office and with the trade. Together, they make a formidable pair.

Advertisement December 17, 1890 showing Finger Bowl

Advertisement December 18, 1890 from *Crockery and Glass Journal* for Flint Blown Stem Ware, etc. showing four examples

⇒CENTRAL GLASS CO.,⇐
Bar, Tableware and Lamps,
·Lead Blown Tumblers and Stem Ware, Plain, Etched and Cut.

Advertisement December 24, 1890 in *China, Glass and Lamps* for E. LeBel, representing various companies including Central Glass Company

• 1891
CENTRAL GLASS NEVER MOVED TO INDIANA

1891 from *C&GJ:*
No little comment has been caused in this city during the past week by the action of the Central Glass Co. following the demand of the Natural Gas Co. for another increase in the price of that fuel. The Central has been paying about $19,000 per year for gas. The increase asked would swell that cost to about $25,000, and at a meeting of the Board last week a committee of five of the principal stockholders and directors, including the manager of the works, was appointed to go to Anderson, Ind., and investigate the plant and surroundings of the American Glass Co., with a view of purchasing and operating it. The plant has been offered to the Central for $35,00, it is said, and this includes a gas well adjacent to the works. The committee left last Monday night, and will spend all of this week there. It is probable, if this deal is concluded, that the Central will only run one furnace here this season.

January 8, 1891 from *AP&GR*, "Local Items:"
Probable Removal
A committee from the Central Glass Co., Wheeling, West Va., has been delegated to inspect the glass plant of the American Glass Co., Anderson, Ind., with a view of purchasing the works, if suitable arrangements for a permanent gas supply can be secured. The Central, under the Presidency of Col. Scott, has been one of the most successful of the Ohio valley glass companies, and have steadily operated three furnaces for many years on fine pressed, blown and special lines of glassware. The reason assigned for their contemplated removal is the partial failure of the gas supply, and an increase in the price which would make their fuel cost $15,000 in excess of present rates.
President N.B. Scott, of the Central Glass Co., is not enthusiastic for removal to the Indiana town, but as the plant there is well equipped and cost $61,000 he believes that its purchase and operation would be good business under existing circumstances.

THE CENTRAL'S REMOVAL
A Talk with President Scott on the Subject
There has been so much speculation and so many false reports concerning the possible removal of the Central Glass Works from this city to Anderson, Indiana, first mentioned in the *Intelligencer* last Monday, that a reporter yesterday called on President Scott and asked him for an authentic statement on the subject. Mr. Scott said the *Intelligencer's* original report was correct as far as it went.
"It is not a pleasure to myself or to any of the gentlemen associated with me," he added, "to contemplate, even, removal from Wheeling. Our associations here are extremely satisfactory, but this is purely a business matter. The stockholders appointed a committee of five of their own number, Mr. James Leasure, a practical and experienced glass man, Mr. Louis Stifel, the lawyer; Mr. Peter Cassel, Mr. W.M. Handlan and Capt. Rolf, who are to go there and look at the American works. Our manager, Mr. Louis Schaub, who has been there, will also go back with the committee. On their report when they return to Wheeling the question of removal will largely depend. The committee will leave for there next Monday night, as the *Intelligencer* said. If they report favorable a part of our factory will be removed there in the spring."
"How fully will you probably continue to run your works here after that?"
"Well, we will probably continue two furnaces on here until we can increase our capacity there."
"In the end will you remove there entirely?"

"That is the idea. But I wish you would correct a false notion. People seem to think we propose to remove the whole plant there. Of course we would take only the machinery and moulds. We will put the factory here in charge of day and night watchman. If the gas ever should give out we have our own coal field here, and could soon be in operation in Wheeling again."

"Do you expect the gas to give out?"

"No. We consider Anderson one of the best points in the gas field, and that is after looking over the whole gas region of Ohio and Indiana. There is a gas well on one corner of the lot, showing a pressure of over 275 pounds to the square inch, and new wells can be sunk there at a cost of $1,200 each, for you only have to go to the Trenton limestone, which is only 1,000 feet down.

"Some people say we will be fooled in the bonds. Why, there is no question of bonus in it. We are offered none, and ask none. But look at the Beauiles, at Tiffin, with the same capacity we have; their fuel costs them nothing, while ours costs us $24,000 for a ten months' run; that is $2,400 a month. Don't you see what that means?"

"Has Anderson good transportation facilities?"

"First rate. Instead of one railroad, as some people assert, she has two, and they are competing lines—the Pennsylvania and Vanderbilt systems. Another advantage is that Anderson is a town of 10,000 population, and we think we will be able to get plenty of boys there. That is a great consideration, as experience has shown."

February 4, 1891 from *CG&L:*

The committee from the Central Glass Co., who visited Anderson, Ind., mentioned in our last, have made no formal report since their return and it is generally believed that the matter will be allowed to rest, for a long time at least. Last Monday (19) saw everything going and a prosperous run is assured. Their No. 999 tableware is just out and is selling rapidly. They report a fine outlook for trade. Mr. Meder is off on a business trip west. Mr. Chas. B. Ott is looking after the wants of the southern buyers.

February 26, 1891 from *AP&GR:*

The Central Glass Works was one of the few in the Ohio Valley which did not suffer by the recent flood.

Advertisement March 19, 1891 from *Crockery and Glass Journal,* showing five pieces of etched glass ware

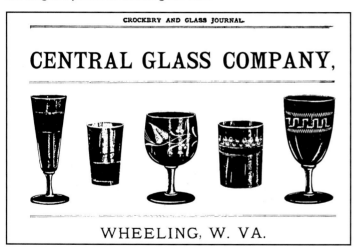

April 23, 1891 from *AP&GR:*

Two new lamps have been introduced by the Central Glass Co., one figured and one plain, with a catch top, and they will doubtless sell well. The Central is constantly adding new things. All of the workmen are at work but business is rather dull.

May 14, 1891 from *C&GJ:*

The Central Glass Co. move along with their usual activity, their great variety of goods being such as to prevent any general dullness, for when one line drops out of season another fills it place. They have an elegant line of lamps for this season, and are already taking orders for these, while in other lines trade is fair.

May 21, 1891 from *C&GJ:*

The Central Glass Company's new line of lamps struck the fancy of the dealers right from the start in such a way as to insure a good season on these goods, and already returns are coming in from the display last week. Trade with the Central is fair in all lines except tableware, which branch of the business seems a little dull all around; yet they are making good shipments right along. Their blown goods and stemware have taken a fine hold with the trade, and are certainly displacing some of the imported lines.

The following is a copy of a Central bill dated June 22, 1891 for payment of an invoice from June first and was signed by the treasurer, William Goering.

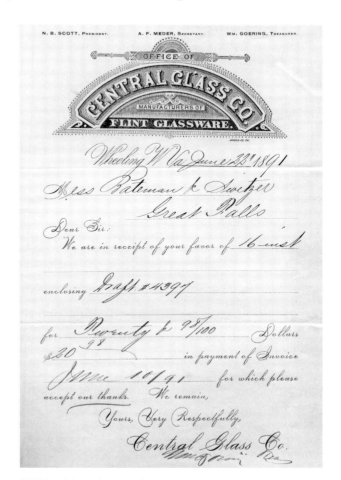

Bill Head Dated June 22, 1891

29

June 29, 1891 from *C&GJ:*

The Central Glass Co. will not go to Anderson, Ind., nor buy the plant of the American Glass Co., though this is not officially announced. That plant was bought in at the recent sale by Mr. Charles L. Henry, who is understood to be one of the creditors. The committee sent out from the Central has not yet made an official report, and just what will be done with the Anderson plant cannot be fully told just now. But it is a desirable plant, and will be operated by some company, perhaps this spring.

July 23, 1891 from *AP&GR:*

THE CENTRAL GLASS CO.

Opened its samples last Wednesday at room 130, in charge of Mr. Chas. B. Ott. The ware of this house has a reputation second to none in this country, and the samples of their light pressed goblets and general bar ware astonished European glass makers as far back as 1878, when it was exhibited at the Paris Exposition in charge of Mr. Charles Colne, and was highlycomplimented in the official report (see 1878 for this report). Their varied and full lines of pressed and blown bar goods and general tableware, stem ware, bar bottles, berry bowls, etc. are well known to the trade, and require no especial description. In all glass lamps with pressed figure feet and blown bowls and their new line of No. 1026 that hand, table and sewing lamps, and their stand lamp furnished with No. 1 or 2 collar, are among the strongest and solidest lamps shown this season.

1891 from *C&GJ:*

The Central Glass Co's. new lines of lamps, numbered 1026 and 1027 just out, and shown in the JOURNAL the past two weeks, are having a big sale. Mr. Albert Meder is in the West and Mr. Chas. S. Ott in the South, both taking flattering orders. General business with the Central is fair, and they are making some good shipments.

President N.B. Scott, of the Central Glass Co., in a talk with the editor of a local daily paper, gave the cause of the present dullness in the glass business and the consequent large stocks on hand at the factories hereabouts very pointedly in this wise: "There are now in existence in the United States enough glass factories to supply the entire annual demand of the country running three months in the year. In spite of this fact new factories are being erected every week in the boom towns. There are a great many glassworkers who think they know more about the glass business than anyone else. Such a man goes to the persons who are booming a town, represents himself to be a valuable and practical man, and proposes to build a glass factory. He values his services as manager at, say, $3,000 a year. Half of this amount he offers to work out in stock. He is asked how much money is required and replies that for $9,000 or $10,000 he can build a 15 pot furnace, which will employ a large number of men, and which can be operated profitably. In this way many towns are imposed upon, but after the factory is built an attempt is made to operate it. These men do not know anything about the business, and are attracted by the comparatively small outlay of money, the number of new families which will be brought to the town, and an erroneous idea that it is very profitable."

1891 from *C&GJ:*

The Central Glass Co. are having a fine trade on their elegant line of blown goods, some of which are taking a place heretofore occupied by imported goods, while their pressed ware lines are also in good request, and all the specialties they are handling are popular with the trade. They soon drop anything that doesn't strike the popular fancy and this is one of the secrets of their good trade.

1891 from *C&GJ:*

The beautiful display of blown goods by the Central Glass Co. strikes the fancy of the trade in a way that leaves no doubt of their appreciation of first-class ware, while at the same time it brings to the Central an enviable business. This, with the excellent trade they have on other goods makes up a volume of business that keeps that large establishment quite busy. Mr. Albert Meader, who will represent this company on the road this season, left last week for a tour.

CENTRAL GLASS JOINS U.S. GLASS COMPANY

The Central Glass Company became FACTORY "O" ("O" for Oesterling) of the United States Glass Company merging with seventeen other firms. It was taken into that corporation on July 1, 1891, however the final consummation was not until November 1891. The new owners operated the factory only a short time, as the Union men would not agree to an open shop, and the glassworks was closed down from 1893 to 1895.

August 26, 1891 from *CG&L,* "The Glass Trade:"

It is definitely decided that the Central Glass Co., of Wheeling, will join the United States Glass Co., just as soon as the necessary valuations are made and other arrangements completed.

September 2, 1891 from *CG&L,* "Wheeling:"

It is understood that the Central Glass Co., has at last become a part and parcel of the United States Glass Co. We cannot yet say by what letter this factory will be designated, but for a long time to come the people will speak of our two large glass factories as the Central and the Hobbs. Trade has been moderately active at the Central and the outlook is very promising.

September 9, 1891 from *CG&L,* "The Glass Trade:"

The Central Glass Co. of Wheeling, are now part of the consolidation (of the U.S. Glass Company).

September 16, 1891 from *CG&L,* "The Glass Trade," "Wheeling:"

The two large tableware houses in this city, the Hobbs and the Central, are now members of the United States Glass Co., and of necessity many changes will have to be made and new arrangements entered into to fit the new order of things. Some departments will be enlarged and others diminished and some changes in the lines of ware heretofore manufactured may be made. It is a little too soon to speak definitely about the matter. In the meantime both factories are at work as of old and making lots of glass. We shall be able to give you a better account of what is doing a little later.

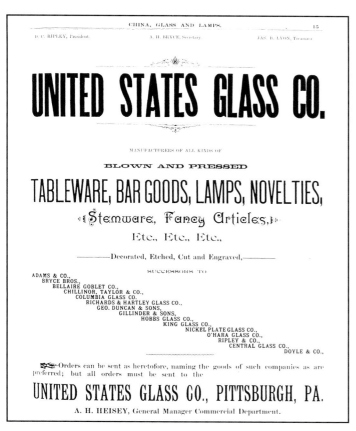

D. C. RIPLEY, President.   A. H. BRYCE, Secretary.   JAS. B. LYON, Treasurer.

UNITED STATES GLASS CO.

MANUFACTURERS OF ALL KINDS OF

BLOWN AND PRESSED

TABLEWARE, BAR GOODS, LAMPS, NOVELTIES,

Stemware, Fancy Articles,

Etc., Etc., Etc.,

————Decorated, Etched, Cut and Engraved,————

SUCCESSORS TO

ADAMS & CO.,
   BRYCE BROS.,
      BELLAIRE GOBLET CO.,
         CHILLINOR, TAYLOR & CO.,
            COLUMBIA GLASS CO.
               RICHARDS & HARTLEY GLASS CO.,
                  GEO. DUNCAN & SONS,
                     GILLINDER & SONS,
                        HOBBS GLASS CO.,
                          KING GLASS CO.,
                            NICKEL PLATE GLASS CO.,
                              O'HARA GLASS CO.,
                                RIPLEY & CO.,
                                  CENTRAL GLASS CO.,
                                     DOYLE & CO.,

Orders can be sent as heretofore, naming the goods of such companies as are preferred; but all orders must be sent to the

UNITED STATES GLASS CO., PITTSBURGH, PA.

A. H. HEISEY, General Manager Commercial Department.

Advertisement September 16, 1891 in *China, Glass and Lamps* for United States Glass Co. with Central Glass Company one of the last to join

The advertisement above from *Crockery, Glass and Lamps* dated September 16, 1891 shows Central Glass in the lower right hand corner as one of the last companies to join U.S. Glass Company at that time. Later the companies that joined U.S. Glass were listed alphabetically.

November 12, 1891 from *C&GJ*, "The Glass Factories," "Wheeling:"

During the past week several of the head officers of the United States Glass Co, were here arranging for the final consummation of the deal for the Central Glass Works. Its business has been controlled by the new company ever since the announcement, though the deal was not fully closed as to the plant until last week. The success of the United States Glass Co. may be guessed at fairly well when it is stated that from three to four per cent on the whole capital stock is saved in the matter of salaries of officers and representatives.

The Central has made some of the largest shipments for years during the past few days, and the good business keeps up in all the lines they handle.

December 17, 1891 from *C&GJ:*

Mr. N.B. Scott, the manager of factory O of the United States Glass Co., is too busy to talk about the trade and from appearances they are as busy as at any time this season. But the blown goods and stemware of this factory always go; the seasons for them never seems to end.

December 23, 1891, Wednesday, from *CG&L:*

There has been no dullness in the tableware trade with the factories "H" and "O" (at Wheeling, W. Va.) of the United States Glass Co., and their product has been demanded as fast as produced. For the particular time of the year business has been rather surprising, but as nearly all of their goods are suitable for Christmas gifts, this may in part account for the sales.

Note: "H" – Hobbs Glass Co. (originally Hobbs, Brockunier & Co.); "O" – Central Glass Co.

December 24, 1891 from *C&GJ*, "The Glass Factories," "Wheeling:"

The Central, or factory O, keeps up its usual appearance of lively trade, their blown goods and stemware seeming to be in especial demand for this season. During the past week they have made as good shipments as when the season was at its best. They have a number of new patterns for the trade not ready.

Ever since the organization of the United States Glass Co., some of the highest paid workmen, notably the mold-makers, have anticipated that some of them would be cut off, and their fears were will grounded. There will be just as many blowers, pressers, gatherers and other employees about each factory, but there will only be from one-half to two-thirds as many mold-makers. As an instance, the mold-shop will do for factory O and factory H in this city, whereas heretofore each had a mold shop of its own. This is one of the ways the company expects to accumulate profits. The same principle applies to agencies, and altogether it foots up a handsome per cent on the capital invested.

• 1892

January 6, 1892, Wednesday, from *CG&L:*

Factories "H" and "O", United States Glass Co., closed down just before the holidays, and will resume when orders are received to do so. Both of these factories have had a very large business, shipping more ware than at any season for several years.

January 20, 1892, Wednesday, from *CG&L:*

"….starting up of factories "H" and "O" of the United States Glass Co., (Wheeling, W. Va.)…."

February 3, 1892, Wednesday, from *CG&L:*

A meeting of representatives of pressed glass factories in the Ohio valley, and a few elsewhere, not included in the United States Glass Co., was held at the Windsor Hotel, Wheeling, on the afternoon of Monday, February 1. The object of the assemblage was to consider the question of the advisability of forming a consolidation similar to that of the above named company. About half a dozen firms were represented, but beyond a preliminary discussion of the matter, nothing specific was done. Another meeting has been called for February 16, when it is expected that a larger representation will be present and more definite conclusions arrived at. A committee was appointed to carry out the views of the meeting and correspond with those who are thought likely to join. It may be said, however, in regard to this project, that the list of probable partakers in the enterprise as published in a morning paper, is altogether imaginary. Some of the firms names are no longer in existence, and others are engaged in the manufacture of such diverse products, that their association would work them no benefit. The movement of capital at the present time is toward amalgamation, in order to economize production and distribution, and this has been to a certain extent forced by the low prices for manufactured goods that have prevailed.

Business has been fairly good at factories H and O, United States Glass Co. and Managers Scott and Waddell seem gratified with the way things are running under the new arrangement. (Waddell Mgr. of "H")

N.B. Scott, of the Central Glass Works, of the United States Glass Co., was registered at the Monongahela House (Pittsburgh, Pa.,) on Monday.

February 10, 1892 from *CG&L:*

Colonel N.B. Scott, of the Central Glass Works, of the United States Glass Co. addressed the assemblage (The National Ass'n of Jobbers in Crockery and Glassware, in convention at the Monongahela House, Pittsburgh, Pa., Feb. 3 and 4) as follows:

"Ten years in the history of America is a half century in Europe. Ten Years in the Northwest are in their results fully equal to half a century east of the Alleghanies.

"It is but a few years since England regarded the manufacturers of American as too insignificant for consideration, but today we are taking not only her markets from her but the markets of the world. We are now the greatest manufacturing country on earth. In 1880 we exceeded Great Britain six hundred and fifty million dollars. I think the Creator when He was making this world concluded to arrange it so we could manufacture for the entire world generations after all others had exhausted themselves. We have coal, gas and oil, raw materials of all kinds, iron ore in 23 states, any one capable of supplying the world's demands….Why we have 18 states, each as large as Spain, 31 each as large as Italy, and cut this vast country up into 60 states, either of them would be as large as England and Wales…."

February 17, 1892, Wednesday, from *CG&L:*

Both of the United States Glass Co.'s factories at this point (Wheeling), "H" and "O", are having a large output and are making large shipments. Everything is going along in a very smooth and regular style and the new order of things seems to be satisfactory to those interested.

Wheeling

The air has been full of rumors of a contemplated combination of all of the tableware houses in this district, not already in the United States Glass Co. The plan has many advocates and some opponents, but one thing is certain it will be thoroughly discussed and investigated before it is finally adopted or rejected. Should the scheme be carried out the headquarters would be in this city, with offices and sample rooms similar to those of the United States Glass Co. in Pittsburgh, and the plan of operations be the same.

• **1893**

March 29, 1893 from *CG&L:*

Wheeling – factories H and O of U.S. Glass Co. are fully engaged on orders and have more to do than every before this season.

July 05, 1893 from *CG&L:*

Factories H and O of U.S. Glass have just completed the busiest season they ever had and both were run to the fullest limits to the last day of the fire (at Hobbs).

July 19, 1893 from *CG&L:*

Orders are fairly plentiful at Factory O.

August 09, 1893 from *CG&L:*

On account of the business depression Factory O of the U.S. Glass Co. will not resume August 15. The mold makers are at work on two new lines.

August 16, 1893 from *CG&L:*

Factory O at Wheeling in operation.

August 16, 1893 from *CG&L:*

The United States Glass Co. have Factories K Pittsburgh, O at Wheeling, and R in Tiffin, Ohio, N in Fostoria, Ohio, and U in Gas City, Ind., in operation.

August 23, 1893 from *CG&L:*

The annual meeting of the U.S. Glass Co. was held at their general offices, 9th and Bingham Sts., S.S., Pittsburgh, on Aug. 16th. The following gentlemen were elected directors of the company for the ensuing year: D.C. Ripley, Wm. C. King, A.H. Heisey, Jas. B. Lyon, Jos Anderson, Jas. D. Wilson, David Challinor, Wm. A. Gorby, Geo. Beatty, Wm. F. Lloyd, C.B. McLean, Ralth Baggaley, and John C. Stevenson, all of Pittsburgh, and N.B. Scott and John H. Hobbs, of Wheeling. The new board met on August 22, and elected Ralph Baggaley president, after which they adjourned without further action.

October 11, 1893 from *CG&L,* "Wheeling:"

Only one furnace running at Factory O.

November 8, 1893 from *CG&L,* "Wheeling:"

Wheeling parties talk of purchasing the idle glass factories of the U.S. Glass Co. here and starting them up.

Col. N.B. Scott, the well known glass manufacturer, for many years president of the Central Glass Co., of Wheeling, and of late with the U.S. Glass Co., has severed his connection with the above named company and will, at an early date, start another factory and at the proper time will be in the market with a full line of goods. Mr. Scott's long years of experience and his knowledge of just what the trade desires, give him quite an advantage, and those who know the Colonel will not doubt nor question that he will have a line that will prove a credit to him. (*Scott had been Supt. Of Factory "O" while it had been in operation by the U.S. Glass Co. – but the firm had closed Factory "O" in October 1893.)

November 29, 1893 from *CG&L*, "Wheeling:"

A largely attended meeting of the citizens of Wheeling was held in the offices of the Chamber of Commerce on Nov. 20 to see what could be done toward purchasing Factories O and H, in this city, of the U.S. Glass Co. A letter from the company stated that O cost them $274,000, including $40,000 for good will, leaving $234,000, and H cost $178,300, including $13,000 for good will, leaving $165,300. Molds and etchings at the former cost $45,584 and molds at the latter $28,177, this to be deducted. The company offers to sell at 25 per cent off, leaving $244,154 for the two plants. Twenty-eight business men subscribed stock. It was decided to apply for a charter at once and buy or build new factories.

December 13, 1893 from CG&L, "Wheeling:"

The men who are at the head of the project to buy factories O and H, (Central and Hobbs) or build two new glass factories, mean business and there seems no doubt but what the scheme is a go. The best men in Wheeling have subscribed liberally and the stock will soon have been all taken. If the two factories mentioned are purchased they will be put into operation at once.

• 1894

September, 26, 1894 from CG&L, "Wheeling:"

Hon. N.B. Scott, Joseph Spiedel, and other Wheeling capitalists are trying to buy the Central Glass Works in Wheeling from the U.S. Glass Co. It is understood that they offered $75,000 which offer has been declined. If bought the works would be put in operation as soon as possible. Over 700 hands were employed at this works at one time.

• 1895

July 10, 1895 from *CG&L:*

Last week the U.S. Glass Co. refused $50,000 for factory "O" at Wheeling, parties of that city wanting to buy it and offering the above price.

October 23, 1895 from CG&L, "Wheeling:"

Wheeling parties have been trying to purchase the old Central glass works owned by the U.S. Glass Co. with the expectation of starting it about the first of the year. It is understood that the parties are offering $85,000 and the company refused to sell for less than $90,000. Nearly all of the molds and machinery have been moved away.

Factory bought from U.S. Glass December 31, 1895

The following is an excerpt from Louis Schaub's diary, one of the workers from Central Glass. He is the one who patented the method of forming hollow stems for glass articles (see November 05, 1890.) It is handwritten and was in possession of the author's grandmother. At the end she had added, "Louis Schaub died January 16, 1911 of Hearts Disease. Buried at Mt. Calvary Cemetary January 19, 1911."

Commenced to Work, the 3 day of September, 1866. I started to work in the Mold Shop, for $15.00 dollars a week. I took big Interst in my work, and after

I was 2 years in the Shop – I was forman of the Shop. I held the position for 14 years. In the year 1880 Mr. Oesterling asked me to take the Job as Manager of the Factory. Mr. Brody Covinson was day manager and Mr. Tom Leasure was Night manager. After considering it, I took the job. We had all 3 furnaces going. Mr. Oesterling died the 22 of October, 1883 In 52 year. The Central Glass Co. made a mistake in 1893. Mr. N.B. Scott recommented, to the Company to join the Trust its name was United States Glass Co.

We sold our Factory for 335,000 and our Good Will. – Not for cash money. We got our certificates. We thought it wouldn't take so many office people, not so many sample rooms, not so many traveling men, and all diferent other clerks and hamauch (how much) money they could save, for the stock holders.

We werent 6 months in the Company until, we saw our mistake. We had a strike for 18 months. We formed a new Company and made The arrangement to buy the old Factory back from the U.S. Glass Co. They asked $40,000 cash, 85 shares of Preferd Stock and $2,800 for the stem ware molds I had sent to Tiffen Ohio. And our stock holders only got a single stock certificate

I had 85 shares of Common Stock and I received 14 cents on the doller. I had 30 shares Prefered Stock. I paid 3000 dollars for them and I received 75 cents on the dollar. They promist to pay 8 per cent, on the prefered stock. We didn't get no divident, and no interest. I lost on that deal over $6,000 dollars. I went all around Wheeling had to make all kinds of promises, the old Company done well and I would work hard to get it in a good paying condition.

We bought the factory the 31 December 1895.

We payed cash	$40,000
85 Shares Prefered Stock	$5,950
Common Stock 200,000.00	$28,000
For Stem Ware Molds	$2,800
	$76,750

We commenced to work in February 1896, and had a hard time the U.S. Glass Co. took our best machines and moulds away and the first sets, John Beltz and all got made, were no good they did not pay for the price of the last iron. Some of the molds did not work at all. We had to depent only, on stemware and Punchtumblers.

The Central had a big fire the 8 day of October 1901. In the evening 6:40. I was setting at the supper table. The entire factory burned only the two ends of the factory was savet (saved). The factory was insured but in a lump for $75,000.00. It was hard to rebuild in winter. It costed the Company $61,000.00 as the factory stands, and only receivet $17,000.00 insurance. We started to work the 17 day of March, Saint Patrick day.

The Company paid in 1904 11 per cent divident. 1905, 11 per cent divident and in 1906, 12 per cent, and declared a stock divident of 50 per cent the 3 day of January 1907, and stock sells at present time at $140 for a share.

I took the job as Manager 1880 Up to the 1est (first) of January 1906 I retired in my 61 age. I still hold 135 shares, of stock, And I am, one of the Directors of the Company. My sonnelow [son-in-law] John Yeager Is at present time Secretary and Treasure. Mr. Albert Meder died in September 1906, he was secretary of the Company.

Worker's Diary detailing buying back the factory from the U.S. Glass Company

November 20, 1948 from *National Glass Budget.*

Note: This obituary for John Yeager in 1948 ties in the connection of the "Glass Worker's Diary", showing John Yeagers relationship to Louis Schaub:

JOHN YEAGER DEAD

John Yeager, retired official of the former Central Glass Company, Wheeling, W.Va., died November 3, 1948. He was born in Wheeling in 1865 and entered the employ of the Central Glass Company in 1879. From the "Wheeling Intelligencer" we read that the Central Glass Company sold their plant to the United States Glass Company in 1891. Four years later the plant was purchased from the United States Glass Company by W.B. Scott, Peter Castle, Louis Schaub and John Yeager, and incorporated under the name of Central Glass Works.

Mr. Yeager was elected treasurer of the concern, then later secretary-treasurer and general manager of the company which he successfully operated until his retirement in 1917. He was one of the widely known manufacturers in the glass industry at that time.

Surviving are his widow, Mary Louise Schaub Yeager; two sons, Louis J. and Clarence J. Yeager. Burial was made in Mt. Calvary Cemetery, Wheeling, W.Va.

CENTRAL GLASS WORKS

• 1896

1896 from U.S. Glass:

Factory "O" at Wheeling, W. Va. Was sold on Jan. 4, 1896 to a Wheeling Stock Co., which re-established the plant as the CENTRAL GLASS WORKS.

1896 from *Wheeling Glass* by Josephine Jefferson:

A new company was formed with a capital stock of $500,000. N.B. Scott, Peter Cassell, L.F. Stifel, and Joseph Speidel were the backers. The name they took was the Central Glass Works. It was difficult to reestablish business but by 1898 the factory was in full production.

January 8, 1896 from *CG&L:*

The Central Glass Co., Wheeling, W. Va., which has remained idle since passing into the control of the U.S. Glass Co., has been sold to a Wheeling stock company, headed by Col. N.B. Scott, president of the old Central Glass Co., the name the works was formerly known by. The transfer of the property was made last Saturday and the first payment made last Monday. The price paid for the works has been thus far carefully suppressed. Work is to be resumed at an early date, and as the factory has been kept in excellent repair, it is believed glass will be made within a month or six weeks. A popular movement has been started to secure favorable municipal legislation to supply the works with natural gas, and the last dollars worth of stock necessary was subscribed last Thursday. An effort is to be made to start a company to purchase and operate the old works of Hobbs, Brockunier & Co. (Hobbs Glass Co. when it was sold to the U.S. Glass Co.), and, as business men, merchants and investors generally seem to have realized that Wheeling and the Ohio valley has lost by and since the departure of their flint and window glass industry, it is probable that Wheeling will soon again be what she was of old, a center or fine art glass manufacture.

[Author's Note: These last two articles from 1896 show that William H. Cassell and Peter Cassell were still very much involved with Central Glass after it reformed.]

January 15, 1896 from *CG&L:*

The Wheeling parties who recently bought the Central Glass Works from the United States Glass Co. have applied for a charter and will organize and get down to business as soon as possible. Mold makers are already at work and the factory is being put in shape to resume. The new company is to get ALL OF THE OLD MOLDS and will manufacture about the same class of goods that were formerly made, such as tableware, bar goods and novelties. The management and force will be practically the same as it formerly was, about as follows: President, N.B. Scott; secretary, Albert F. Meder, late of A.H. Heisey & Co., Newark, Ohio; Charles B. Ott, traveling salesman; Will H. Cassell, chief shipping and bill clerk; John Yeger, Chief bookkeeper, succeeding Major Boering, who is with the German Bank; Louis Schaub, factory manager.

January 15, 1896, Wednesday, an advertisement in *CG&L:*
"Richards's Himself Again"

The old reliable Central Glass Works will resume the making of its former line of Bar Goods under the old management. Glass will be made January 27th, 1896. We will be glad to hear from all our friends, former patrons and the glass trade generally.

Central Glass Works,
Wheeling, W.Va.

Note: Another ad from the same issue ran almost the same thing except it said they have resumed the making of its former line of Fine Lead Blown Stemware, Etched and Engraved Blown and Pressed Tumblers, and a complete line of Bar Goods under the old management.

January 29, 1896 from *CG&L:*

Glassmaking was resumed at the Central Glass Works this week and everything is moving along satisfactorily. The management is much pleased with the start made. Only one furnace is in operation but the others will be started when the trade justifies it. Some handsome orders have already been received from old customers of the Central and others promise to remember the company. Several of the former customers have already written words of encouragement, saying that they will be glad to renew their relations. The outlook seems very bright. C.B. Ott, the traveling salesman, has started out with a full line of samples. At a meeting of the stockholders on Saturday these directors are elected: N.B. Scott, W.E. Goering, Louis F. Stifel, James Steadman, Joseph Sheidel, Peter Cassell and R.H. Hazlett.

February 12, 1896 from *C&GJ:*

Matters are beginning to move along at the old time gait at the Central Glass Works. This makes the third week the works has been in operation. The pay roll on last Saturday numbered 200 persons, which is a large force, considering that the works is just starting. Many of the old employees stepped into their former places, and with Hon. N.B. Scott as president and Albert Meder as secretary, everything is moving along like clock work. The product is about the same as it formerly was, consisting of tableware, bar goods, etc. and will surely please the trade. Quite a number of orders are being received from the old customers, some sending orders four weeks ago. C.B. Ott, the traveling salesman, is having a satisfactory trip.

September, 1906 from *Glass and Pottery World*

The following obituary for Albert Meder who died from "overwork" shows his devotion to Central Glass. He was also mentioned in the "Glass Worker's Diary" as well as other articles as he was the secretary of the company.

Albert F. Meder

Albert F. Meder, Secretary of the CENTRAL GLASS WORKS, Wheeling, W. Va., died last week, aged 45 years.

Overwork was the prime cause of the loss to the trade of this most capable, forceful, modest, kindly man.

Senator Scott, President of the company, virtually compelled Secretary Meder to take his first real vacation early this year. A trip to the Bermudas revived his strength for a time, but he had postponed rest too long, his zeal for work was too great, and his life was sacrificed through devotion to a business to which he had given thirty years of loyal service. Only on his prime when the spirit left for a better country.

After the Central Glass Works were sold to the United States Glass Co., Mr. Meder assumed for two or more years the secretaryship of the Ohio Valley China Co., then engaged in making or experimenting with the problem of producing fine translucent china. Subsequently he joined Senator Scott and his associates in buying back the old glass plant from the United States Glass Co. and became again the Secretary and active manager of its affairs. To regain the scattered trade and put the plant upon its present prosperous footing required tact, sound business judgment and executive ability. The whole glass trade knows how well the task was done and now also realizes that in the doing this conscientious, industrious, manager gave his life.

Albert Meder was always cordial and friendly, because he was essentially sincere and really felt a human interest in those brought into contact with him. Workmen, close business associates, competitors in the industry, the people of Wheeling, all knew him as just and generous, one whose motives were right and actions those of a high-minded gentleman, ever considerate in business and social life.

To the widow and children words at this time may count for little, but as the years pass those nearest and dearest can take some slight comfort in knowing that his memory is revered by very many who learned his rare worth and lovable qualities even in the prosaic walks of business.

The last obituary is for Peter Cassell, with text that pertain to his long term connection with the Central Glass Company. These were taken from two different articles in the author's grandmothers scrapbook. He was a resident of Wheeling since 1841 and was active in the management of other business and was a stockholder and on the board of directors of several Wheeling companies. Not only was he one of the founders of the Central Glass Company, but he was also one of the founders of the Nickel Plate Glass works at Fostoria, Ohio.

Death of Peter Cassell Shocks Whole Community

PETER CASSELL, one of the founders of the Central Glass Works, and father of Wm. H. Cassell, the present sales manager of that concern, died at his home in Wheeling, West Virginia, Monday, July 22. Mr. Cassell was eighty-two years of age and was a pioneer manufacturer in that city. He followed various lines of business in his early days and subsequently entered the glass trade as a presser, and after a service of seven years took charge of the press in the Barnes & Hobbs factory, where he continued to work until 1861. In that year, with others, Mr. Cassell organized the Central Glass Works, which in 1863 was made a stock company. Mr. Cassell was one of the heaviest stockholders in the company and although interested in many other business enterprises he turned his attention particularly to the Central Glass plant, maintaining an active interest up to the time of his death.

Another obituary added:

…he learned the trade of glass blowing, and after a service of several years he took charge of a press in the works of Barnes & Hobbs, where he was engaged at his trade until 1861. He was one of the original projectors of the Central Glass company, which was established in 1861 and made a stock company in 1863, and since then he has been a director.

In recent years, however, he retired from all active business connections, only retaining his membership on the board of directors of the Dollar Savings and Trust Company and the Central Glass Works.

DEATH OF PETER CASSELL SHOCKS WHOLE COMMUNITY

July 22, 1912.

AND CAME PEACEFULLY AT 8:50 O'CLOCK LAST NIGHT.

Was Pioneer Resident of Community and Prominent in Business Circles. Much Regret Expressed.

Peter Cassell, one of the pioneer residents of this city and one of its most prominent citizens, died at 8:50 o'clock last evening, at the Cassell home, No.

extent of it will never be known as he never talked of his charitable work and the secret died with him.

In the business world he was a prominent figure and everywhere his word was taken as quickly as his signature. He was always honest and straightforward in all his dealings and he was held in the highest esteem by the business element.

He was a devout member of the First Presbyterian church and was prominent

THE LATE PETER CASSELL.

76 Fourteenth street, after an illness with heart trouble and pneumonia. Mr. Cassell was 82 years of age and came to this city last fall from Atlantic City, where he had spent the greater part of the last six or seven years. For some time past he has been a sufferer from heart trouble and a short time ago suffered an acute attack of pneumonia, from which he never fully recovered. For several days past he had been confined to his bed and last evening asked to be placed in a chair so that the change of position would give him a rest. He sat in the chair for some time and finally requested to be put into bed and just as they were laying him down he gasped and expired. The end came peacefully and the members of his family were present at his bedside, including a niece, Mrs. William Haupt, of Oakland, Pa.

The news of his death spread quickly and it occasioned many expressions of regret throughout the city. He is survived by his widow, two sons and one daughter, all of whom have the sympathy of their many friends in their bereavement.

Interesting Career.

Mr. Cassell was born near Millvale, N. J., June 26, 1830, and was the son of Levi and Martha (Watson) Cassell, of German and English descent, respectively, and who settled in what is now Ohio county in 1837. They made their home in West Union, where the father, who was a blacksmith by trade, was engaged at the same until his death in 1840. He left a family of five children—Joseph, Peter, Nathaniel, Levi and Mary A., wife of John D. Jones. Peter Cassell, from his seventh year, was raised in Ohio county, and received a very limited education. At an early age he went upon the river as an employe on a passenger boat, in which occupation he was engaged three years. Subsequently he learned the trade of glass blowing, and after a service of seven years he took charge of a press in the works of Barnes & Hobbs, where he was engaged at his trade until 1861. He was one of the original projectors of the Central Glass company, which was established in 1861 and made a stock company in 1863, and since then he has been a director. He was also a stockholder in the Wheeling Steel and Iron company and the Carnegie Steel company, and is a stockholder and director in the Nickel Plate Glass works at Fostoria, Ohio.

Mr. Cassell has been a resident of Wheeling since 1841, and in his many years of residence here has gained the respect and esteem of the community. In 1862 he was married to Elizabeth J. daughter of John and Mary (Conley) Henderson, of Wheeling, by whom he had four children, three of whom survive him, in addition to his widow. They are William H., sales manager of the Central Glass works; Levi, of Atlantic City, and Virginia, wife of Frank H. Stamm, of this city, and Miss Elizabeth Stamm, a granddaughter.

Mr. Cassell was also one of the founders of the old North Wheeling pottery, the Neuralgine Company and the Dollar Savings and Trust Company, and for many years was active in the management of the business affairs of each. In recent years, however, he retired from all active business connections, only retaining his membership on the board of directors of the Dollar Savings and Trust Company and the Central Glass Works.

In addition to his many business interests, Mr. Cassell found time to look after charities and in his death many of the local institutions have lost an earnest and liberal supporter. One of his favorite charitable institutions was the City Hospital, but his contributions were not confined to this alone, but many others have received aid from his liberal hand. Being quiet and unostentatious, he did the most of his charitable work in a quiet way and the in the church councils. He was at all times earnest and sincere and in his death the community has lost a man whose place it will find hard to fill.

No arrangements for the funeral had been made last evening, but they will be announced to-day.

PETER CASSELL

PETER CASSELL, one of the founders of the Central Glass Works, and father of Wm. H. Cassell the present sales manager of that concern, died at his home in Wheeling, West Virginia, Monday, July 22. Mr. Cassell was eighty-two years of age and was a pioneer manufacturer in that city. He followed various lines of business in his early days and subsequently entered the glass trade as a presser, and after a service of seven years took charge of the press in the Barnes & Hobbs factory, where he continued to work until 1861. In that year, with others, Mr. Cassell organized the Central Glass Works, which in 1863 was made a stock company. Mr. Cassell was one of the heaviest stockholders in the company and although interested in many other business enterprises he turned his attention particularly to the Central Glass plant, maintaining an active interest up to the time of his death.

Peter Cassells Obituary July 22, 1912

PATTERNS

Central Glass Company numbered their patterns starting with number 1 to over 1000 before they joined the U.S. Glass Company. When a pattern was replaced by the company, because it may not have been a good seller or for whatever reason, the new pattern was given to the old number. An article in *Crockery and Glass Journal* from 1891 mentioned: "They soon drop anything that doesn't strike the popular fancy and this is one of the secrets of their good trade." In other words, if a pattern was not a good seller it was discontinued. A couple of patterns have the same number because they were drawn from several different catalogs of the 1870s and 1880s.

The names used in this book for the patterns are the same as Central used, if known. The colors used were crystal (for clear glass), amber, blue, and canary. The canary color is now referred to as vaseline glass. There are variations in some of the colors, like honey amber, and sometimes blue is called "electric blue" but the catalogs did not go into color variations. Etched meant acid etched, sometimes called satin or matte today.

They used Nappy or Nappies, being a term used by early glass factories for a bowl, round or oval, footed or without a foot, covered or without a cover to hold food. Instead of compotes they were called bowls. Central used high foot and low foot for compotes instead of high standard or low standard, the terms most commonly used today. Cake plates were called Salvers. Sugar sifter is the name Central used, but it is also called sugar shaker or sugar duster. A shober is a salt shaker. Molasses can was used instead of syrup.

Most of the patterns had high and low foot bowls in at least three sizes (the diameter), either covered or "open" without a cover. When added up this would make the total of twelve pieces and this is the reason why so many of the patterns have so many pieces.

Several of the stemware terms are no longer in use today as we no longer serve drinks in all the individual glasses. Not only did they make goblets in more than one size, they had wines (and later Rhine wines), sham wines with heavy bottoms, cordials, sherries, champagnes, and clarets. They used egg when referring to eggnog, although some of their "egg" pieces were probably egg cups.

Central was famous for bar ware and made several very large beer mugs. Among them were pattern No. 162 Milwaukee Standard holding 36 ounces, pattern No. 117 Good Templars Pony holding 38 ounces, pattern No. 135 Cincinnati Tea Cup holding 56 ounces, and the largest pattern No. 270 Rubicon holding 69 ounces.

Three Mugs, (left to right) No. 117 Good Templars; No. 35 Cincinnati Tea Cup; No. 270 Rubicon

Barware (left to right, top to bottom)
1. No. 456 Weiss Beer 16 oz.; No. 270 Rubicon Beer Mug 69 oz.; No number Punty (Pilsner) Beer; No. 481 Weiss Beer; No. 455 Centennial Ale; No. 481 Weiss Beer; No. 806 Weiss Beer 29-1/2 ounces
2. No. 745 Ringed Stem Ale; No. 415 Ale; No. 622 Ale; No. 532 Ale; No. 117 Good Templars Pony Beer Mug; No. 431 Ale; No. 649 Ale; No. 431 Pony Ale
3. No. 594 Beer Mug; No number, Knights of Labor Beer Mug; No. 427 Beer Mug; No. 773 Ale, No. 733 Etched Beer Mug; No. 113 Beer Mug 7 oz.; No. 444 Centennial Beer Mug 9 oz.
4. No. 521 Beer Mug; No. 686 Beer Mug 5 oz.; No. 444 Centennial Pony Beer Mug 5 oz.; No. 528 Beer Mug; No. 441 E Pluribus Unum Beer Mug; No. 338 Beer Mug 8-1/2 oz., med.; No. 336 Beer Mug 4-1/2 oz. Pony; No. 335 Beer Mug 3 oz. Toy

They had different size beer glasses named Weiss Beers and Pony Beers. Ales (which were usually footed) were sometimes called Schoppens and they were also made in a Pony Ale size. Many of their barware designs are still in use today.

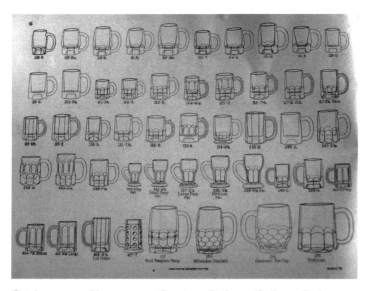

Catalog page of beer mugs. *Courtesy Bethany College, Bethany, WV*

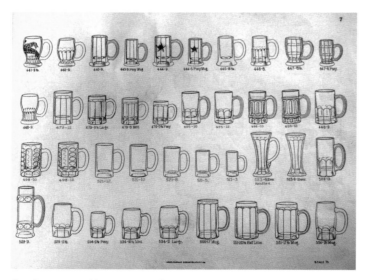

Catalog page of beer mugs. *Courtesy Bethany College, Bethany, WV*

Oil lamps are called either Stand Lamps or Hand Lamps. Finger lamp is the term used today instead of hand lamp. Peg is a type of oil lamp with a round shaped bowl that was "pegged" on marble or metal stands instead of glass. It had a "peg" on the bottom for fitting into the stand and it usually fit into the stand with a brass collar.

The catalog pages illustrated in this chapter are from The Museums of Oglebay Institute in Wheeling, West Virginia unless otherwise attributed.

The photography in this chapter with multiple pieces is credited to Dave Richardson, *The Glass Press*, Marietta, Ohio, unless otherwise noted.

The following gives a description of the patterns and shows either a catalog cutout for identification, a copy of an original catalog page, or a photograph. Sizes are given when known and would be in diameter for compotes, in ounces for tumblers and other drinking wares, and in height to emphasize a pattern.

Some of the last patterns that Central made before joining the U.S. Glass Company are identified in this text from a 1900 Central Glass Works catalog. This catalog used many of the same pattern numbers that were used in the late 1800s. Some of the novelty pattern numbers were replaced with lead blown ware. This catalog is very large as the illustrations show the exact sizes of the patterns. The first half (up to page 76) of this Central Glass Works catalog has the new pattern pages printed in blue ink, with the older Central Glass Company patterns printed in black ink (pages 77 through 120).

The descriptions given in this book are from the actual patterns or from catalog illustrations. Sometimes it is difficult to give an accurate description without seeing the pattern. Hopefully there are not any misrepresentations.

Price Guide

It is difficult to put a price guide in a book with such a multitude of patterns since prices fluctuate with the market. A lot of the pattern values are unknown.

If the patterns in this section do not have a number in brackets means that a price is unknown. Central made numerous tumblers, barware, and stemware and the majority of these patterns have never been located so it is impossible to put a price on them. Tumblers are either plain or fluted and were fairly common. They were made by Central as well as other companies and the styles haven't changed in over 100 years. Prices for tumblers would be under $25. Stemware came in various sizes holding different amounts and their price range is unknown. Ales and beer mugs come in a $25 to $50 range with the more decorative or unusual ones bringing more. Only the more important pieces will have a price code.

All the major patterns have a break down of prices when the pieces are known. Stand and hand lamps as well as novelties have a price code.

The price code is broken down into A, B, C, etc. order instead of using dollar amounts. The price range is below.

A– $10-25
B– $25-50
C– $50-75
D– $75-100
E– $100-135
F– $135-170
G– $170-200
H– $200-250
I– $250-300

The price for a pattern over $300 is marked "R " in brackets for rare. For colored pieces add: 20 percent for amber, 30 percent for blue, and 40 percent for canary (vaseline).

Cruet bottles are priced as sets. Some patterns have double letters for a price code (for example D & E) which means they are in the lower price range for smaller sizes and in the higher price range for larger pieces. On the stand and hand lamps the first price code letter indicates stand lamps and the second one is for hand lamps.

If there is an A, B, C, etc. letter in brackets at the end of the description it is a suggested price only. Colored pieces are always higher than the crystal ones and canary (vaseline) patterns bring the highest prices. If there is nothing in brackets at the end of the description means a price is unknown. If the piece is an ale or beer mug and there is nothing in brackets at the end of the description means they are in the "B" price range of 20 to 50 dollars. These prices are given on the availability of the patterns and can go either higher or lower. In ten years of looking the author has not found many of the pieces in the pattern sets.

The first 75 patterns were Tumblers of various sizes and shapes. The catalog page shows the first 62 patterns made by Central Glass. They are either plain or fluted the majority of them having heavy bottoms. Please note that there were three major patterns with different numbering than the pattern numbers usually used when referring to these patterns, they are, number 55 Oak Leaf, number 56 Rose, and number 60 Janus.

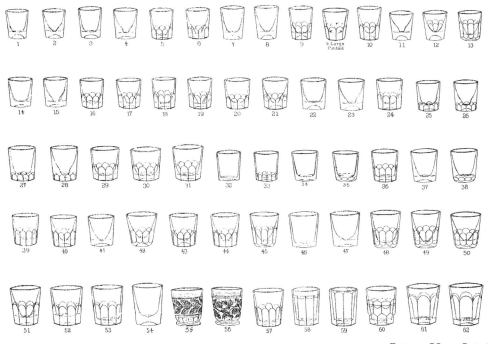

Pattern 1	3 ounce plain tumbler	
Pattern 2	2-1/2 ounce plain tumbler	
Pattern 3	plain 3-1/2 ounce tumbler	
Pattern 4	plain 3 ounce tumbler	
Pattern 5	fluted tumbler	
Pattern 6	fluted 3-1/2 ounce tumbler	
Pattern 7	plain 4 ounce tumbler	
Pattern 8	plain 3-1/2 ounce tumbler	
Pattern 9	fluted large 5 ounce and Puntied 4 ounce tumbler	
Pattern 10	fluted 3-1/2 ounce tumbler	
Pattern 11	plain 3 ounce tumbler	
Pattern 12	plain tumbler with inside flutes	
Pattern 13	fluted tumbler	
Pattern 14	There are two number 14 patterns, one 14 is a plain tumbler and the other is a 1-1/2 ounce fluted Cordial on a spool stem	
Pattern 15	plain 3-1/2 ounce tumbler	
Pattern 16	There are also two number 16 patterns, one 16 is a fluted 4 ounce tumbler and the other is a Carriage Candy Tray and Individual Salt	
Pattern 17	fluted 3-1/2 ounce tumbler	

Pattern 18	fluted 5-1/2 ounce tumbler
Pattern 19	fluted 4 ounce tumbler
Pattern 20	fluted 4-1/2 ounce tumbler
Pattern 21	fluted 4 ounce tumbler
Pattern 22	plain 5 ounce tumbler
Pattern 23	plain 4-1/2 ounce tumbler
Pattern 24	fluted 5-1/2 ounce tumbler
Pattern 25	fluted tumbler
Pattern 26	fluted tumbler
Pattern 27	fluted tumbler
Pattern 28	fluted tumbler
Pattern 29	fluted tumbler
Pattern 30	fluted 8 ounce tumbler
Pattern 31	8-1/2 ounce fluted tumbler
Pattern 32	plain 6-1/2 ounce tumbler
Pattern 33	6-1/2 ounce fluted tumbler
Pattern 34	plain tumbler
Pattern 35	tumbler with a horizontal thumbprint band on the bottom
Pattern 36	fluted tumbler
Pattern 37	plain tumbler
Pattern 38	with a horizontal thumbprint band on the bottom like pattern 35

Pattern 39	fluted tumbler
Pattern 40	fluted tumbler
Pattern 41	plain tumbler
Pattern 42	fluted 5 ounce tumbler
Pattern 43	fluted 6-1/2 ounce tumbler
Pattern 44	fluted 6 ounce tumbler
Pattern 45	fluted tumbler
Pattern 46	plain 8-1/2 ounce tumbler
Pattern 47	plain 8 ounce tumbler
Pattern 48	fluted 8 ounce tumbler
Pattern 49	fluted 7 ounce tumbler
Pattern 50	fluted 6 ounce tumbler
Pattern 51	fluted 8 ounce tumbler
Pattern 52	fluted tumblers
Pattern 53	fluted tumblers
Pattern 54	plain 9 ounce tumbler
Pattern 55	Oak Leaf 9 ounce tumbler
Pattern 56	Rose 9 ounce tumbler
Pattern 57	fluted tumbler
Pattern 58	tumbler with tall flutes
Pattern 59	Huber 8 ounce tumbler
Pattern 60	Janus tumbler
Pattern 61	fluted 9-1/2 ounce tumbler
Pattern 62	fluted 12 ounce tumbler.

There were duplicate numbers of 14 and 16. Whether these were added later to replace the original pattern or whether they were just given the same numbers in error is unknown. Since the first 200 patterns were made in the 1860s and a duplicate pattern is in color (which was from the 1880s) it is logical to assume it was a pattern replacement.

The Pattern 14 Tumbler is plain with a heavy bottom. It is illustrated in the tumbler catalog page (numbers 1-62) above. The other number 14 pattern is a Cordial. It holds 1-1/2 ounces and has a fluted bowl and is on a spool stem. If Central made more stemware like this cordial is not known, however, there are other stemware pieces produced at a later date very similar to this pattern.

There are two number 16 patterns which are quite different. One is a Tumbler and the other is a Carriage pattern and was probably an 1880s replacement for the tumbler since it was made in colors.

The Pattern 16 Tumbler holds 4 ounces and has a fluted bowl with heavy bottom. It is illustrated in the tumbler catalog page (numbers 1-62) on the previous page.

The other Pattern 16 is the Carriage Candy Tray and Individual Salt in the shape of an old fashioned horse drawn open Carriage. They were made in crystal and colors. Both pieces have an inverted diamond point pattern on the bottom. The candy is 7 inches long and 3-1/2 inches wide and the salt is slightly under 3 inches long and about 1-1/2 inches wide. The salt has been reproduced but the reproduction is larger than the Central pattern and has a notch to hold a cigarette. See Colored Novelties photo page 166 bottom row on left for Salt and on right for Candy Tray. Also see Salts and Miscellaneous Ware photo page 69 row three pattern number 4 for Salt. (Candy Tray R, Salt E)

Pattern 14, Cordial

Pattern 16, Candy Tray and salts in crystal, blue, and amber

Pattern 16, Carriage candy tray and salt

Patterns 63 through 75 are Tumblers.

Pattern 63	fluted 12 ounce tumbler	Pattern 70	plain 10 ounce tumbler
Pattern 64	fluted 10 ounce tumbler	Pattern 71	plain 11 ounce tumbler
Pattern 65	fluted 9-1/2 ounce tumbler	Pattern 72	plain 12-1/2 ounce tumbler
Pattern 66	fluted 10 ounce tumbler	Pattern 73	11 ounce plain tumbler with tapered top
Pattern 67	fluted 10 ounce tumbler		
Pattern 68	plain 11 ounce tumbler	Pattern 74	11 ounce plain tumbler with tapered top
Pattern 69	fluted 10 ounce tumbler (also came etched with Band 200)		
		Pattern 75	fluted 13-1/2 ounce tumbler.

Patterns 76 through 83 are Ales of various sizes and shapes with heavy bottoms. Many of these tumblers and ales were reissued by the U.S. Glass Company and were also made by other glass companies.

Pattern 76	fluted 5-1/2 ounce ale	Pattern 80	plain 9-1/2 ounce ale
Pattern 77	fluted 7-1/2 ounce ale	Pattern 81	fluted 8 ounce ale
Pattern 78	plain 7 ounce ale	Pattern 82	plain 6 ounce ale
Pattern 79	plain 8 ounce ale	Pattern 83	plain 8 ounce ale.

Pattern 84 is a Huber Handled Mug. It holds 6 ounces and has a wide foot.

Pattern 84, Huber Handled Mug

Pattern 86 consists of Weiss Beers. They are plain and cylindrical. The Weiss Beer holds 16 ounces and the Sham Weiss Beer with heavy bottom holds 14 ounces.

Pattern 86, Weiss Beer & Sham

Pattern 85 is an Ale. It holds 7 ounces and is cylindrical and has a horizontal oval band below the rim with elongated vertical notches around the middle. The bottom of the bowl is fluted and it has a wide ringed foot.

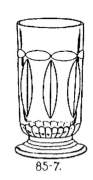

Pattern 85, Ale

Patterns 87 and 88 are unknown. Could they have been more Ales or Tumblers or a major pattern?

Patterns 89 through 104 are Handled Tumblers. The two most important ones are number 99 Oak Leaf and number 100 Rose. They have early pattern numbers not usually associated with the pattern.

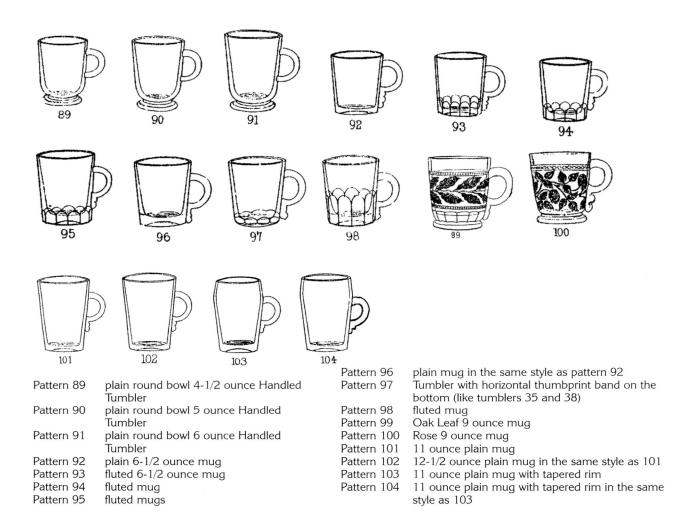

Pattern 89	plain round bowl 4-1/2 ounce Handled Tumbler	
Pattern 90	plain round bowl 5 ounce Handled Tumbler	
Pattern 91	plain round bowl 6 ounce Handled Tumbler	
Pattern 92	plain 6-1/2 ounce mug	
Pattern 93	fluted 6-1/2 ounce mug	
Pattern 94	fluted mug	
Pattern 95	fluted mugs	

Pattern 96   plain mug in the same style as pattern 92
Pattern 97   Tumbler with horizontal thumbprint band on the bottom (like tumblers 35 and 38)
Pattern 98   fluted mug
Pattern 99   Oak Leaf 9 ounce mug
Pattern 100   Rose 9 ounce mug
Pattern 101   11 ounce plain mug
Pattern 102   12-1/2 ounce plain mug in the same style as 101
Pattern 103   11 ounce plain mug with tapered rim
Pattern 104   11 ounce plain mug with tapered rim in the same style as 103

Number 105 is an Egg. It holds 4 ounces and has a round cup bowl with a handle and is footed. This is the first of several patterns called "Egg." and refers to eggnog instead of eggs.

Patterns 106 and 107 are unknown.

Patterns 108 through 134 are all Beer Mugs. There are several mugs of the same shape but each one holds different ounces ranging from 3-1/2 to 9-1/2 ounces. The most significant beer mug of this group is pattern 117, the Good Templars Pony, which holds 38 ounces, and is the Janus pattern. The name "Good Templars Pony" is engraved in the bottom of the mug. See the Barware photo page 39 for pattern 117 on the second row, number 5 and for pattern 113 on the third row, number 6.

Pattern 105, Egg

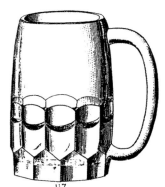

Pattern 117, Good Templars Pony

Good Templars Mug, Pattern 117, showing wording in the bottom of the mug

Numbers 108-134 Beer Mugs

108-6.
109-9½.
110-10.
111-8.
112-9½.
113-7
114-9.
115-10
116-8.
118-5.
119-9.
120-9½.
121-3½.
122-5.
123-8.
126-7½.
126 Block Handle. 8 oz.
124-4½.
125-8.
127 Block Handle
128-4½.
129-8.
117 Good Templars Pony.
127-10 old

**117 GOOD TEMPLARS PONY
32 oz**

130-5.
131-7½.
132-8.
133-9.
134-9½

Patterns 108 to 112 beer mugs are the same with tapered rims and fluted flat heavy bottoms

Pattern 108   6 ounces beer mug with tapered rim and fluted flat heavy bottom

Pattern 109   9-1/2 ounces beer mug with tapered rim and fluted flat heavy bottom

Pattern 110   10 ounces beer mug with tapered rim and fluted flat heavy bottom

Pattern 111   8 ounces beer mug with tapered rim and fluted flat heavy bottom

Pattern 112   9-1/2 ounces beer mug with tapered rim and fluted flat heavy bottom

Pattern 113   7 ounces mug with tapered rim and rounded bottom

Pattern 114   9 ounces mug with tapered rim and rounded bottom

Pattern 115   10 ounces mug with tapered rim and rounded bottom

Pattern 116   8 ounces mug with tapered rim and rounded bottom

Pattern 118   5 ounces plain cylindrical mug

Pattern 119   9 ounces plain cylindrical mug

Pattern 120   9-1/2 ounces plain cylindrical mug

Pattern 121   3-1/2 ounces cylindrical fluted mug

Pattern 122   5 ounces cylindrical fluted mug

Pattern 123   8 ounces cylindrical fluted mug

Pattern 124   4-1/2 ounces mug with double flute bands

Pattern 125   8 ounces mug with double flute bands

Pattern 126   two sizes of flutes, 7-1/2 ounces in one mug and 8 ounces in the other with a Block Handle.

Pattern 127   fluted mug with a 10 ounce "Old" mug with more flutes and the 9-1/2 ounce mug with Block Handle.

Pattern 128   4-1/2 ounces Huber mug

Pattern 129   8 ounces Huber mug

Pattern 130   fluted 5 ounce mug

Pattern 131   fluted 7-1/2 ounce mug

Pattern 132   fluted 8 ounce mug

Pattern 133   large thumbprint band 9 ounce mug

Pattern 134   9-1/2 ounce mug with fluted bowl on a rounded foot

There are two patterns for number 135. One is Stemware in a thumbprint pattern called "Argus" in the catalog from Island Mould. It has a round bowl with a double thumbprint band on paneled stem. It was made in four sizes, 11 ounce goblet, 6 ounce champagne, 3-1/2 ounce claret and 2 ounce wine. This was a popular pattern and made by other glass companies. (B & C)

The other pattern 135 has a very large Beer Mug called "Cincinnati Tea Cup". It holds 56 ounces and has a honeycomb pattern. (E)

135 Champ
6 oz.

135
Cincinnati Tea Cup.

Pattern 135, two different patterns with the same number. Left: Argus Stemware (Thumbprint); right: Cincinnati Tea Cup, 56 ounce beer mug, Honeycomb pattern.

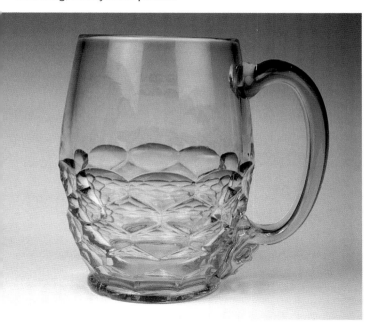

Pattern 135, Cincinnati Tea Cup. Holds 56 ounces.

Pattern 136 is a Honeycomb pattern. This pattern was called Cincinnati[1] by Central. This was a name used for overall honeycomb and was also used by other glass companies. Sometimes it is called Vernon. Central made several honeycomb patterns and gave them all different pattern numbers. Many of the glass factories made identical honeycomb patterns so it is quite difficult to attribute them. These stems came in a 10 ounce goblet, 5 ounce champagne, and a 2 ounce wine. (B)

Pattern 136, Honeycomb Stemware

136 Goblet.
10 oz.

Pattern 137 was named "Janus"[2] by Central, and is sometimes called Colonial or Inverted Thumbprint. This was Central's first line with complete tableware and had some 57 pieces[3] even though some of the patterns had different numbers. From a clear top the pattern has inverted thumbprints in panels tapering down toward the bottom of the piece. The stems were made in a 10 ounce large goblet, 5-1/2 ounce champagne, 4 ounce claret, 2-1/2 ounce wine, 1 ounce cordial, and a 5-1/2 ounce egg. Other Janus patterns included pattern 117 Good Templars Pony mug, 157 Celery, 158 Pickle, 160 a 7" low foot saucer, 161 a 8" low foot Saucer, 173 in a roll top bitter bottle for cork and a screw top for "Screw Tube," 175 Decanter, and 188 a master salt. These are included in the list below. Compotes were called "Bowls."[4]

Sugar (C)
Cream (C)
Spoon (C)
Butter (called Covered Nappie) it had a drainer with notched rim (D)
Celery (No. 157) (D)
Bitter Bottle (No. 173) (D)
Decanter (No. 175) (E)
Pickle (No. 158) (C)
Salt (master) footed (No. 188) (B)
Nappies (round) in 4, 5, 6 and 7 inches (B)
Saucer (No. 160) 7 inch low foot small saucer (B)
Saucer (No. 161) 8 inch low foot large saucer (B)
Ovals in 7, 8 and 9 inches (B)
Bowls (shallow bowls) in 7 and 8 inch high foot and low foot open or covered (C)
Bowls in 6, 7, 8 and 9 inch high foot deep bowls open or covered (C)
Bowls in 7, 8 and 9 inch low foot bowls open or covered (C)
Bowls in 9 and 10 inch shallow open bowl (D)
Salvers (cake plates) in 9, 10, 11 and 12 inches (D)
Stemware in 6 sizes (B & C)
Tumbler footed (B)
Good Templar Pony Mug (No. 117) (E)
Pitcher (E)

137
Goblet, large.
10 oz.

Pattern 137, Janus

47

Pattern 137, Janus (left to right, top to bottom)
1. Bowls 7" HF Covered, 7" HF Open, Celery, Decanter No. 175
2. Goblet, Master Salt, Egg., Footed Tumbler, Spoon, Wine, Cordial
3. Nappy 7" HF Shallow Bowl, 8" LF Saucer No. 161, 7" LF Saucer No. 160
4. Salver 10", Good Templars Pony Mug No. 117

Pattern 137, Janus bowls from Island
Mold catalog.

| JANUS BOWLS. | 6 inch H. F. covd. | 7 inch L. F. cov'd. | 8 inch L. F. covd. | 9 inch L. F. covd. |

Patterns 138 and 139 are Huber Stemware. As many glass companies produced these they are difficult to attribute. Examples are in this catalog page.

Catalog page of stemware showing Huber and other stemware. *Courtesy Bethany College, Bethany, WV*

Pattern 138 has a round bowl with straight paneled stem in 5 sizes. It was made in a 9-1/2 ounce large goblet, 6 ounce champagne, 4 ounce claret, 4 ounce egg., and 2-1/2 ounce wine. (B & C)

Pattern 139 is Huber Stemware. The round bowl has a joined paneled stem and came in a 10 ounce goblet, 6 ounce champagne, 4 ounce claret, 2-1/2 ounce wine and 3/4 ounce cordial. (B & C)

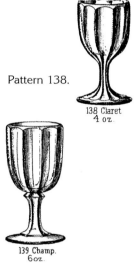

Pattern 138.

138 Claret
4 oz.

139 Champ.
6 oz.

Pattern 139, Huber Stemware

Pattern 140 was called "Rose" by Central but since it is commonly called Cabbage Rose we will keep that name, but for the book Rose will be used.

Rose was a patented pattern and very popular. It was one of Central's earliest patterns and continued being produced by them up until they joined the U.S. Glass Company. It is made up of cabbage roses, stems and leaves going around the pieces, and has a rose bud finial. The majority of the pieces have a small bead band below the rim. The pattern had some 57 pieces.

The goblets have been reproduced.
Sugar (D)
Cream (D)
Spoon (D)
Butter 6 inch flat bottom (called Covered Nappie) (E)
Celery (E)
Bitter bottle (E)
Ovals in 7, 8, and 9 inches (D)
Nappies (round) in 4, 5, 6 and 7 inches (D)
Nappie 7 inch without feet covered (D)
Nappies in 6, 7, and 8 inch shallow bowls HF & LF open or covered (E)

Bowls in 8, 9, and 10 inch shallow bowls high and low foot open or covered (G)
Bowls in 7, 8 and 9 inch deep bowl high and low foot open or covered (G)
Salt (master) (C)
Stemware in 8 oz. goblet, 4-1/2 oz. champagne, 4-1/2 oz. egg, and 2-1/2 oz. wine (C)
Tumbler 9 ounces (Table Tumbler No. 56, Handled Tumbler No. 100) (C)
Pitchers in 3 pint and quart sizes (F)
Salvers in 10, 11 and 12 inches (G)

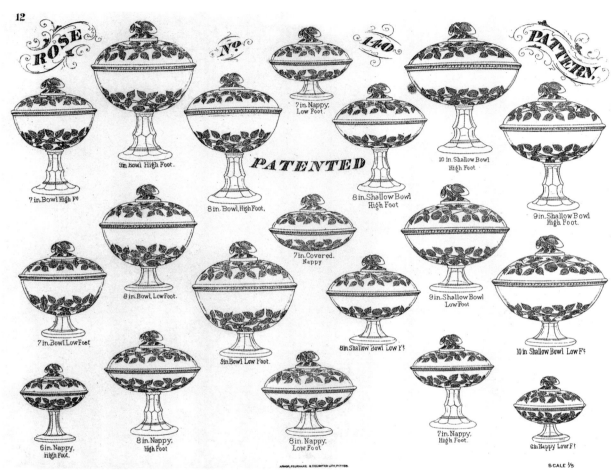

Catalog page with Rose, Pattern 140, bowls

Pattern 140, Rose

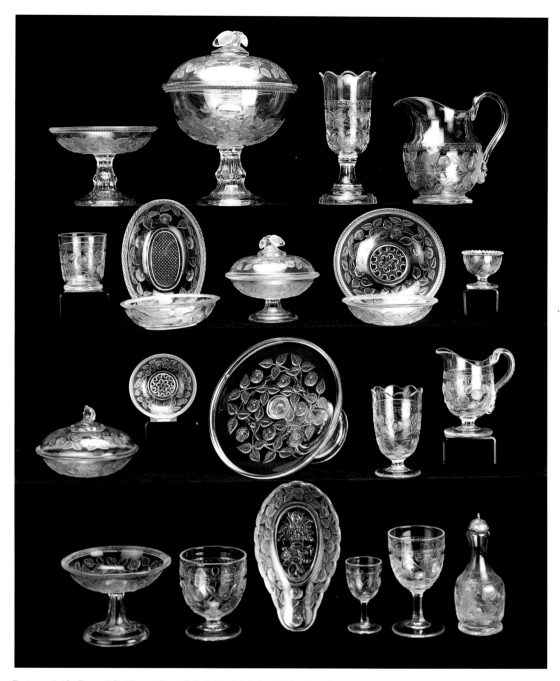

Pattern 140, Rose "Cabbage Rose" (left to right, top to bottom)
1. Comport HF Shallow Bowl Open, Bowl 9" HF Covered, Celery, Pitcher 3 pt.
2. Tumbler No. 56, Ovals 7" & 8", Nappy 6" LF Cov'd., Nappy Round 6" & 4", Master Salt
3. Butter, Nappy 4" Round, Salver 10", Spoon, Cream
4. Nappy 7" Straight Stem, Egg., Pickle, Wine, Goblet, Bitter Bottle

JOHN OESTERLING, OF WHEELING, WEST VIRGINIA.

Design No. 4,263, dated July 26. 1870.

DESIGN FOR GLASS-WARE.

The Schedule referred to in these Letters Patent and making part of the same

To all whom it may concern :

Be it known that I, JOHN OESTERLING, of Wheeling, in the county of Ohio and State of West Virginia, have invented a new and original Design for Pressed Glass-Ware; and I do hereby declare that the following is a full, clear, and exact description thereof, which will enable others skilled in the art to make and use the same, reference being had to the accompanying drawing forming part of this specification.

The nature of my design is fully represented in the accompanying drawing, to which reference is made, the said design being a continuous rose-wreath for pressed glass-ware.

Having thus described my invention,
I claim as new and desire to secure by Letters Patent—

The design for pressed glass-ware, as shown.

JOHN OESTERLING.

Witnesses:
A. P. HALL.
Wᵐ H. BRINTON.

Patent No. 4,263 Design For Glass-Ware for Rose Pattern 140.
Designed by John Oesterling, July 26, 1870

4263   *Design*   PATENTED JUL 26 1870

John Oesterling. Pressed Glass Ware.

Witnesses:

Inventor:
John Oesterling
PER

Attorneys.

Patent showing design for Rose Pattern 140

Pattern 141 was named "Royal"[5] by Central. It is a honeycomb band pattern and came in a complete line of table ware. This is an early 1860s pattern and would not have been known except for the catalog from Island Mould; the Central catalogs had the pattern illustrated with only a small and large goblet. The pattern had at least 40 pieces and did not show a celery or a pitcher. The honeycomb band is around the middle of the pieces and the rim of the bowls has a thin horizontal diamond band (several of Central's early bowls had this diamond band rim). The bottom of the bowls have round flutes that look like

flower petals. The finial is oval in the shape of an acorn with a tiny stem. It has indented octagon panels with three leaves on the round bottom of the finial. The stem and feet are the same as on 137 Janus, and 140 Rose bowls.

Sugar (D)
Cream (C)
Spoon (C)
Butter 6 inch flat bottom (called Covered Nappie) (D)
Ovals were 7, 8 and 9 inches (C)
Nappies (round) in 4, 5, 6 and 7 inches (C)
Nappies in 6 and 7 inch covered without feet (C)
Nappy 7 inch low foot covered and open (C)
Bowls (shallow) in 6, 7 and 8 inch high foot covered or open (D & C)
Bowls (deep) in 7 and 8 inch low foot covered or open (E & D)
Bowls (deep) in 6, 7 and 8 inch high foot covered or open (E)
Stemware (B)
Tumbler footed (B)
Salvers in 9, 10, 11, and 12 inches (E)

141 -2½OZ.

Pattern 141, Royal
(stemware only
shown)

Pattern 141, Royal
covered bowl

ROYAL BOWLS.   8 inch L. F.   7 inch L. F.   8 inch H. F.   6 inch H. F.

Royal Bowls

ROYAL SET.   Sugar.   Cream.   Spoon.   6 in. Nappie & Cov.

Royal Set

52

Royal, Honeycomb, and O'Hara Patterns (left to right, top to bottom)
1. Royal No. 141 Spoon and Cream, Honeycomb No. 146 Cream, Honeycomb No. 153 Pitcher 3 pint
2. Royal No. 141 Open Bowls, 7" HF Shallow Bowl, 8" HF & 8" LF Deep Bowls
3. O'Hara No. 145 Goblet, Spoon, Pitcher, Cream

Pattern 142 is a Huber Cordial. It holds 1 ounce and has a paneled stem.

14.2 Cordial.
1oz.

Pattern 142,
Huber Cordial

Pattern 143 is unknown. Could this have been the Cord and Tassel pattern or a pattern from the Island Mould catalog called "Central"?

The next two patterns do not have numbers.

"Central" pattern is illustrated in the Island Mould catalog with only two bowls showing. It does not have a pattern number. The bowls are plain and may have a honeycomb pattern in the bottom but it is unclear. They join above the stem with a pointed band. Both bowls are 9 inches, high footed, with deep bowls. One is open with a plain rim and the other is covered and has the diamond band rim. The finial comes to a point and is six- or eight-sided with an indentation in each side. The stems and feet are the same as patterns 137 Janus, 140 Rose, and 141 Royal. It is not known whether this was a complete line of table ware.

Cord and Tassel does not have a pattern number and it was not in the Central catalog from Island Mold. It was patented in 1872 by Andrew Baggs, one of the founders of Cen-

tral Glass. Mr. Baggs left Central in 1872 to start his own company (LaBelle Glass) and whether he took the pattern with him or the pattern was made before he left Central is unclear. Cord and Tassel has been attributed to Central in the 1870s but I think they made it earlier as it is similar to the 1860 patterns. It came in a complete line of tableware including stand and hand lamps. How many pieces were made is not known, but it would probably number in the fifties with open and covered bowls and all the high foot and low foot bowls. Some of the patterns have different designs as the foot can be plain or have a cable design and the bottoms of the ovals have a Cord and Tassel design and others have 4 oval rings. The pattern has a scalloped cord band with hanging tassels with a thin cord band above and below it. The stems and feet are like the previous patterns. The finial is an open triangle.

Sugar (D)
Cream (D)
Spoon (D)
Butter 6 inch covered with flat bottom (E)
Butter Oval covered with low foot (E)
Celery (D)
Ovals (with different designs in the bottom) (C)
Nappies (C)
Bowls high foot and low foot, shallow and deep bowls (E & F)
Bitter Bottle (D)
Molasses Can (E)
Salt (C)
Pitcher half gallon (F)
Stemware in goblet, egg., wine and cordial (C & D)
Tumbler with and without handle (C)
Salvers (F)
Stand and Hand Lamps (Stand F, Hand E)
Stand and Hand Lamps (hand lamps with no foot or footed)

CENTRAL BOWLS.   9 inch H. F.   9 inch H. F. Cov'd.

Island Mold catalog page showing Central Bowls

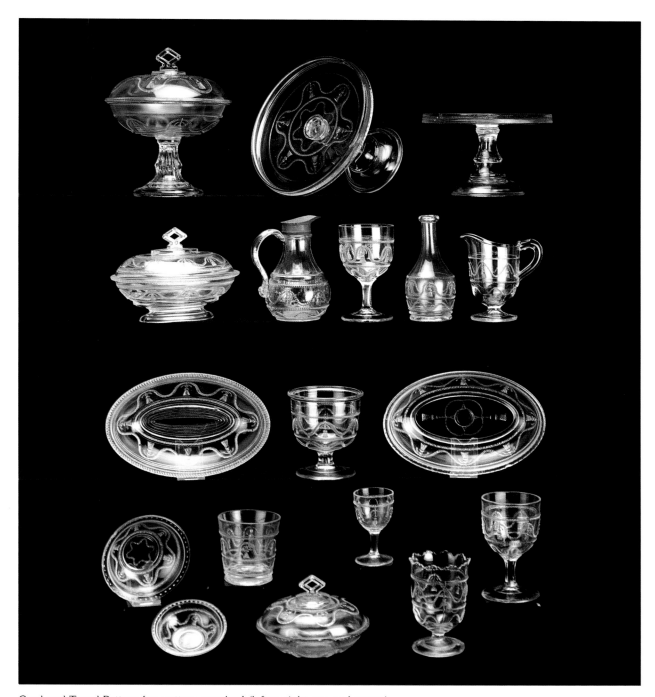

Cord and Tassel Pattern [no pattern number] (left to right, top to bottom)
1. Bowl 8" HF Covered, Salver 10" showing pattern, Salver
   9-1/4"
2. Oval Butter, Molasses Can, Goblet, Bitter Bottle, Cream
3. Oval Bowl 9", Sugar (missing cover), Oval Bowl 9" (note different bottoms)
4. Nappy 5", Nappy 4", Tumbler, Butter 6", Wine, Spoon, Goblet

Patent No. 6,002 for Design For Ornamentation of Glass-Ware for Cord and Tassel Pattern, designed by Andrew H. Baggs, July 23, 1872.

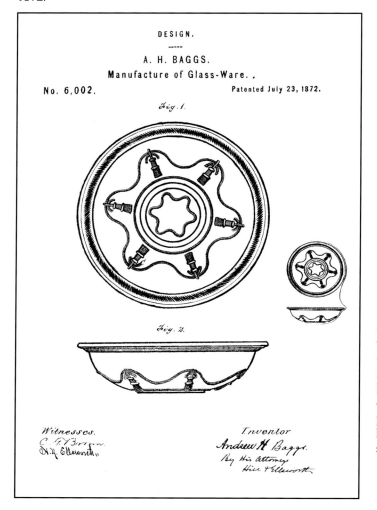

Patent showing design of Cord and Tassel Pattern

Pattern 144 consists of the "Oak Leaf" Goblets. Oak Leaf[6] is the name Central gave the pattern but it is usually referred to as Oak Wreath as there were several oak leaf patterns made by other glass companies. The Oak Leaf tumbler had an early pattern number of 55 and the handled tumbler was number 99. This pattern number is only for a small and large goblet and other sizes were not illustrated. The pattern number associated with Oak Leaf is number 152; see that number for price suggestion.

Pattern 144, Oak Leaf Goblets

Pattern 145 is called "O'Hara" by Central[7] which is a loop pattern commonly called Petal and Loop or Loop and Petal. This is a difficult pattern to attribute as several other glass companies also produced it. The pattern came in stemware in a 10 ounce goblet; 9 ounce small goblet, 5 ounce champagne, 3-1/2 ounce claret, and a 2 ounce wine. This probably was a complete table service but I do not have catalog pages to back it up. See Royal, Honeycomb, and O'Hara patterns photograph on page 53 on the bottom row for the goblet, spoon, pitcher, and cream. (B)

Pattern 145, O'Hara Stemware

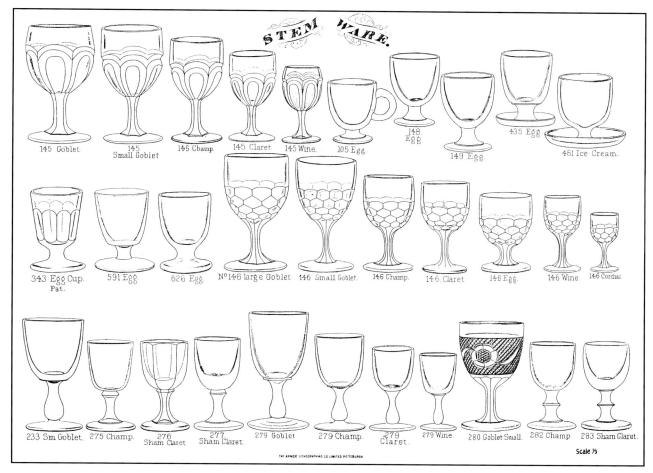

Catalog page of Stem Ware with O'Hara Pattern No. 145 and other early Stem Ware

Pattern 146 is a Honeycomb pattern named "New York" by Central[8]. In the New York Honeycomb pattern the upper third of the bowl is plain above the honeycomb pattern. Honeycomb was produced by the majority of early glass companies thus it is very difficult to identify which company produced a piece. It also came in many variations in the placement of the honeycomb. The stemware came in a 9-1/2 ounce large goblet, 9 ounce small goblet, 5-1/2 ounce champagne, 5 ounce egg, 3-1/2 ounce caret, 2-1/2 ounce wine, and 1 ounce Cordial. See Royal, Honeycomb, and O'Hara patterns photo page 53 top row number 3 for cream pitcher. (B)

146 Small Goblet.

Pattern 146,
Honeycomb

Pattern 147 is a Goblet. The pattern may be referred to as Paneled Diamonds and Flower. It holds 10 ounces and has a design around the bowl of a stemmed flower with two leaves inside an oval panel next to two diamond point diamonds inside an oval panel with a ribbed scalloped band above and below the oval panels. It is on a paneled stem. The flower looks like the rose in Pattern 140's Rose. This is a large goblet and it is unknown if there are other sizes. See Pitchers, Molasses Cans, and Misc. photo on page 65 third row, second pattern. (C)

147
Goblet.

Pattern 147,
Goblet

Patterns 148 and 149, Eggs

Patterns 148 and 149 are Eggs. They are plain with round footed bowls and are identical except for size. Number 148 holds 4 ounces.

Pattern 150 is called "150 Ware" and does not have a name. It is a heavy plain pattern with hollow stem salvers. This hollow stem design was used in many other patterns. The stems are joined to the bowls or salvers then come out in an hourglass shape above a narrow ring followed by another longer hourglass shape above a narrow ring with a shorter hourglass shape above a narrow ring on top of the foot. They have wide plain bowls and cover. The finial has a round knob that is slightly pointed at the top. Pattern 350 has the same shaped bowls and hollow stems; the main difference is that the bowls are engraved and the finial is flat on the top.

Sugar (C)
Cream (C)
Spoon (B)
Butter (C)
Nappies (round) 3-1/2, 4, and 6 inch (B)
Nappy 6 inch covered low foot with shallow wide bowl (C)
Bowls in 6, 7, and 8 inch high foot covered bowl (D)
Bowls in 7 and 8 inch low foot covered bowls (D)
Hollow Stem Salvers in 8, 9, 10, 11, 12, and 14 inches (G)

8 in.150 Hollow Stem Salver.

Pattern 150, Heavy Plain Salver

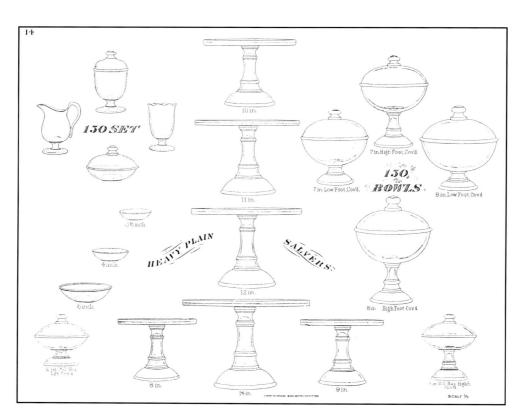

Catalog page of No. 150 ware with Heavy Plain Salvers

Plain Ware Patterns No. 150 and No. 350 (left to right, top to bottom)
1. No. 150 Bowls 8 inch LF, 9 inch HF, 7 inch HF
2. No. 350 Salvers Patented 9 inch, 10 inch
3. No. 150 Heavy Plain Salvers 10 inch

Pattern 151 is missing.

Pattern 152 is a "Oak Leaf" 3-pint Water Pitcher. This is the number I use when referring to this pattern as Central gave different pattern numbers to six different pieces of this pattern. Oak Leaf is also called Oak Wreath or Oak Leaf Band. The pattern has a clear top then a very thin band of beads above two rows of oak leaves going around the pattern to the right. The finial is an acorn with a half acorn on top of a leaf. There are some 57 pieces in the Oak Leaf pattern including Pattern 55 tumbler; Pattern 99 handled tumbler; Pattern 144 goblets; Pattern 156 celery; Pattern 181 oval individual salt; and Pattern 191 footed master salt. These are in the list below.

Sugar (D)

Cream (D)

Spoon (C)

Butter 6 inch flat bottom (called a Covered Nappy) (D)

Celery (No. 156) (D)

Ovals in 7, 8, and 9 inch (C)

Nappies (round) in 4, 5, 6, and 7 inch (no foot) (C)

Nappies in 6 and 7 inch covered (no foot) (C)

Nappies in 6 and 7 inch high and low foot covered or open (D)

Bowls (deep bowls) in 7, 8, and 9 inch high foot covered or open (F)

Bowls (deep bowls) in 8, 9, and 10 inch low foot covered or open (F)

Bowls (shallow bowls) in 8, 9, and 10 inch, high and low foot, covered or open (F)

Salt (No. 191 footed master salt and No. 181 individual oval salt) (C)

Stemware with large and small goblets (No. 144) (C)

Tumblers 9 ounces (No. 55 Tumbler and No. 99 Handled Tumbler) (C)

Pitcher (F)

Salvers in 9, 10, 11, and 12 inch (G)

Pattern 152, Oak Leaf pitcher

152 3 Pint

OAK LEAF BOWLS.   10 in. L. F.   9 in. L. F.   8 in. L. F.
Cov'd.   Cov'd.   Cov'd.

Pattern 152, Oak Leaf Bowls, page 93 Island Mold Catalog

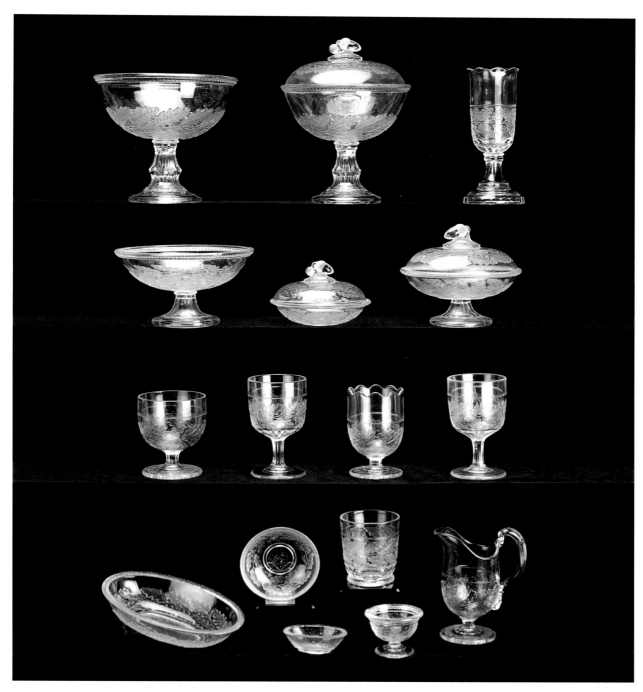

Pattern 152, Oak Leaf (left to right, top to bottom)
1. Bowl 9" HF Deep Bowl Open, 8" HF Deep Bowl Cov'd, Celery No. 156
2. Bowl 8" LF Shallow Bowl Open, Butter, Bowl 7" LF Shallow Bowl Open
3. Egg., Goblet No. 144, Spoon, Goblet No. 144
4. Oval, Nappy, Salt Oval No. 181, Tumbler No. 55, Master Salt No. 191, Cream

Pattern 153 is a Pitcher in a Honeycomb pattern. It holds three pints. See Royal, Honeycomb, and O'Hara patterns photo on page 53 on the top row pattern number four. (E)

Pattern 153, Honeycomb Pitcher

Patterns 154 and 155 are Pitchers. They are plain and have a slightly bulbous shape and applied handles. They are the same except number 154 holds a quart and 155 holds a half gallon. They can be "cut" (engraved). See Pitchers, Molasses Cans and Misc. photo page 65 top row on the right. (D)

Pattern 154, Plain Pitcher, Quart; Pattern 155, Plain Pitcher, half-gallon

Pattern 156 is the "Oak Leaf" Celery. The price suggestion is in with pattern 152.

Pattern 156, Oak Leaf Celery

Patterns 157, 158, 160, and 161 are Janus patterns. Pattern 157 is a Janus Celery. Pattern 158 is a Janus Pickle and is oval with one end longer. The bottom has an oval design of a figure eight with diamond points inside it with lines on the outside. The long end has a notched oval. Pattern 160 is the Janus low foot Saucer with shallow bowl and scalloped rim on a short round knop stem, 7 inches in diameter. Pattern 161 is the Janus low foot Saucer with shallow bowl and scalloped rim on a short round knop stem, 8 inches in diameter. See Janus Pattern 137 photograph on page 48. Price suggestions are under pattern 137.

Pattern 157, Janus Celery

Pattern 158, Janus Pickle

Pattern 160, Janus Saucer

Pattern 161, Janus Saucer

Janus Celery.   Janus   Huber   Janus   Janus
   Decanter.   Bitter.   Bitter.   Pickle.

Janus patterns from Island Mold catalog with a Huber bitter bottle

Pattern 159 in unknown.

Pattern 162 is the "Milwaukee Standard" Beer Mug in a honeycomb pattern. It holds 36 ounces. Do not confuse this mug with pattern 135 Cincinnati Tea Cup which holds 56 ounces. (E)

Pattern 162, Milwaukee Standard Beer Mug

Pattern 163 is a Butter in the Ripple pattern. It has a ripple design on the bowl and cover. The rim is flanged and the finial is pointed and looks similar to an arrow. It was on a catalog page with other butters including a flanged pattern 234 Wheat In Shield, and is similar in shape and size to it. Whether there are more pieces in this pattern is unknown. This was a popular pattern and made by other glass companies.

Pattern 163, Ripple Covered Butter

Catalog Page of Pitchers and Molasses Cans

Pattern 164 is missing.

The next five patterns are Molasses Cans[9]. Their names were found in the catalog from Island Mould. They are all around 6-1/2 inches tall and have hollow applied handles. Sometimes they will have a metal lid without the spout.

Pattern 165 is called "Delta" and has flutes in the middle and bottom. See Pitchers, Molasses Cans and Miscellaneous photograph on page 65 the first pattern in the second row. (F)

Pattern 165, Delta Molasses Can

Pattern 166 is called "Texas" it has a fluted neck and plain bulbous bottom. See Pitchers, Molasses Cans and Miscellaneous photograph on page 65 the second pattern in the second row. (F)

Pattern 166, Texas Molasses Can

Pattern 167 is called "Venus" and has a fluted neck like the Texas pattern but with a honeycomb bottom. See Pitchers, Molasses Cans and Miscellaneous photograph on page 65 the third pattern in the second row. (F)

Pattern 167, Venus Molasses Can

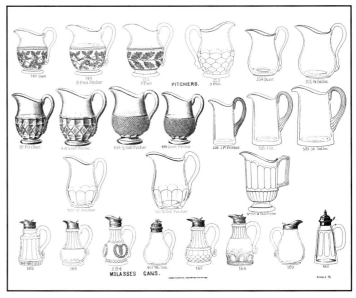

Pattern 168 is called "Central" and has a fluted neck then plain bowl with an arch band over cable band foot. (F)

Pattern 168, Central Molasses Can

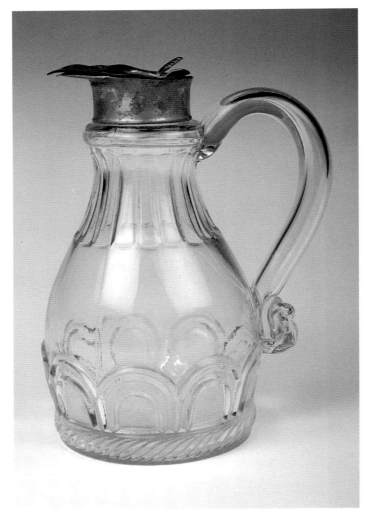

Central Molasses Can pattern 168

Pattern 169 is a plain molasses can in a pear shape. See Pitchers, Molasses Cans and Miscellaneous photograph on on the next page the fourth pattern in the second row. (E)

Pattern 169, Molasses Can

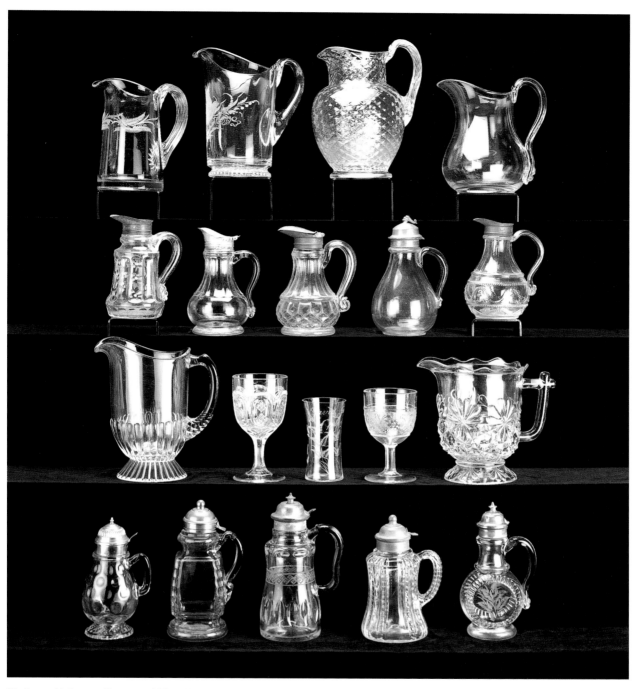

Pitchers, Molasses Cans, and Miscellaneous (left to right, top to bottom)
1. Water Pitchers: No. 518 Water Pitcher, Eng. 109; No. ? with Central's Eng. No. 142 Bird Etching; No. 799
      Water Pitcher; No. 154 Water Pitcher
2. Molasses Cans: No. 165, No. 166, No. 167, No. 169, No. 731
3. No. 877 Water Pitcher, No. 147 Goblet, No. 929 Blown Tumbler, No number Vine Goblet, No. 830 Water
      Pitcher
4. Molasses Cans: No. 796, No. 720, No. 585, No. 895, Cord & Tassel

Pattern 170 is a Wine Bottle. It has a roll top and a fluted bottom. (E)

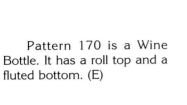

Pattern 170, Wine Bottle

The next four patterns are Bitter Bottles for cork or screw tube. They have roll-tops with the cork bottles having a narrow ring slightly below the top.

Pattern 171 is in a Huber pattern with a plain neck. (C)

Pattern 171, Bitter Bottles, screw tube and cork tops

Pattern 172 is a plain bottle with fluted bottom. (C)

Pattern 172, Bitter Bottles, screw tube and cork tops

Pattern 173 is in the Janus pattern. (D)

Pattern 173, Janus Pattern Bitter Bottles, screw tube and cork tops

Pattern 174 is in the Rose pattern. (E)

Pattern 174, Rose Pattern

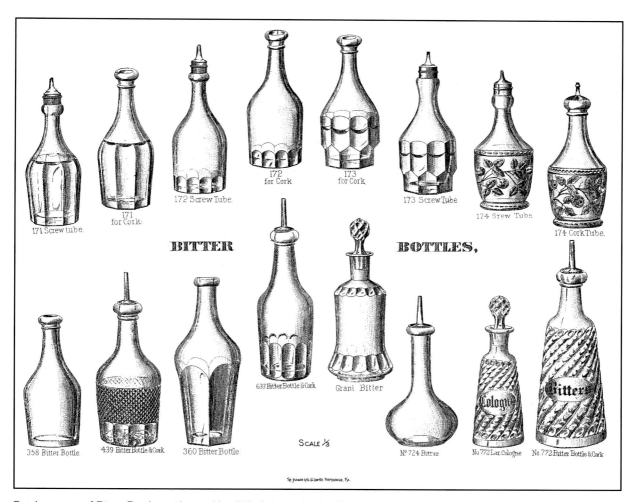

Catalog page of Bitter Bottles with one No. 772 Cologne and a Grant Bitter Bottle

The Grant Bitter Bottle and Grant Bar Bottle are two of the patterns with a missing pattern number that are listed in the "Easy Pattern Identification Guide". These have a hourglass shape with a thumbprint band below the neck around the top of the bottles and around the bottom. They were also made without a pattern number under Central Glass Works. The Grant Bitter Bottle is illustrated in the above catalog page. Also see Salts and Miscellaneous Ware photograph on the top row the third pattern for a Grant Bar Bottle.

Pattern 175 is a Decanter in the Janus pattern. It is 9 inches high and very heavy. It has a roll top with a thin ring slightly below it above the neck. (E)

Grant Bitter & Bar Bottle

Pattern 175, Janus Decanter

Pattern 176 is a Decanter in a Honeycomb pattern. It has a roll top with a thin ring slightly below it above the neck. (E)

Pattern 176, Honeycomb Decanter

Patterns 177 through 197 are Salts[10]. Note that pattern 183 is the Florence pattern and the salt was the only reference in the Central catalogs to this pattern which had a complete line of tableware. The Florence pattern is listed below after the salts.

177 Individual

178.

179 Individual

180 Individual Salt

181

182

183

184.

185.

186.

187

188.

189.

190

191

192

193

194

195.

196.

197.

Patterns 177 to 197, Salts

The first four salts are individual salts.
Pattern 177   round in a honeycomb pattern called "Diamond"
Pattern 178   "Baltimore"
Pattern 179   square
Pattern 180   "Octagon Footed"

The next seven salts are oval master salts.
Pattern 181   "Oak Leaf"
Pattern 182   fluted
Pattern 183   "Florence"
Pattern 184   "Cincinnati" in a honeycomb pattern
Pattern 185   "Split" with flutes on the bowl
Pattern 186   "Buffalo" in plain clear glass
Pattern 187   "Dobson" with a narrow fluted bottom.

The next five salts are all footed master salts.
Pattern 188   "Janus"
Pattern 189   "Curtain" often called Stippled Swag
Pattern 190   "Frosted" with a stippled bowl
Pattern 191   "Oak Leaf"
Pattern 192   "Rose".

The next five are master salts to go with the individual salts.
Pattern 193   "Arch"
Pattern 194   "Baltimore"
Pattern 195   "Octagon Footed"
Pattern 196   Albany
Pattern 197   "Diamond" in a honeycomb pattern.

Note that pattern 193 "Arch" did not have an individual salt illustrated in the catalogs. See Salts and Miscellaneous Ware photograph on the next page for most of these salts except numbers 182, 184 and 185. (B & C)

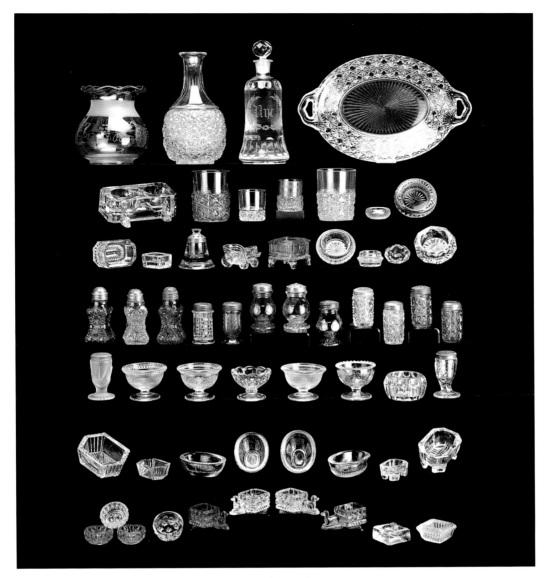

Salts and Miscellaneous Ware (left to right, top to bottom)
1. No number Oregon Etch'd. Globe, No. 835 D&B Water Bottle, No number Grant Bar Bottle, No. 775 Bread Plate
2. No. "K" Bankers Ink Stand, Single Pen Rack, No. 835 Daisy & Button Tumblers various sizes, No. 439 Diamond Point Ind. & Master Salts
3. No. 196 Albany Master & Ind. Salt, No number Liberty Bell Salt, No. 16 Carriage Salt, No. 822 Stove Salt, No. 194 Baltimore Master Salt, No. 178 Baltimore Ind. Salt, No. 177 Diamond Ind. Salt, No. 197 Diamond Master Salt
4. No. 782 D&B Hourglass Salts (3), No. 870 Brick Window Salt, No. 800 Leaf & Rib Salt, No. 796 Rope & Thumbprint Salts (3), No. 775 Pressed Diamond Salts (4)
5. No. 579 Hand Salt (Etched), No. 189 Curtain Footed Salt, No. 191 Oak Leaf Footed Salt, No. 188 Janus Footed Salt, No. 190 Frosted Footed Salt, No. 192 Rose Footed Salt, No. 193 Arch Master Salt, No. 579 Hand Salt (Crystal)
6. No. 730 Panel Rib & Shell Master and Ind. Salts, No. 186 Buffalo Oval Salt, No. 181 Oak Leaf Oval Salt, No. 183 Florence Oval Salt, No. 187 Oval Salt, No. 180 Octagon Ft'd. Ind. Salt, No. 195 Octagon Ft'd. Master Salt
7. No. 775 Pressed Diamond Ind. Salts (3), No. 876 Star Ind. Salt, No. 860 Dog Salts (4), No. 179 Square Ind. Salt, No. 572 Ind. Salt

Catalog page of Salts

Pattern 183 was named "Florence"[11] by Central. The design of Florence has a clear top then a stippled narrow band above stippled bar bands with wide panels getting smaller toward the bottom (resembling fan blades) in between clear ribbed panels. There is also a stippled ring band around the foot. The finial is an acorn with a half acorn on top of a leaf identical to pattern 152 Oak Leaf. This is another pattern that would have gone unidentified had it not been for the catalog from Island Mould as the only reference to this pattern was the salt and that is the pattern number used. This pattern had some 52 pieces including the master and individual salt, but a celery was not pictured.

Sugar (D)
Cream (C)

Spoon (C)
Butter 6 inch flat bottom (called a Covered Nappie) (D)
Ovals in 7, 8, and 9 inches (C)
Nappies in 6 and 7 inch covered without feet (C)
Nappies in 6 and 7 inch high foot and low foot covered or open footed (D)
Bowls (deep) in 7, 8, and 9 inch high foot or low foot covered or open (E)
Bowls (shallow) in 8, 9, and 10 inch high foot or low foot, covered or open (D)
Salt in master and individual oval shape (B)
Stemware (only a goblet shown) (B)
Salvers in 9, 10, 11, and 12 inches (F)

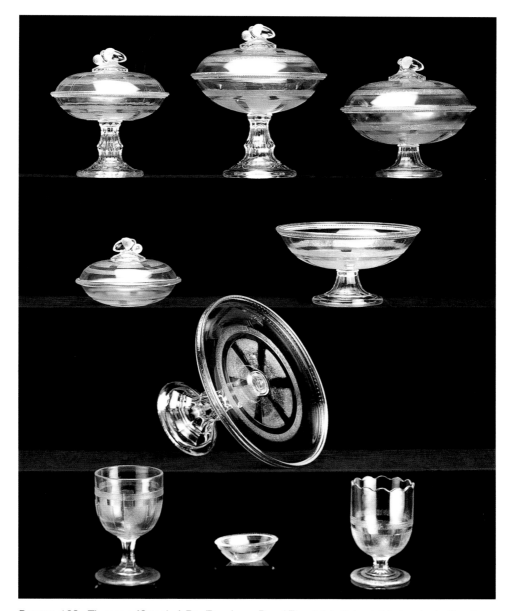

Pattern 183, Florence [Stippled Bar/Bands or Panel/Bands] (left to right, top to bottom)
1. Bowls all Shallow and Covered, 7" HF, 8" HF, 8" LF
2. Butter, Bowl 8" LF Shallow Bowl Open
3. Salver 10 inch
4. Goblet, Salt Oval, Spoon

FLORENCE SET.   Sugar.   Cream.   Spoon.   6 inch Nappie & Cov.

Florence Set from Island Mold catalog

Florence Salvers

FLORENCE SALVERS.   9 inch, 10 inch 11 inch and 12 inch,

The next 10 patterns are Oil Lamps. The stand lamps were made in four sizes with size 'A' being quite small and the 'D' size very large. The smaller lamps had a number one collar while the larger lamps had a number two collar. Unless noted, they are in A, B, C and D sizes.

72

Oil Lamps (left to right, top to bottom)
1. No. 203 Central Stand Lamp, No. 219 Bullseye Stand Lamp, No. 220 Bullseye Stand Lamp, No. 199 West Stand Lamp, No. 202 Double Diamond Stand Lamp
2. No. 469 Oesterling Stand Lamp, No. 425 Stand Lamp, No. 790 Hive Hand Lamp, No. 311 Mountain Laurel Stand Lamp, No. 207 Stand Lamp
3. No. 240 Wheat In Shield Hand Lamp, No. 221 Troy Hand Lamp, No. 207 Etch'd Font Stand Lamp, No. 219 Delta Hand Lamp, No. 225 Hand Lamp
4. No. 385 Central Rib Hand Lamp, No. 234 Wheat In Shield Stand Lamp, No. 201 Ohio Stand Lamp, No. 246 Wheat In Shield Footed Hand Lamp

Pattern 198 is called "Brilliant"[12]. It has a round font with vertical diamond point panels between clear panels from top to bottom and is on a scalloped foot. This font was also a peg so it will be found on a variety of stands. (F)

Pattern 198, Brilliant Stand Lamp

Pattern 198, Brilliant Stand Lamp with Star Foot

Pattern 200 was called "Band" by Central[14]. It has a round font with a rick-rack looking band a little above the middle with a honeycomb variant in the bottom of the bowl which looks like large ovals. It came on a scalloped foot.

200.
B.

Pattern 200, Band Stand Lamp

Pattern 201 is called "Ohio"[15]. The first three-fourths of the font is round and bulbous above a narrow ring followed by flutes that taper in on the bottom. It came on a plain or scalloped foot. It was also a peg so it will be found on other stands. This font was also made in hand lamps under patterns 248, 249, and 250. See Oil Lamps photograph on page 73 on the bottom row number the third lamp. (F)

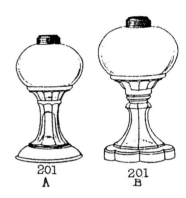

201
A

201
B

Pattern 201, Ohio Stand Lamp

Pattern 199 is called "West"[13]. This oil lamp has been called Buckle, but West is the correct name. There is a lamp that looks very similar, but the design is more oval with a clear oval panel inside the diamond point oval. The Central lamps have a slant center where the inside panel comes to a point at each corner. It came on a scalloped foot. This font was also a peg so it will be found on a variety of stands. See Oil Lamps photograph on page 73 on the top row pattern number four. (F)

Pattern 199, West Stand Lamp

Pattern 202 is a Double Diamond pattern with a round font with two raised diamond point diamonds above each other in a panel between ribs and clear panels. It came on a scalloped foot. See Oil Lamps photograph on page 73 on the top row the fifth pattern. (G)

202
D

Pattern 202, Double Diamond Stand Lamp

Pattern 203 is called "Central"[16]. It has a round font with a cable band in the middle and honeycomb in the bottom of the bowl. It came on a scalloped foot. It was also a peg so it would be found on other stands. See Oil Lamps photograph on page 73 on the top row the first lamp. (F)

Pattern 203, Central Stand Lamp

203
B

74

Pattern 204 is called "Star"[17]. It has a round font with three stars inside hearts going in a circle around the font. The catalog page shows tiny stars at the bottom between the points of the hearts, however, the Island Mold catalog shows a diamond point triangle coming up from the bottom in between the heart points alternating with a single star at the bottom between the points of the hearts. It came on a scalloped foot. It was also a peg so it would be on different stems. (G)

204
B

Pattern 204, Star

Pattern 204, "Star" Peg and Hand Lamp (Hearts and Stars)

Star stand lamp on metal stand and marble foot number 011

Pattern 205 is called "Diamond"[18]. The shape is a large diamond made up of four small diamond shapes with diamond point inside arched panels halfway down on the bowl. It came on a straight stem with a round foot with notches on the inside. It is also a peg and would be found on other stands. (F)

205
A

Pattern 205, Diamond stand lamp

Pattern 206 is called "Panel"[19]. The font has a double bar band with two rows of bars in the middle of an oval font. It also came as a peg so it would be on other stands. This font was also made in a hand lamp under pattern 220. (F)

206
B

Pattern 206, Panel stand lamp

Pattern 207 is a Hollow Stem stand lamp with a plain round font. The stems vary slightly with the rings. The stem comes down from the font in a hourglass shape onto a narrow single or double ring with a shorter hourglass shape above the foot. It came in 6 sizes, A, B, C, D, E, and F. This font was also made in hand lamps under patterns 223, 224, and 225. See Oil Lamps photograph on page 73 in the third row lamp number three (in the middle) with an etched font and in the second row the fifth lamp with a plain font. (E)

Pattern 207, Hollow Stem Stand Lamp

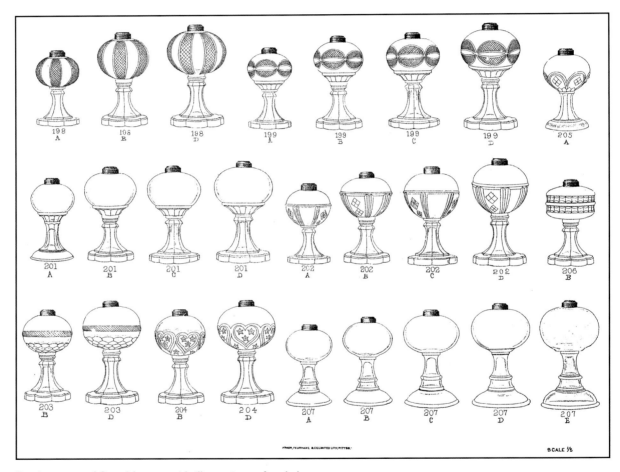

Catalog page of Stand Lamps with illustrations of early lamps

Patterns 208 through 217 are fonts. Some were made with filler (a opening to pour kerosene into the font without having to remove the chimney and burner) and without filler. Some are "bracket" lamps made to sit in a metal frame that extended out from the wall or used in chandeliers. The names for some of the fonts were found in the Island Mould Central catalog. Prices are unknown.

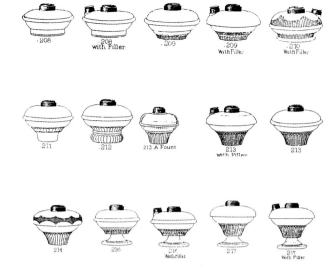

Pattern 208   "Troy." Came with or without filler. The bowl is plain, short, and squatty with a protruding ring around the middle and a flat base.

Pattern 209   "Huron". The bowl without the filler looks similar to 208 except for a fluted flat base. The bowl with filler did not have the protruding ring around the middle but has the fluted flat base.

Pattern 210   I named this "Rick-Rack" as it has a rick-rack or picket fence pattern on the top of the bowl.

Pattern 211   "Basket".

Pattern 212   "Footed Basket".

Pattern 213   "Baltic Basket". It came with a small "A Fount" and with and without filler.

Pattern 214   I named "Rick-Rack Band".

Pattern 215   Pattern unknown.

Pattern 216   "Huron Footed" and is identical to font pattern 209 with a foot added. It came with or without filler.

Pattern 217   "Baltic Basket Footed" and is identical to font pattern 213 with a foot added. It came with or without filler.

Pattern 211, Basket Font

The next four pattern numbers, 218 through 221, contain two different patterns. They each have a different Hand and Stand lamp. The reason for two separate patterns with the same pattern number is not known.

There are two patterns with number 218. Both are from the 1860s and in the Island Mould catalog. The first one is a "Troy"[21] Hand Lamp. It has a plain round lamp with star bottom and applied handle. (D)

The other 218 pattern is a Stand Lamp called "Virginia"[22] and has never been located so a price is unknown.

Pattern 218, Troy Hand Lamp and Virginia Stand Lamp

There are two patterns for 219. Pattern 219 is a Hand Lamp called "Delta"[23]. See Oil Lamps photograph page 73 in the third row the fourth lamp. (D)

The other 219 pattern is a Stand Lamp called Bullseye and came in five sizes on a scalloped foot. See Oil Lamps photograph page 73 on the top row the second lamp. (F)

Pattern 219, Delta Hand Lamp and Bullseye Stand Lamp

There are two patterns for 220. The first pattern is also the Bullseye Stand Lamp like the previous pattern, but in the 'F' size which has a number 2 collar. The stem and foot are different from the 219 lamp as it has a straight paneled stem on a diamond band foot. See Oil Lamps photograph on page 73 on the top row in the middle. (G)

The other 220 pattern is a "Panel"[24] Hand Lamp. This is the same pattern as the 206 Panel stand lamp. I am not sure why this pattern had the same number as the above large Bullseye pattern. (E)

Pattern 222 is another "Troy" Hand Lamp. (D)

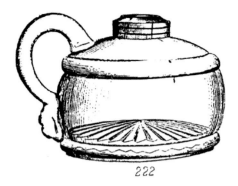

Pattern 222, Troy Hand Lamp

Patterns 223, 224, and 225 are Hand Lamps in different sizes. They have a round font with applied handle and plain stem and foot. These would have been the hand lamps to match pattern 207 stand lamps. See Oil Lamps photograph on page 73 in row three the fifth lamp. (D)

Pattern 220, Bullseye Stand Lamp and Panel Hand Lamp

Pattern 220, Panel Hand Lamp

Patterns 223, 224, and 225, Hand Lamps

The are two patterns for 221. One is the "Troy"[25] Hand Lamp. For some unknown reason Central gave the Troy hand lamp three different pattern numbers, 218, 221, and 222 and called the 208 fount Troy also. The only difference in the hand lamps is their size. See Oil Lamps photograph on page 73 on the third row the second lamp. (D)

The other 221 pattern is a large plain round 'F' size Stand Lamp with the same stem and foot as pattern 220. The font is round and plain like in 207 lamps. (F)

Patterns 226 and 227 are Ales also called "Schoppens". Pattern 226 holds 4-1/2 ounces and 227 holds 8 ounces. They are fluted halfway up with heavy bottoms.

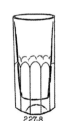

Patterns 226 and 227, Ales

Pattern 221, Troy and Stand Lamps

Patterns 228 and 229 are Ales. They have a Honeycomb pattern in the lower fourth of the bowls. They have tall tapered cylindrical bowls on a paneled stem. Pattern 228 holds 5 ounces and 229 holds 3 ounces.

Patterns 228 and 229, Honeycomb ales

Patterns 230, 231, and 232 are Tumblers. They have fluted bowls with heavy bottoms. Pattern 230 holds 3-1/2 ounces, 231 holds 4-1/2 ounces, and 232 holds 3-1/2 ounces.

Patterns 230, 231, and 232, Tumblers

Pattern 233 is a Goblet. It is a small goblet and holds 8 ounces. It has a plain tapered cylindrical bowl and is on a bulbous stem. There were probably other sizes but the small goblet is the only one illustrated.

Pattern 233, Goblet

Patent 5,269 for the design for the oval foot for glassware was used on several stand lamps with different fonts and can be found in cobalt blue. Whether Central produced these or the U.S. Glass Company reissued them is unknown. They are very rare in cobalt. See the Colored Oil Lamps photograph on page 161 for examples.

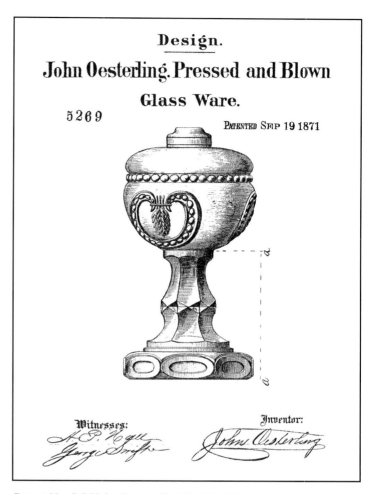

Design.
John Oesterling. Pressed and Blown
Glass Ware.
5269

PATENTED SEP 19 1871

Witnesses:

Inventor:

Patent No. 5,269 for Design For Feet For Glassware, September 19, 1871

5,269

UNITED STATES PATENT OFFICE.

JOHN OESTERLING, OF WHEELING, WEST VIRGINIA.

DESIGN FOR FEET FOR GLASSWARE.

Specification forming part of Design No. 5,269, dated September 19, 1871.

To all whom it may concern:

Be it known that I, JOHN OESTERLING, of Wheeling, in the county of Ohio and State of West Virginia, have invented a new and original Design for Pressed and Blown Glassware; and I do hereby declare that the following is a full, clear, and exact description thereof, which will enable others skilled in the art to make and use the same, reference being had to the accompanying drawings forming part of this specification.

The nature of my design is fully represented in the accompanying drawings, to which reference is made, the said design being a pressed-glass foot, as shown by the red line *a a* on said drawings.

Having thus described my invention, I claim as new and desire to secure by Letters Patent—

The design for pressed-glass feet, as shown.
JOHN OESTERLING.

Witnesses:
A. P. HALL.
JNO. CORMICK.

(41.)

Patent showing Design For Feet by John Osterling for pressed and blown glass ware.

Pattern 234 is the "Wheat In Shield" pattern. This design was Patent No. 5,318, patented October 17, 1871 by John Oesterling. It represented "a bunch of wheat hanging in a shield". The "shield" looks more like a horseshoe with three sheaves of wheat hanging from the middle. The stand oil lamps have the stem with diamond pattern in the middle with oval foot (which was patented by John Oesterling) except for the largest lamp, which has the straight stem and diamond band pattern foot. The stand lamps also have a thin band of dots above the wheat while the hand lamps have the same band below the wheat. The set consisted of cream, spoon, sugar (footed) and butter (no foot). Pieces included nappies, bowls, molasses can, stemware, and numerous other pieces which I am unable to list due to lack of catalog illustrations. If this pattern were like the other earlier patterns the pieces would have been numerous as Central counted each high foot and low foot piece separately as well as each one covered or without cover. The Wheat In Shield cruet set with five bottles was illustrated in a 1800s Montgomery Ward & Company Catalogue No. 57, page 197 in an extra plate silverware caster. See Oil Lamps photograph on page 73 for the stand lamps on the bottom row the second lamp. The hand lamps have different pattern numbers.

Sugar (E)
Cream (E)
Spoon (D)
Butter (E)
Nappies (E)
Bowls (F)
Stemware (C)
Cruets (F)
Molasses Cans (F)
Stand Lamps (G & H)

Pattern 234, Wheat In Shield

Patent No. 5,318 for Design For Ornamentation of Glass-Ware for Wheat-In-Shield patter by John Osterling, October 17, 1871.

Wheat in Shield Pattern (left to right, top to bottom)
1. Stand Lamp, Molasses Can, Hand Lamp No. 240, Hand Lamp Footed No. 246
2. Nappy LF Covered, Caster Set in Holder, Caster Bottles (2)
3. Egg, Nappy 4", Spoon, Cream

Design.
John Oesterling. Pressed and Blown
Glass Ware.

No. 5,318.

Patented Oct. 17, 1871.

Witnesses:

Inventor:

Patent No. 5,318 for Design For Ornamentation of Glass-Ware for Wheat-In-Shield Pattern by John Oesterling, October 17, 1871

There is a pattern that is similar in style to the Wheat In Shield pattern and it is called "Corn In Shield". The main difference in these two patterns is that an ear of corn with husks is hanging in the middle instead of wheat sheaves. The oil lamps and other pieces are identical to Wheat In Shield pieces so we can attribute this pattern to Central although I was unable to find a catalog pattern number for it. Prices are unknown.

Corn in Shield Stand
and Hand Lamps

Patterns 235, 236, 237, 238, and 239 are Tumblers. They are fluted with heavy bottoms. Pattern 235 holds 3 ounces, 236 holds 3-1/2 ounces, 237 holds 4-1/2 ounces, 238 holds 3-1/2 ounces, and 239 holds 3-1/2 ounces.

Patterns 235-239, Tumblers

Patterns 240 and 241 are Wheat In Shield Hand Lamps without feet. Lamp 240 is approximately 3 inches high and number 241 is 3-1/2 inches high. See Oil Lamps photograph on page 73 in row three the first lamp. (F)

Patterns 240 and 241, Wheat in Shields

Pattern 242 is a Cruet Bottle with three different shapes, shaker, flare top for stopper, and condiment. The necks on the bottles have a narrow ring below the screw tops followed by a hourglass shape with a narrow ring in the middle with another hourglass shape and ring before joining the body of the bowl. The bowls have an overhanging middle with narrow bottom so they will fit in casters. They came plain or engraved. See Casters, Urn Pattern 560, and Miscellaneous photograph on page 119 in the middle row the first pattern. An example of 242 cruet bottles is in the catalog page below. (C)

Pattern 242, Cruets

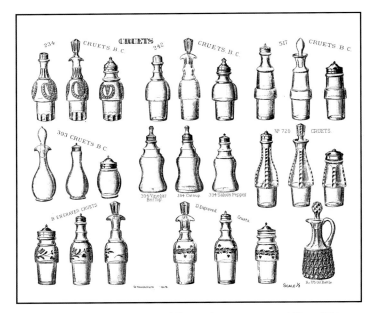

Cruets with No. 242 in the middle on the top row, and Nos. 234, 617, 393, 394, 720 Cruets and a No. 775 Oil Bottle

Patterns 243 and 244 are Tumblers. They are fluted with heavy bottoms. Pattern 243 holds 8 ounces and Pattern 244 holds 6 ounces.

Patterns 243 and 244, Tumblers

Patterns 245, 246 and 247 are Wheat In Shield footed Hand Lamps. Pattern 245 lamp is 4 inches, Pattern 246 is 4-1/2, and Pattern 247 is 5 inches high. See Oil Lamps photograph on page 73 in the bottom row the fourth lamp. (F)

Patterns 245-247, Wheat In Shield footed hand lamps

Patterns 248, 249 and 250 are Ohio footed Hand Lamps. This hand lamp has the same font as pattern 201. (E)

Patterns 248-250, Ohio footed hand lamps

Pattern 251 consists of Cruets in three different shapes. These are ribbed from the neck down with rings below the neck and at the bottom before it tapers down. They have a bulbous shape. See Casters, Urn Pattern 560, and Miscellaneous photograph on page 119 in the middle row the three bottles in the center. (D)

Pattern 251, Cruets

Pattern 251, Cruets

Patterns 252 to 264 are Tumblers of various sizes. Most of them have heavy fluted bottoms and shallow bowls. Pattern 252 has tall flutes and holds 6 ounces and has a heavy bottom. Pattern 253 has a fluted bottom and holds 10 ounces. Patterns 254 and 255 are fluted in a similar style with heavy bottoms. Patterns 256 and 257 are fluted in a similar style with heavy bottoms. Pattern 257 holds 5 ounces. Pattern 258 is plain and holds 8 ounces. Pattern 259 is fluted and holds 8 ounces. Pattern 260 is plain with a heavy bottom. Patterns 261, 262, 263 and 264 are fluted with heavy bottoms.

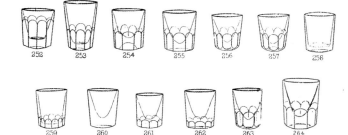

Patterns 252-264, Tumblers

Patterns 265 through 269 are Beer Mugs with heavy bottoms. Pattern 265 is a 12 ounce Huber mug. Pattern 226 is a 11 ounce plain mug. Pattern 267 is a 11-1/2 ounce fluted mug. Pattern 268 is a 10 ounce mug with large thumbprints above a fluted bottom. Pattern 269 is a 10-1/2 ounce mug with elongated oval thumbprints above a fluted bottom.

Patterns 265-269, Beer Mugs

Pattern 270 is the Rubicon Beer Mug. It is the largest mug that Central made holding 69 ounces. Rubicon is engraved in the bottom of the mug. See Barware photograph on page 39 on the top row the second mug. (E)

Pattern 270, Rubicon beer mug

Pattern 270, Rubicon Mug showing wording in the bottom of the mug. Holds 69 ounces

Patterns 271, 272, 273 and 274 are unknown. Could they be more bar ware or stemware?

Pattern 275 is a Champagne. It holds 4-1/2 ounces and has a plain conical bowl with a plain flared stem joined at the bottom of the bowl.

Pattern 275, Champagne

Pattern 276 is a Sham Claret. It holds 4 ounces and is in the Huber pattern on a paneled stem.

Pattern 276, Sham Claret

Pattern 277 is a Sham Claret. It holds 3-1/2 ounces and is a plain pattern with round heavy bottom bowl on a plain flared stem..

Pattern 277, Sham Claret

Pattern 278 is a Salt. It is round and has a notched bottom.

Pattern 278, Salt

Pattern 279 is plain Stemware. It has a plain conical bowl and is on a bulbous stem in 11 ounce goblet, 5-1/2 ounce champagne, 3-1/2 ounce claret, 2 ounce wine, and 1 ounce cordial.

Pattern 279, Stemware

Pattern 280 is a Goblet in the Mountain Laurel pattern. It has a flower band on a diamond point background. It was made in a small 9-1/2 ounce goblet and other sizes are not known. The pattern was also made in stand lamps under pattern 311. (C)

Pattern 280, Mountain Laurel goblet

Pattern 281 is a Tumbler. It holds 6 ounces and is fluted with heavy bottom.

Pattern 281, Tumbler

Pattern 282 is a Champagne. It holds 4 ounces. Pattern 283 is a Sham Claret with heavy bottom and holds 3-1/2 ounces. They both have plain round bowls and are on spool stems joined in the middle.

Pattern 282, Champagne, and Pattern 283, Sham Claret

Pattern 284 is a Huber Wine. Pattern 285 is a Huber Sham Wine with heavy bottomed bowl holding 2-1/2 ounces. They are on paneled stems and in the same style as pattern 139.

Pattern 284, Huber Wine, and Pattern 285, Sham Wine

Pattern 286 is a Beer Mug. It holds 7-1/2 ounces and is fluted with a heavy bottom.

Pattern 286, Beer Mug

Pattern 287 is a Cordial holding 1-1/2 ounces. Pattern 288 is a Sham Cordial with heavy bottomed bowl holding 1 ounce. They have round bowls and are on spool stems.

Pattern 287, Cordial, and Pattern 288, Sham Cordial

Pattern 289 consists of Weiss Beers. They are trumpet shaped and hold 18-1/2 ounces or 16 ounces in the heavy bottomed Sham. They have heavy hollow feet.

Pattern 289, Beer Mug & Sham

Pattern 290 is Stemware. It has a plain conical shape on a plain stem. It came in a 11 ounce large goblet, 5 ounce champagne, 3-1/2 ounce claret, 2-1/2 ounce wine, and 1 ounce cordial.

Pattern 290, Stemware

Pattern 291 is Stemware. It has a plain conical shape on a paneled stem. It came in a 11 ounce large goblet, 5 ounce champagne, 3-1/2 ounce claret, 2-1/2 ounce wine, and 1 ounce cordial.

Pattern 291, Stemware

Pattern 292 is a Cordial. It holds 1 ounce and is in the Huber pattern and is on a paneled stem.

Pattern 292, Cordial

Pattern 293 is a Cordial and holds 1-1/2 ounces. Pattern 294 is Sham Cordial with a heavy bottom and holds 1 ounce. The have round fluted bowls on spool stems.

Pattern 293, Cordial, and Pattern 294, Sham Cordial

Patterns 295 and 296 are Ales. Pattern 295 holds 6 ounces and pattern 296 holds 10 ounces. They have a tall cylindrical shape and heavy fluted bottom.

Pattern 295 and Pattern 296, Ales

Pattern 297 is a Tumbler. It is a plain blown tumbler called a "punch tumbler" and came plain or engraved. Some of Centrals other blown tumblers with lettering from, A, B, C, etc., instead of numbers are below.

Pattern 297, Tumbler

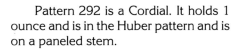

Blown Tumblers without numbers A – Z. F, I, J, and V are unknown.

Pattern 298 is unknown.

Pattern 299 is a Tumbler. It is plain in a barrel shape and holds 13 ounces.

Pattern 299, Tumbler

Pattern 306 is unknown.

Pattern 307 is a Cocktail. It holds 3 ounces and has a plain cup shaped bowl and straight stem.

Pattern 307, Cocktail

There are two patterns for 300. The first one is a Tumbler. It is plain with cylindrical shape and heavy bottom. It probably was a 1860s pattern then discontinued.

Pattern 300, Tumbler

Pattern 308 is a Claret. It holds 4-1/2 ounces and has a plain round bottomed bowl and straight stem.

Pattern 308, Claret

The other 300 pattern is a Night Lamp. It is 4-1/2 inches high and was made in crystal, amber, and blue. It would have been a replacement pattern for the tumbler as it is in color. See Colored Oil Lamps photograph on page 161 in the bottom row in the middle. It is also illustrated in the colored catalog page from Bethany College on page 188 with patterns 310 night lamp and 858 stand lamps. (E)

Pattern 300, Night Lamp

Pattern 309 is Patented Stemware including a large and small celery. The celery rim has 8 scallops and the plain bowls taper down to the straight stem. The stemware included a large and small goblet, a 4 ounce small champagne, 3 ounce wine, and a 1/2 ounce cordial. If there were more pieces in this pattern is not known.

Pattern 309, Stemware and Celery

Pattern 301 is a Master Salt and pattern 302 is the Individual Salt. They are round with plain bottoms.

Pattern 301, Master Salt

Pattern 302, Ind. Salt

There are two patterns for 310. The first one is Stemware with plain round bottomed bowls and tapered stems in a large goblet and 1/2 ounce cordial.

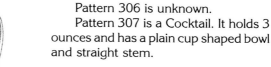

Pattern 310, Stemware

Patterns 303 and 304 are Tumblers. They both hold 1-1/2 ounces and are cylindrical with heavy fluted bottoms. The only difference is the flutes as 303 has wide flutes and 304 has narrow flutes.

Patterns 303 & 304, Tumblers

Pattern 305 is a Cocktail. It holds 3 ounces and has a plain cup shaped bowl on a paneled stem.

Pattern 305, Cocktail

The other pattern 310 is a Night Lamp. It has a rib band in the middle of the font with a wide rib next to three thin ones. The stem has three narrow rings above a rib band with a narrow ring before the foot. The foot has narrow ribs on top and a rib band around the bottom. It was made in crystal, amber, and blue. See Colored Oil Lamps photograph on page 161 on the bottom row numbers two and four. It is also illustrated in the colored catalog page from Bethany College on page 188 with pattern 300 night lamp and 858 stand lamps. (F)

Pattern 310, Night Lamp

Pattern 311 is a Stand Lamp called Mountain Laurel. It has a clear top and loop bottom with a flower band and swags. The flower has six petals with a hexagon center. The center of the flower and background of the band are diamond point. Five sizes were made on the oval foot and center knopped stem with notched diamonds and the largest lamp had the straight stem on diamond band foot. This lamp is in three different oil lamps photographs. See Oil Lamps photograph on page 73 for the largest (diamond band foot) Mountain Laurel lamp in the third row the fourth lamp. It is also in the Oil Lamps and Whirlpool Cologne photograph on page 135 on the top row in the middle. Also see Colored Oil Lamps photograph on page 161 in the third row the fifth lamp with a cobalt stem and base. (F)

Pattern 311, Mountain Laurel
Stand Lamp

Pattern 312 is a Font with filler. It has a ribbed bottom and would fit in a holder.

Pattern 312, Font

Patterns 313 and 314 are patented Champagnes. They have plain funnel shaped bowls with hollow stems.

Patterns 313 and 314,
Champagnes

Pattern 315 is a Champagne. It holds 4-1/2 ounces and has a plain cup shaped bowl and solid straight stem.

Pattern 315, Champagne

Pattern 316 is a Champagne. It holds 4-1/2 ounces and has a plain cup shaped bowl and wavy stem. It came either plain or engraved.

Pattern 316, Champagne,
Plain & Eng.

Pattern 317 is a Champagne. It holds 4-1/2 ounces and has a cup bowl with loop pattern in bottom on sold straight stem.

Pattern 317, Champagne

Pattern 318 is a Champagne. It holds 4-1/2 ounces and has a cup bowl with loop pattern in bottom. It came either plain or engraved.

Pattern 318, Champagne,
Plain or Eng.

Pattern 319 is a small Goblet. It has a plain round bowl with straight stem. Pattern 320 is a small goblet and has a plain round bowl with wavy stem.

Patterns 319 and 320,
Goblets

Pattern 321 is a Salt. It has an octagon shape with oval bowl and flat bottom. (B)

Pattern 321,
Salt

Pattern 322 consists of Ales. They hold 7-1/2 ounces and have plain tall trumpet shaped bowls on two different stems. One has a straight stem and the other has a cut stem.

Pattern 322, Ale & Cut
Stem Ale

Pattern 323 is patented Stemware. They have plain rounded bowls on wavy stems in large goblet, champagne, claret, and wine.

Pattern 323, Stemware

Patterns 324 and 325 are patented Stemware. They have rounded bowls with a loop pattern in the bottom and are on a wavy stem. Pattern 324 came in large goblet, champagne, claret, and wine. Pattern 325 is the small goblet that matches pattern 324.

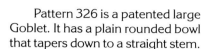

Patterns 324 and 325, Stemware

Pattern 326 is a patented large Goblet. It has a plain rounded bowl that tapers down to a straight stem.

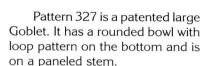

Pattern 326, Goblet

Pattern 327 is a patented large Goblet. It has a rounded bowl with loop pattern on the bottom and is on a paneled stem.

Pattern 327, Goblet

Pattern 328 is a Cocktail. It holds 3 ounces and was in the catalog under "Miscellaneous Stem ware". This pattern has a plain rounded bowl on a wavy stem and came plain or engraved. There were five different engravings of roosters, two of dogs, one of a horse, and other decorative engravings. The many engravings are illustrated in the catalog page below.

Pattern 329 is a Cocktail. It holds 3 ounces and has a rounded bowl with a loop pattern on the bottom and a wavy stem.

Pattern 329, Cocktail

Pattern 330 is a Champagne. It holds 5 ounces and has a hollow paneled stem. It came either plain or engraved.

Pattern 330, Champagne, Plain & Eng.

Pattern 331 is a patented Champagne. It holds 6 ounces and has a hollow paneled stem. It came either plain or engraved. It is similar in style to the above pattern and holds an ounce more.

Pattern 331, Champagne, Plain & Eng.

Catalog page showing Miscellaneous Stem Ware and Pattern 328 Engravings

87

Patterns 332, 333 and 334 are unknown.

Patterns 335, 336, 337, 338 and 339 are patented Beer Mugs. They were patented by John Oesterling, Design No. 6,383, dated February 04, 1873. They are the same pattern in different sizes with the plain upper half barrel shaped and the lower half is narrower with fluted bottoms on wide foot. The handle comes out from below the top and joins above the foot. Pattern 335 is a toy mug and holds 3 ounces. Pattern 336 is a small pony and holds 4-1/2 ounces. Pattern 337 is a large pony and holds 6-1/2 ounces. Pattern 338 is medium pony and holds 8-1/2 ounces. Pattern 339 holds 9-1/2 ounces. See Barware photograph on page 39 on the bottom row the last three mugs (numbers 6, 7 and 8). (B & C)

Pattern 340 is a patented Claret. It holds 3-1/2 ounces and has plain rounded bowls and was made with two stems. One is a plain stem and the other a cut stem.

Pattern 340, Claret & Cut Stem Claret

Pattern 341 is unknown.

Pattern 342 is a patented Pony Ale. It holds 4 ounces and has a plain tall trumpet shape and straight stem.

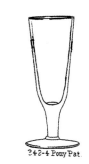

Pattern 342, Pony Ale

Patterns 335 to 339, Beer Mugs

Patent No. 6,383 Design For Beer-Mugs by John Oesterling, February 04, 1873 for patterns 335-339

UNITED STATES PATENT OFFICE.

JOHN OESTERLING, OF WHEELING, WEST VIRGINIA.

DESIGN FOR BEER-MUGS.

Specification forming part of Design No. **6,383**, dated February 4, 1873.

To all whom it may concern:

Be it known that I, JOHN OESTERLING, of Wheeling, in the county of Ohio and State of West Virginia, have invented a new and useful Design for Beer-Mug; and I do hereby declare the following to be a full, clear, and exact description thereof, reference being had to the accompanying drawing forming a part of this specification, in which—

Figure 1 is a side view of a beer-glass made after my improved design, and Fig. 2 is a sectional view of the same.

Like letters of reference in the separate figures indicate like parts.

My improved design consists in making the upper half of the body of the beer or ale glass barrel shaped, and the lower half of a reduced diameter, with straight or slightly-concave sides, so as to present the appearance of a stem.

To enable others skilled in the art to make and use my improved design, I will describe it more specifically.

The upper half of the bowl a—viz., from the line x x—is barrel-shaped. Below the line x x the bowl a is reduced in diameter, and its sides are straight or slightly concave or slightly tapering down to the projecting foot c. A handle, which may or may not be attached at pleasure, is shown at d. The cavity of the bowl a conforms in shape to the general outline.

What I claim as my invention, and design to secure by Letters Patent, is—

The design for beer or ale glass herein described and shown.

In testimony whereof I, the said JOHN OESTERLING, have hereunto set my hand.

JOHN OESTERLING.

Witnesses:
WM. GORING.
WM. L. EWING.

Patent showing design for Beer Mugs for Patterns 335 to 339.

Pattern 343 is a patented Egg., Ale and Weiss Beer. The pattern has a fluted bowl on short stem. It came in a 4 ounce egg cup (note that this piece was called "cup", but since this is all barware it probably is an eggnog), and in a 10 ounce beer, large 9 ounce, medium 6-1/2 ounce, large pony 5 ounce, and small pony 3-1/2 ounce.

Pattern 343, Egg Cup, Ales & Weiss Beers

Patterns 344 and 345 are unknown.

Pattern 346 consists of Beer Mugs. They hold 5 ounces and have heavy fluted bottoms and were made with two different handles. One is in a 'C' shape and the other is a block handle.

Pattern 346, Beer Mug

Pattern 347 is a patented Wine. It has a flute band around the middle of the bowl and is on a solid straight stem.

Pattern 347, Wine

Pattern 348 is a Champagne. It holds 5 ounces and has a cup shape bowl and is on a hollow loop paneled stem.

Pattern 348, Champagne

Pattern 349 is patented Stemware. It has plain rounded bowls on a loop paneled stem and was made in a goblet, champagne, and wine.

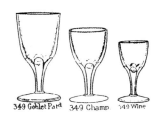

Pattern 349, Stemware

Pattern 350 is a plain pattern and is referred to as "350 Ware" and "350 Solid Stem Salvers". It does not have a name. The 350 Salvers Stem was patented by John Oesterling. It came under Manufacture of Stemmed Glass Ware and was covered by number 143,777 September 09, 1873 and granted October 02, 1873. They have solid stems with a protruding ring (or knop) in the middle. The Central stems join the top with a flare instead of coming straight down. These are being reproduced today so be careful. The butter is only 6 inches and looks like a toy cake plate. If there was a 7 inch salver is not known. See Plain Ware 150 and 350 photograph on page 59 showing two Salvers in the middle row.

The bowls are not on the same stem as the salvers. The high foot bowls are on the hollow stem similar to the 150 pattern. The bowls are identical to pattern 150 with wide plain bowls. The cover has a short round finial that is flat on top. The bowls came in high or low foot and were engraved with six different engravings. .

Bowls 7 and 8 inch high foot and low foot covered (D)

Butter Salver 6 inch on low foot (R)

Salvers in 6, 8, 9, 10, 11, 12 and 14 inches (F)

Pattern 350, Butter

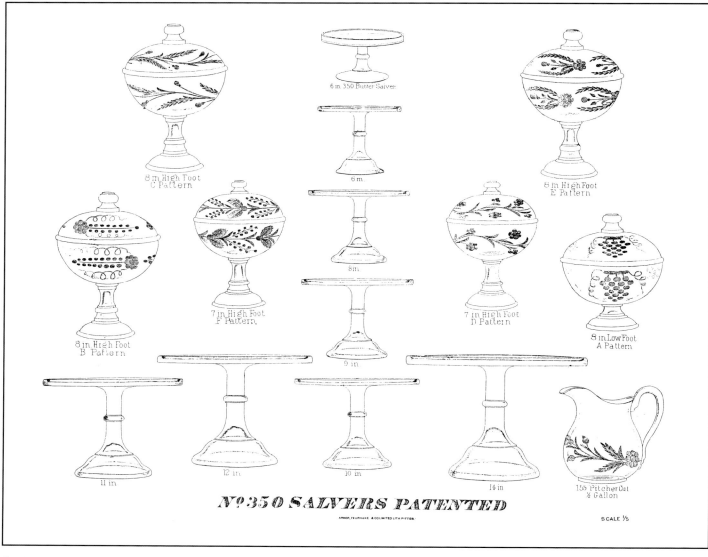

Catalog Page with patented 350 Salvers showing engravings

Pattern 351 is patented Stemware. It has plain rounded bowls on bulbous stems in a 10-1/2 ounce goblet, 5-1/2 ounce champagne, and 3 ounce wine.

Pattern 351, Stemware

Pattern 352 is a Beer Goblet. It holds 10 ounces and has a tall rounded bowl with a thumbprint band around the bottom of the bowl and is on a spool stem.

Pattern 352, Beer Goblet

Pattern 353 is a Tumbler. It holds 8 ounces. This tumbler was reissued by the U.S. Glass Company under pattern number 764 for "Factory O".

Pattern 353, Tumbler

Pattern 354 is a Beer Mug. It holds 10 ounces and has a heavy fluted bottom.

Pattern 354, Beer Mug

Pattern 355 is a patented Jelly Saucer. It has a short wide bowl that resembles a champagne glass and came either plain or engraved and are on either a straight or cut stem

Pattern 355, Jelly Saucers

Pattern 356 is a light Weiss Beer. It holds 14 ounces and has a trumpet shaped bowl with heavy bottom and is on a wide hollow foot.

Pattern 356, Weiss Beer

Pattern 357 is unknown.
Pattern 358 is a Bitters Bottle. It is plain with a roll top with a narrow ring slightly below the top. (B)

Pattern 358, Bitter Bottle

Pattern 359 is a patented Sherry. It holds 1-1/2 ounces and has a trumpet shaped bowl and was made on three different stems in plain, medium cut, or full cut. The plain bowl has a plain stem. The medium cut has narrow flutes in the lower half of the bowl, and the full cut has wide flutes slightly below the rim and they both are on a cut (paneled) stem.

Pattern 359, Sherries, Plain, Medium & Full Cut

Pattern 360 is a Bitter Bottle. It has a roll top with plain sides and 6 flutes on the lower three-fourths that taper at the bottom. (C)

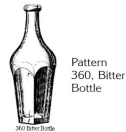

Pattern 360, Bitter Bottle

Pattern 361 consists of Ales. They have a trumpet shaped bowl and came in a 7 ounce large and 3-1/2 ounce pony. The stem is fluted with knop in lower part of the stem.

Pattern 361, Ales

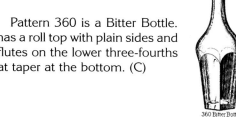

Pattern 362 consists of Ales. They have a trumpet shape bowl and came in a 7 ounce large and 3-1/2 ounce pony. The fluted stems are straight.

Pattern 362, Ales

Patterns 363 and 364 are Tumblers. They are fluted with heavy bottoms.

Patterns 363 and 364, Tumblers

Pattern 365 is patented Stemware. They have conical bowls with a large single honeycomb pattern at the bottom of the bowl on a paneled stem. They were made in a 9 ounce goblet, 6 ounce champagne, 4 ounce claret, 2-1/2 ounce wine, and a 1 ounce cordial.

Pattern 365, Stemware

Patterns 366 and 367 are patented Goblets. They both have round bowls. Pattern 366 has a loop pattern at the bottom of the bowl with a paneled stem. Pattern 367 has the large single honeycomb pattern (like pattern 365) at the bottom of the bowl on a paneled stem.

Patterns 366 and 367, Goblets

Pattern 368 consists of Weiss Beers. They are tall cylindrical glasses in the Huber pattern in a 19 ounce beer and 15 ounce heavy bottom pony sham.

Pattern 368, Weiss Beers

Pattern 369 is a patented Weiss Beer. It holds 19-1/2 ounces and has a trumpet shape with heavy bottom. It is fluted half way up and is on a wide foot.

Pattern 369 Weiss Beer

91

Pattern 370 is a plain pattern and is referred to as "370 Ware", it does not have a name. Because the pattern has a loop pattern in the bottom of the bowl above the stem I call it "370 Loop Pattern". This pattern is the same as number 390 except, the compotes are shallow bowls and open, they do not have covers. If they are covered, they would be pattern 390. They have plain shallow wide bowls with loop fluted stem and a knop (it resembles a washer) in the middle of the high foot bowls only. The ovals have a wide fluted bottom with star center. The bowls came in high and low foot.

Ovals in 7, 8, and 9 inch (C)

Bowls in 6, 7, 8, 9, and 10 inch high foot and low foot open (D)

Pattern 370, Ware (Loop) pattern

Catalog Page with 370 Bowls

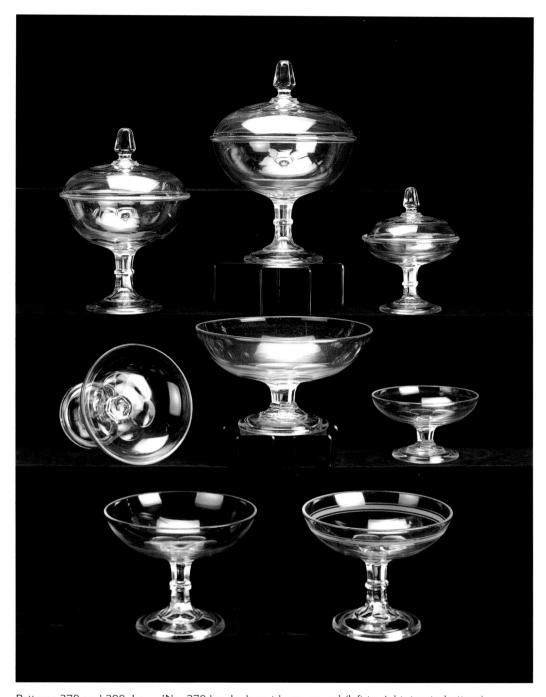

Patterns 370 and 390, Loop [No. 370 bowls do not have covers] (left to right, top to bottom)
1. No. 390 Deep Bowls covered, 8" & 9" Deep Bowl, 6" Shallow Bowl
2. No. 370 Bowls 7" showing Loop design, 10" LF Deep Bowl, 6" LF Shallow Bowl
3. No. 370 Shallow Bowls, 8", and 8" Engraved with Plain Band

Pattern 371 is a patented Wine. It holds 4 ounces and has a round bowl and is on a straight stem with round knop in the middle.

Pattern 371, Wine

Pattern 372 is a Wine. It holds 4 ounces and has a round bowl with loop fluted bottom and is on a stem with round knop in the middle.

Pattern 372, Wine

Pattern 373 is a Cocktail. It holds 5 ounces and has a plain round bowl on wavy stem.

Pattern 373, Cocktail

Patterns 374 to 383 are Tumblers. All are cylindrical and they are either plain or fluted. Pattern 374 is plain and holds 5 ounces. Pattern 375 is also plain and holds 4-1/2 ounces. Pattern 376 is fluted and holds 5-1/2 ounces. Pattern 377 is fluted and holds 4-1/2 ounces. Pattern 378 is plain and holds 6 ounces. Pattern 379 is plain and holds 5 ounces. Pattern 380 is fluted and holds 6 ounces. Pattern 381 is fluted and holds 5-1/2 ounces. Pattern 382 is fluted and holds 3 ounces. Pattern 383 is plain and holds 13 ounces and also came etched.

Pattern 374 to 383, Tumblers

Pattern 384 is an Ale. It is conical with long flutes from below the rim to the bottom of the bowl on a stocky stem.

Pattern 384, Ale

Pattern 385 consists of Central Rib Stand and Hand Lamps sometimes called Filly Font. It has a notched band around the middle of the font. The stand lamp has a hollow stem and foot like pattern 207. See Oil Lamps photograph on page 73 on the bottom row the first lamp. (D)

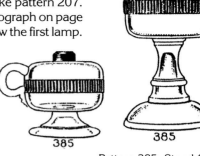

Pattern 385, Stand & Hand Lamps

Patterns 386, 387 and 388 are Tumblers. Pattern 386 holds 18 ounces and 387 holds 16-1/2 ounces. They are plain conical tumblers. Pattern 388 holds 5 ounces and is a fluted conical tumbler with heavy bottom.

Patterns 386 to 388, Tumblers

Pattern 389 consists of Ales. They have fluted conical shapes in a 6 ounce large Vienna Beer with narrow flutes and a 4-1/2 ounce Vienna Pony with wider flutes. The bowls taper in before the wide foot.

Pattern 389 Ales

Pattern 390 is a plain pattern and was referred to as "390 Bowls." It does not have a name. Because this pattern has a loop pattern in the bottom of the bowls I call this "390 Loop Pattern". It has the same bowls as pattern 370 except these are deep bowls and covered. The cover has a loop pattern on the top under the finial. The finial has tall flutes with round top. See Loop Patterns 390 and 370 photograph on page 93 on the top row.

Bowls in a 6, 7, 8, and 9 inch
high and low foot (E)
Sweetmeat 6 inch squatty bowl
in high and low foot (D)

Pattern 390, Loop Pattern Bowls

Catalog Page with 390 Bowls

Patterns 391 and 392 are Ales. They have fluted cylindrical bowls with very heavy bottoms. Pattern 391 holds 5-1/2 ounces.

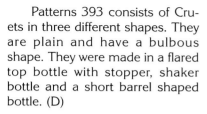

Pattern 391, Ale, and Pattern 392, Ale

Patterns 393 consists of Cruets in three different shapes. They are plain and have a bulbous shape. They were made in a flared top bottle with stopper, shaker bottle and a short barrel shaped bottle. (D)

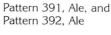

Pattern 393, Cruets

Pattern 394 consists of Cruets. They are plain in a hourglass shape and were made in a Vinegar "Brit Top", Catsup and Saloon Pepper. The necks are similar to pattern 242 cruets. (D)

Pattern 394, Cruets

Pattern 395 is a patented Ale. It holds 9 ounces and is conical with fluted bottom half of the bowl and is on a short stem. Pattern 397 is in the same style.

Pattern 395, Ale

Pattern 396 is an Ale. No picture is available as it was on a list in a Central catalog for shipping orders.

Pattern 397 is a patented Ale. It holds 7-1/2 ounces and is conical with fluted bottom half of the bowl and is on a short stem. It is the same style as pattern 395.

Pattern 397, Ale

Pattern 398 is a patented Wine. It holds 3-1/2 ounces and has a plain round bowl and tapered straight stem.

Pattern 398, Wine

Pattern 399 is a Catsup Bottle. It is plain and has a hourglass shape and was made with either a roll top for cork or a screw top. See pattern 417 for a catsup bottle in the same style. (B)

Pattern 399, Catsup Bottle & Catsup for Cork

Pattern 400 has two patterns. One pattern is a Goblet called a "heavy foot goblet". It has a plain round bowl and is on a bulbous stem. There are other stemware pieces that match this goblet with different pattern numbers.

The other 400 pattern is a Weiss Beer. It holds 15 ounces and has a tall cylindrical fluted bowl with heavy bottom.

Pattern 400, Goblet and Weiss Beer

Pattern 401 is an Octagon Salt. It is plain with curved bowl and heavy bottom. It has the same shape as No. 196 and was marked "N.M." for new model, perhaps it replaced pattern 196. It could be the master salt to pattern 321. (B)

Pattern 401, Salt

Pattern 402 is a Stand Lamp in four sizes. It has a plain round font with the center knopped stem with notched out diamonds and oval band foot. It came in four sizes. (E)

Pattern 402, Stand Lamp

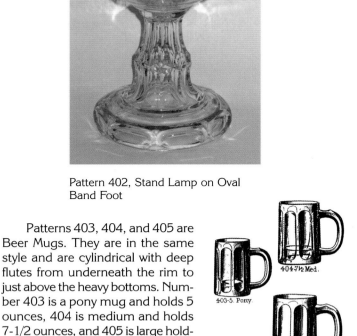

Pattern 402, Stand Lamp on Oval Band Foot

Patterns 403, 404, and 405 are Beer Mugs. They are in the same style and are cylindrical with deep flutes from underneath the rim to just above the heavy bottoms. Number 403 is a pony mug and holds 5 ounces, 404 is medium and holds 7-1/2 ounces, and 405 is large holding 9-1/2 ounces. From research found at the Corning Museum of Glass this mug was designed by John Oesterling.

Patterns 403, 404,. and 405, Beer Mugs

Pattern 406 is a Huber Beer Mug. It has a heavy bottom and came in six sizes holding 14, 12, 10, 8, 5, or 3 ounces.

Pattern 406, Beer Mug

Pattern 407 is a Molasses Can. It is plain in a pear shape (or light bulb-shape) and has an applied handle. (D)

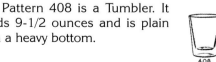

Pattern 407, Molasses Can

Pattern 408 is a Tumbler. It holds 9-1/2 ounces and is plain with a heavy bottom.

Pattern 408, Tumbler

Pattern 409 is a Cocktail. It holds 2-1/2 ounces and has a plain round bowl with flared rim and is on a baluster shaped stem.

Pattern 409, Cocktail

Pattern 410 is a Tumbler. It holds 18 ounces and is in the Huber style.

Pattern 410, Tumbler

Pattern 411 is a Goblet. It has a plain conical bowl on a straight stem.

Pattern 411, Goblet

Patterns 412 and 413 are plain Tumblers. Pattern 412 holds 5-1/2 ounces and pattern 413 holds 5 ounces and has a heavy round bottom.

Patterns 412 and 413, Tumblers

Pattern 414 is an Ale. It holds 7 ounces and has a tall cylindrical bowl with ribs on the bottom of the bowl that taper down to a round knop stem.

Pattern 414, Ale

Pattern 415 is an Ale. It has a bucket shaped fluted bowl and is on a round knopped stem in a 9-1/2 ounce large, 7 ounce medium, and 5 ounce pony size. See Barware photograph on page 39 in the second row the second Ale.

Pattern 415, Ale

Pattern 416 is a Tumbler. It holds 5-1/2 ounces and is fluted with a heavy bottom.

Pattern 416, Tumbler

Pattern 417 is a Catsup Bottle. It has a hourglass shape with roll top for cork and a screw top. This pattern is almost identical to pattern 399. (B)

Pattern 417, Catsup

Patterns 418, 419, 420 and 421 are Tumblers. They are all fluted with heavy bottoms. Pattern 418 holds 4-1/2 ounces, pattern 419 holds 3-1/2 ounces, pattern 420 holds 6 ounces, and pattern 421 holds 5 ounces.

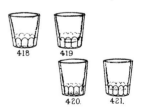

Patterns 418 to 421, Tumblers

Pattern 422 is a Cocktail. It holds 4 ounces and has a plain round bottomed bowl. The stem is straight with round knop slightly under the bowl.

Pattern 422, Cocktail

Pattern 423 is unknown
Pattern 424 consists of Stand and Hand Lamps. The font has a plain band at the top then curves in before joining the stem. The stand lamps stem and foot are the hollow stem similar to pattern 207 except for the largest lamp which has the straight paneled stem and diamond band foot. The stand lamps are in six sizes and hand lamps are in four sizes. (F)

Pattern 424, Hand & Stand Lamps

Pattern 425 consists of Stand and Hand Lamps. The font has a band of vertical and horizontal notches on the lower half of the bowl and has the same shape as 424 lamps with a plain band at the top then it curves in before the stem. The stand lamp is on the center knop stem with notched out diamonds on the oval band foot except for the largest which is on the straight paneled stem with the diamond band foot. The stand lamps are in five sizes and hand lamps are in four sizes. See Oil Lamps photograph on page 73 in the second row the second lamp. (F)

Pattern 425, Stand & Hand Lamps

Pattern 426 is a Font with and without filler. It has six vertical rings down from the top with a clear bottom on a fluted base.

Pattern 426, Font

Pattern 427 is a Beer Mug. It holds 7 ounces and is cylindrical with a heavy bottom and a pattern of four thumbprints in vertical oval panels from below the rim to above the foot. See Barware photograph on page 39 in the third row the third mug.

Pattern 427, Beer Mug

Patterns 428 and 429 are Tumblers. They both hold 3 ounces and are plain with heavy bottoms.

Patterns 428 and 429, Tumblers

Pattern 430 is a Butter Plate. It has with a star bottom and wide flanged rim.

Pattern 430, Butter Plate

Pattern 431 consists of Ales. They have a bucket shaped bowl with flutes from below the rim to the bottom of the bowl and are on a round knopped stem. The large ale holds 9-1/2 ounces and the pony holds 5 ounces. See Barware photograph on page 39 in the second row number six for the large ale and number eight for the pony ale.

Pattern 431, Ales

Pattern 432 consists of Ales and a Weiss Beer. They have trumpet shaped bowls and are fluted from below the rim to above the stocky stem. The ales hold 15 ounces, 10 ounces, and a large 7-1/2 ounce, and pony 4-1/2 ounce. The weiss beer holds 18-1/2 ounces.

Pattern 432, Ales

Pattern 433 is a Tumbler. It holds 6 ounces and is fluted.

Pattern 433, Tumbler

Pattern 434 is an Ale. It holds 8 ounces and has a plain trumpet shaped bowl on stocky stem.

Pattern 434, Ale

Pattern 435 is an Egg. It holds 4-1/2 ounces and is plain with a short stem and attached to a saucer foot. It looks more like an egg cup instead of eggnog.

Pattern 435, Egg

Pattern 436 is a Tumbler. It holds 9-1/2 ounces and is fluted with a heavy bottom.

Pattern 436, Tumbler

Pattern 437 is a Pickle Jar. It is cylindrical with a star design on the bottom and star design on the cover. It has a knob finial. It was either plain or engraved. The catalog shows a number 12 engraving which consists of an etched band with a thin line above and one below. (B & C)

Pattern 437, Pickle Jar

Pattern 438 is the Prism and Diamond Band pattern. It has flat panels with a wide horizontal band in the middle of diamonds with diamond points. This pattern was one of the ones made for the San Francisco Exhibition in 1881. It came in a complete line of tableware including octagon bowls, two butters, and cheese plates. It had at least 32 pieces, probably more with open or covered bowls.

Sugar (E)
Cream (E)
Spoon (D)
Butter (F)
Butter 5 inch flange butter and cover (F)
Celery (D)
Cheese Plate in 7 and 8 inch with star bottom (C)
Pickle octagon with tapered pointed ends and star bottom (E)
Saucer 6 inch footed and covered (E)
Jelly footed (C)
Octagon Bowls in 7, 8, 9 inch with star bottom (D)
Nappy 6 and 7 inch covered (D)

Nappies 4 and 5 inch round (C)
Bowls in 6, 7, 8, 9 inch low foot and high foot covered (F)
Stemware came in goblet, champagne, claret, a patented
   wine, & cordial (D)
Pitchers in quart and half gallon (D & E)

Pattern 438, Prism and Diamond Band

Catalog Page with Prism and Diamond Band Pattern 438

Pattern 438, Prism & Diamond Band Pattern
1. Bowls Covered 7", 9", 8" Deep Bowls
2. Spoon, Bowl 9" Deep Bowl Open, Celery
3. Nappy footed 5-1/2", Sauce 4", Sugar (missing cover)

Pattern 439 is the Scalloped Diamond Point pattern. It has also been called Panel with Diamond Point and Late Diamond Point. It is usually found in crystal except for a few rare compotes in cobalt or with either cobalt bowls and crystal stem and foot or cobalt stem and foot with crystal bowls. Some stemware (usually wines) was made in colors in the 1880s as this pattern was around a long time. The pattern has a wide diamond point band in the middle or bottom of the bowls and a fine thin band of cording within scallops on the rims. A few of the patterns that do not have the cord band in scallops are the bitter bottle, pickle jars, finger bowl, quart and half gallon pitchers, master and individual salts, tumblers, toothpick, "flange" covered butter, stemware with a 10-1/2 ounce goblet, 3 ounce claret, and 2 ounce patented wine. The set consisted of sugar, cream, spoon, and butter, however, there were three different butter bowls. All had covers, one was without a foot, another was a 6 inch footed, and the last was the 5 inch flanged butter. There were two sugar bowls, a tall covered one and a large open sugar. There are some 60 pieces in this pattern and it probably has the most pieces of any of the Central patterns.

Sugar tall with cover (D)
Sugar large open (C)
Spoon (C)
Cream (D)
Butter no foot (D)
Butter "flange" 5 inches and cover (no foot) (E)
Butter 6 inch footed (paneled low foot no knop in middle) (E)
Bitter bottle (E)
Celery (D)

Pickle dish (oval with flange) (C)
Horseradish or mustard on saucer foot with knob finial (D)
Finger bowl (C)
Nappy round in 4, 5, 7, 8, 9 inches (C & D)
Nappy footed (no cover) in 4 and 5 inches (C & D)
Oval bowls in 6, 7, 8, 9 inches (D)
Cheese cover with flame finial (F)
Sweetmeat 6 inch high foot and low foot covered (D)
Pitchers quart and half gallon (E & F)
Bowls covered with low foot in 7, 8, 9, and 10 inches (F)
Bowls covered with high foot in 7, 8, 9, and 10 inches (F & G)
Bowls shallow bowls in high foot and low foot in 8, 9, and 10 inches (E)
Plates in 5, 6, 7, 8, 9 inches (D)
Pickle jar with ground stopper (has a neck with flanged rim, the round stopper is flat with diamond point in the center) (D)
Pickle jar and cover (has ground top, cover has knob finial) (D)
Tumblers in 7 ounce and small 3-1/2 ounce with pattern on bottom half of bowl and N.M. (new model) 7 ounce with pattern up three-fourths on bowl (C)
Toothpick (2-1/2 ounces) (B)
Salt master and individual salt (See Salts and Miscellaneous Ware photograph on page 69 on row six number six and seven.) (B)
Salvers in 8, 9, 10, 11, 12 inches (F & G)

Pattern 439, Scalloped
Diamond Point

Catalog Page with Scalloped Diamond Point Pattern 439

Scalloped Diamond Point Pattern 439 and No. 437 Pickle
(left to right, top to bottom)
1. Sweetmeat 6" HF, Pitcher 1/2-gallon, Wine, Bowl 9" HF,
   Toothpick, Cobalt Bowl 9" HF Open
2. Pickle No. 437 Eng. 12, Pickle, Pickle, Spoon, Cream,
   Goblet, Pitcher quart
3. Tumbler, Master Salt, Ind. Salt, Plate 7", Pickle Oval,
   Butter, Nappy 3", Horse Radish or Mustard
4. Nappy 5", Celery, Nappy 8", Sugar, Nappy 4" Footed

The next pattern does not have a number. It is a Shell pattern that has been attributed to Central because it is so similar to pattern 439, Scalloped Diamond Point. The shape of the bowls, stems, rims are identical, only the design is different. The pickle is the same shape as number 439 and Central used this same shape for other pickles. The finial has the same shape as pattern 439 except it has the shell design on it. With all these similarities it should be attributed to Central. It was made in a complete line of table ware. If it was made in stemware is unknown. Some of the known pieces are below.

Sugar (C)
Cream (C)
Spoon (C)
Butter (D)
Celery (D)
Nappies round (C)
Nappies footed (C & D)
Bowls high foot and low foot
    covered or open (E)
Pickle (C)
Salvers (F)

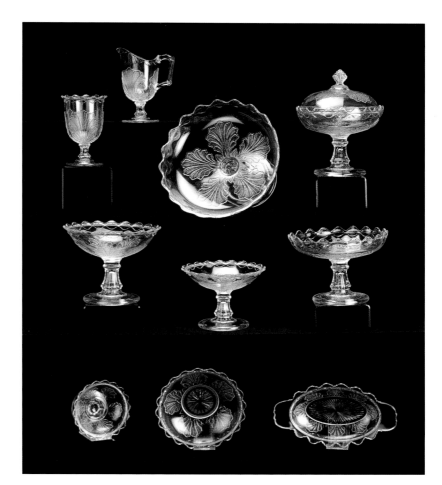

Shell Pattern [No pattern number; similar to No. 439 Scalloped Diamond Point] (left to right, top to bottom)
1. Spoon, Cream, Bowl 10" Showing Pattern, Bowl 7" HF Shallow Bowl Covered.
2. Bowl 7-1/2" Deep Bowl Open, Bowl 6" Shallow Bowl, Bowl 7" with Crimped Rim
3. Pickle, Nappy 4" Footed, Butter 6" (missing cover)

Pattern 440 is miscellaneous ware with Octagon Bowls, Cheese Plates and Covers. The octagon bowls included a pickle dish with tapered pointed ends and the bowls are 7, 8, and 9 inches. The bowls and pickle have the same shape as 438 octagon bowls. The flanged cheese plates were 7 or 8 inches. The plain cover has a flame finial. The bowls and cheese cover were either plain or engraved. The octagon bowls and cheese plates have star bottoms.

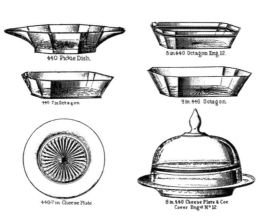

Pattern 440

Pattern 440, 9" Octagon Bowl

Patterns 441 through 448 are Beer Mugs.

Pattern 441 is the E Pluribus Unum mug. It holds 9-1/2 ounces and it has a pattern of three arrows going through a shield which is on a banner in the middle of the mug. The words E PLURIB are on one side of the shield and US UNUM is on the other side. The upper half is barrel shaped and the lower half has narrow oval ribs above a wide foot. See Barware photograph on page 39 on the bottom row the fifth mug. (D)

Pattern 441, E Pluribus Unum beer mug

Pattern 442 is a 6 ounce barrel shaped fluted beer mug with a notched oval band on the stem above the foot.

Pattern 442, Beer Mug

Pattern 443 is a heavy bottomed Huber mug in 9 ounce and 5 ounce pony.

Pattern 443, Beer Mug

Pattern 444 is the Centennial mug in the Huber style. This was patented by John Oesterling who registered his design for a simple beer mug, with or without a handle on February 04, 1872. On April 11, 1876 John Oesterling and Julius Palme received a joint design patent for a "Centennial Beer Mug". The design consisted of a star-shaped emblem on both side of the mug with the dates 1776 and 1876 in the center of each star. They were made in a 9 ounce and 5 ounce pony mug size. The Centennial Ale is pattern 455. See Barware photograph on page 39 the 9 ounce mug is on the third row the seventh mug and the 5 ounce pony is on the bottom row the third mug. (D)

Pattern 444, Centennial Beer Mug

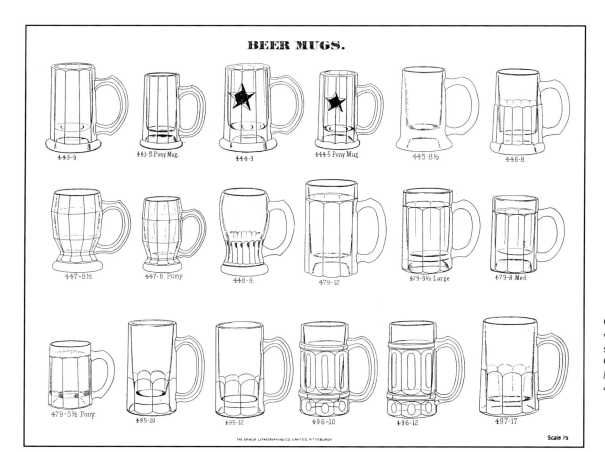

Catalog Page with Beer Mugs showing Centennial Beer Mugs Pattern 444

Pattern 445 is a plain heavy bottomed cylindrical mug holding 8-1/2 ounces.

Pattern 445, Beer Mug

Pattern 446 is a ribbed cylindrical 8 ounce heavy bottomed mug.

Pattern 446, Beer Mug

Pattern 447 is a barrel shaped mug with panels broken up by horizontal lines a fourth and three-fourths way down the bowl in a 8-1/2 ounce and 6 ounce pony size. (C)

Pattern 447, Beer Mug

Pattern 448 is a 9 ounce beer mug with the upper half barrel shaped and the lower half narrower with flutes on wide foot.

Pattern 448, Beer Mug

Pattern 449 is Custard. It is plain and cup shaped with a handle.

Pattern 449 Custard

Pattern 450 is a Huber Cordial and Sham Cordial. The cordial holds 1-1/4 ounces and the sham cordial holds 1 ounce. This pattern was also called Brandy and Brandy Sham. They are on a short stocky stem.

Pattern 450, Cordial

Pattern 451 is a Pepper. No picture is available as the catalog page only showed the bottom half of the pattern which looked like a hourglass shape.

Pattern 451, Pepper, partial image

Pattern 452 is a Goblet. It holds 9 ounces and has a plain tapered cylindrical bowl and is on a straight stem.

Pattern 452, Goblet

Pattern 453 is Stemware. It has plain tapered cylindrical bowls on straight stems in a goblet, champagne, claret, large wine, small wine, and cordial.

Pattern 453, Stemware

Pattern 454 is Stemware. It has plain tapered cylindrical bowls on bulbous stems in a 12 ounce goblet, 6-1/2 ounce champagne, 4 ounce claret, and 2-1/2 ounce wine.

Pattern 454, Stemware

Pattern 455 is the Centennial Ale. This was produced to commemorate the nation's Centennial in 1876. John Oesterling and Julius Palme patented the ale and beer mugs April 11, 1876. The patent describes it as a pilsner but the catalog called it an ale. The design has a star shaped emblem on each side with 1776 or 1876 in the center of each star. It holds 8 ounces and has a tapered cylindrical shape tapering toward the stem on a short paneled stem that flares out at the base. Pattern 444 has the Centennial beer mugs. See Barware photograph on page 39 on the top row number five. (E)

Pattern 455, Centennial Ale

Pattern 456 consists of Weiss Beers. They have trumpet shaped bowls with a thin ring at the bottom before joining a heavy flared foot in a 14 ounce light and 10-1/2 ounce sham. See Barware photograph on page 39 on the top row the first pattern.

Pattern 456, Weiss Beers

Pattern 457 consists of Weiss Beers. They have fluted trumpet shaped bowls with a thin ring at the bottom before joining a heavy flared foot in a 14 ounce light and 10-1/2 ounce sham beer.

Pattern 457, Weiss Beer & Sham

Pattern 458 is a Champagne. It holds 4-1/2 ounces and has a plain cup bowl on a hollow straight stem.

Pattern 458, Hollow Stem Champagne

Pattern 459 is an Ale. It holds 9 ounces and has a tall tapered cylindrical bowl with flutes from below the rim to the bottom of the bowl and thick walls on a bulbous stem.

Pattern 459 Ale

Pattern 460 is a Tumbler. It holds 14-1/2 ounces and is plain with a tapered cylindrical bowl.

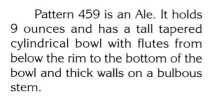 Pattern 460, Tumbler

Pattern 461 is an Ice Cream Bowl. It holds 6 ounces and looks very much like pattern 435 in an egg cup. It has a plain rounded bowl on a short stem with attached saucer foot.

Pattern 461, Ice Cream

Pattern 462 is a Molasses Can. It is trumpet shaped with the base being wider than the top and has deep tall flutes and a flat bottom. (E)

Pattern 462, Molasses Can

Pattern 462, Molasses Can

Patterns 463 and 464 are Sherries. They have fluted trumpet shaped bowls on straight tapered stems. Pattern 463 holds 1 ounce and pattern 464 holds 1-1/2 ounces.

Patterns 463 and 464, Sherry

Pattern 465 is a Champagne. It holds 4-1/2 ounces and has a hollow loop paneled stem.

Pattern 465, Champagne

106

Pattern 466 is a Sherry. It holds 1 ounce and has a fluted trumpet shaped bowl on a straight tapered stem like patterns 463 and 464.

Pattern 466, Sherry

The next three patterns are stand and hand lamps. The stand lamps were made in five sizes of A, B, C, D, and E and the hand lamps were in three sizes of A, B, and C. They have a similar style font and have the same stem and foot.

Pattern 467 consists of Stand and Hand Lamps. This pattern was called "Central Rounds"[27] by Catherine M.V. Thuro. The font has a wide plain flat top that tapers in toward the bottom. It came plain or "roughed and cut". The roughed and cut font has a pattern of three horizontal circles between tall vertical panels around the bowl. The stand lamps are on a bulbous paneled stem on two different feet, either a round hollow foot or a cup foot. The hand lamps also came on a plain hollow foot or cup foot. See Oil Lamps and Whirlpool Colognes photograph on page 135 in row three the fourth lamp. (F)

Pattern 467, Stand & Hand Lamps

Pattern 468 consists of Rope Band Stand and Hand Lamps. The font has a large rope band design around the middle of the font. The stand lamps are on a bulbous paneled stem on two different feet, either a round hollow foot or a cup foot. The hand lamps also came on a plain hollow foot or cup foot. (F)

Pattern 468, Stand & Hand Lamps

Pattern 469 consists of Stand and Hand Lamps named "Oesterling" by Catherine M.V. Thuro[28]. The font has a design of a scallop band of diamond point with a thin protruding ring in the middle. The stand lamps are on a bulbous paneled stem on two different feet, either a round hollow foot or a cup foot. The hand lamps also came on a plain hollow foot or cut foot. See Colored Oil Lamps photograph on page 161 in row three the first lamp with cobalt stem and foot. Also see Oil Lamps photograph on page 73 in row two the first lamp. (F)

Pattern 469 Stand & Hand Lamp

Pattern 470 is a Bullseye Stand Lamp. The font is similar to patterns 219 and 220 except this lamp is on a different stem and foot. It is on the paneled stem with oval foot. If there was a hand lamp in this pattern is unknown. (F)

Pattern 470, Stand Lamp

Patterns 471 and 472 are Tumblers. They are cylindrical and have fluted bowls. Pattern 471 holds 5-1/2 ounces and pattern 472 holds 4-1/2 ounces.

Patterns 471 and 472, Tumblers

Pattern 473 is a Butter and Cover. It is fluted from top to bottom including the cover. It came with or without handles. The bowl has a scalloped rim and the cover has a round knob finial (like a mushroom cap). There is a star design in the bottom of the bowl. (D)

Pattern 473, Butter & Cover

Pattern 474 is a Butter and Cover. The design around the bowl is a flute and notch pattern with a star design in the bottom. It has the same cover as pattern 473. (D)

Pattern 474, Covered Butter & Cover

Patterns 475 and 476 are Blown Tumblers. They are cylindrical with thin walls and came plain or etched. Number 475 held 10 ounces and number 476 held 8 ounces. Some of the etchings used were band 40, 75, 90 and 200. See engravings on the next page.

Pattern 475 and 476, Blown Tumblers

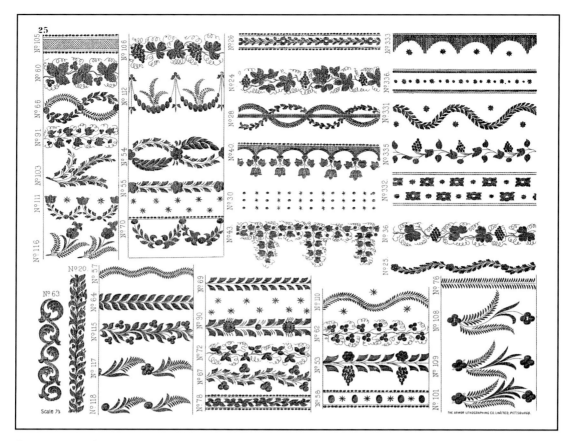

Catalog page of engravings

Pattern 477 is a Tumbler. It holds 8 ounces and is cylindrical with fluted bowl.

Pattern 477, Tumbler

Pattern 478 consists of Ales and a Beer. They are plain with a tall cylindrical bowl on round knopped stems. They came in a 12 ounce ale, 10 ounce beer, 9 ounce ale and 5-1/2 ounce pony ale.

Pattern 478, Ales & Beer

Pattern 481 consists of Weiss Beers. They hold 10 ounces and have fluted bowls a third below the rim to the ring above the heavy flared foot and came in three different styles. Two are trumpet shaped and came with or without a handle. The other beer has a handle and the rim is "cupped" in. See Barware photograph on page 39 on the top row numbers four without a handle and number six with a handle.

Pattern 481, Weiss Beer

Pattern 479 consists of Beer Mugs. They are cylindrical with heavy bottoms and flutes from below the rim to the bottom in a 12 ounce, 9-1/2 large, 8 medium, and 5-1/2 ounce pony sizes.

Pattern 479, Beer Mugs

Pattern 482 is a Huber Tumbler. It holds 2 ounces.

Pattern 482, Tumbler

Pattern 480 is an Ale. It holds 11 ounces and has a trumpet shape fluted bowl on stocky stem.

Pattern 480, Ale

Pattern 483 is a Cocktail. It holds 3-1/2 ounces and has a tapered cylindrical bowl on loop paneled stem.

Pattern 483, Cocktail

108

Pattern 484 is a Champagne. It holds 6 ounces and is on a loop paneled stem.

Pattern 484, Champagne

Pattern 485 is a Tumbler. It holds 2-1/2 ounces and is plain and cylindrical.

Pattern 485, Tumbler

Pattern 486 consists of Stand and Hand Lamps called "Central Plain Panel"[29] by Catherine Thuro. The font is similar to 468 and 469 lamps except this font has panels from top to bottom. The stand lamp came in five sizes on paneled stem and the hand lamp in three sizes both came on the plain round foot or cup foot. See Colored Oil Lamps on photograph page 161 in row three the second lamp. (F)

Pattern 486, Stand & Hand Lamps

Pattern 487 consists of Stand and Hand Lamps. The font is more oval than round and has a pattern of alternating vertical notched panels and large plain oval panels. The stem is a knop stem and the lamp is on a cup foot. There are five stand lamps sizes and three hand lamp sizes. (F)

Pattern 487, Stand & Hand Lamps

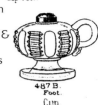

Pattern 488 consists of Stand and Hand Lamps. They are similar to pattern 487 except for a plain oval font. They came in five sizes of stand lamps and three of hand lamps on the knobbed stem and cup foot. See Oil Lamps and Whirlpool Colognes photograph on page 135 in row three the first lamp. (E)

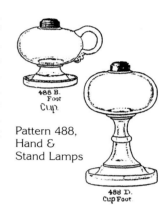

Pattern 488, Hand & Stand Lamps

Pattern 489 is a Tumbler. It holds 10 ounces and is cylindrical with fluted bowl.

Pattern 489, Tumbler

Pattern 490 is an Ale. It holds 11 ounces and has a trumpet shaped fluted bowl on short stocky stem.

Pattern 490, Ale

Pattern 491 is Stemware. It has a trumpet shaped fluted bowl on spool stems. It came in a 10-1/2 ounce goblet, 5-1/2 ounce champagne, 3-1/2 ounce claret, 2-1/2 ounce wine, and 2 ounce wine sham (with heavy bottom).

Pattern 491, Stemware

Pattern 486, Panel Stand Lamps and Hand Lamp. The first Lamp has a Cobalt Stem and Foot

Patterns 492 and 493 are Individual Butters. No picture is available as they were on a shipping order list in a Central catalog from the 1880s

Pattern 494 is a Sherry. It holds 2-1/2 ounces and has a fluted trumpet shaped bowl on straight stem. This pattern is the same as 463, 464, and 466.

Pattern 494, Sherry

Pattern 495 consists of Beer Mugs. They hold 10 and 12 ounces and are fluted cylindrical mugs. They are the same size in height except the 10 ounce mug has thick walls and a very heavy bottom.

Pattern 495, Beer Mugs

Pattern 496 consists of Beer Mugs. They were designed by John Oesterling. The mugs hold 10 and 12 ounces. The pattern has an elongated oval panel between a projecting ring below the rim and above the foot with a smaller oval panel around the foot. They are the same height size except the 10 ounce mug has thick walls and a heavier bottom. (C)

Pattern 496, Beer Mugs

Pattern 497 is a Beer Mug. It holds 17 ounces and is cylindrical with a fluted bowl and heavy bottom.

Pattern 497, Beer Mug

Pattern 498 consists of Beer Mugs. They were designed by John Oesterling. The mugs hold 10 and 12 ounces. They have heavy hollow bottoms and are cylindrical shaped with a pattern of five horizontal thumbprints next to elongated oval panels on a fluted base. They are the same size in height except the 10 ounce mug has thick walls. (C)

Pattern 498, Beer Mugs

Pattern 499 is a Beer. This beer is usually referred to as a Pilsner and was made by other glass companies. It holds 10-1/2 ounces. It is trumpet shaped on stocky stem with a pattern of five oval thumbprints next to narrow elongated flutes. This pattern was also made in a 16 ounce Weiss Beer called "Punty" and a 14 ounce Pony Punty Beer. The punty beers do not have catalog numbers and are illustrated in the section missing pattern numbers. See Barware photograph on page 39 on the top row the third pattern. (C)

Pattern 499, Pilsner Beer

Patterns 500 through 509 are all Tumblers, some with heavy bottoms. Patterns 500 and 501 have arched flutes and Patterns 502, 503, 504, and 505 are fluted. Pattern 506 is a Huber style. Pattern 507 has pointed ribs, 508 has narrow flutes, 509 is plain and all have thick walls.

Patterns 500-504, Tumblers

Patterns 505-509, Tumblers

Pattern 510 is a Goblet. It has a honeycomb pattern three-fourths up on the bowl on a paneled stem.

Pattern 510, Goblet

Pattern 511 is a Goblet. It has a trumpet shaped bowl with flutes starting a little under the rim tapering in above the stem. The stem has a diamond knop slightly below the bowl and is fluted.

Pattern 511, Goblet

Pattern 512 is a Goblet. It has wide panels starting a little under the rim tapering down to the paneled stem above the foot.

Pattern 512, Goblet

Pattern 513 is a Tumbler. It holds 2-1/2 ounces and is plain with a heavy bottom and thick walls. It is similar to pattern 509.

Pattern 513, Tumbler

Pattern 514 is a Hot Whiskey. It holds 5-1/2 ounces and has a tapered cylindrical fluted bowl on a spool stem.

Pattern 514, Hot Whiskey

Pattern 518 consists of Pitchers. They came in 1/2 gallon, quart, and pint sizes. They are cylindrical tapering in slightly toward the top with reeded handles and came either plain or engraved. One of the engravings shown in the catalogs on this pitcher is number 148 of a bird and is quite lovely and was used on other pitchers. See Pitchers, Molasses Cans and Miscellaneous on page 65 on the top row the first pitcher with engraving 109 (the next pitcher has the bird engraving). (D & E)

Pattern 518, Pitchers

Pattern 515 is a Punch Tumbler. It holds 4 ounces and is fluted and looks like any number of tumblers but was called "Punch". It does not have a handle.

Pattern 515, Punch Tumbler

Pattern 516 consists of an Ale and a Square Whiskey. The ale holds 8 ounces and the square whiskey holds 3-1/2 ounces. The pattern has 6 wide flutes from below the rim to the bottom of the bowl. The ale is on a stocky stem and the square whiskey is on a spool stem.

Pattern 516, Ale and Square Whiskey

Pattern 519 is an Ale. It came in a 7 ounce medium and 4 ounce pony. It has a tall cylindrical bowl on a plain stem that flares out slightly before joining the foot. It came plain or etched Band 40.

Pattern 519, Ale

Pattern 517 consists of Cruets in three different shapes. They have tall cylindrical shapes with a wide protruding band of thick glass in the middle for fitting into casters. They came in shaker bottle, stopper bottle with plain stopper that looks like a flame, and in a condiment bottle. (D)

Pattern 517, Cruets

Pattern 520 was named "Central 520" by Kamm[30] but as it is a loop pattern it should be named "Central Loop 520". This pattern was in the Central catalog with samples made for the San Francisco Exhibition in 1881. It has plain bowls with a loop pattern in the bottom with paneled bulbous stems that has a protruding ring at the bottom of the bowls on high foot compotes. The finial is fluted with a ring before a round top. There are two different spooners, butters, and half gallon pitchers. There were probably other pieces of this pattern as not all the pieces were in the catalogs.

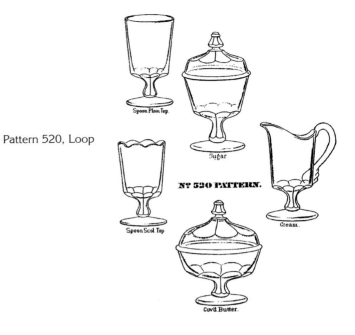

Pattern 520, Loop

Sugar footed (D)
Cream (C)
Spoon with plain top (C)
Spoon with scalloped top (C)
Butter footed with cover (D)
Butter 6 inch with cover (flat bottom) (D)
Nappy 4 inch round (B)
Nappy 4-1/2 inch footed (B)
Ovals (these were on a shipping order list in a 1880s Central catalog) (B)
Bowls 6, 7, 8, 9 inch high foot (C)
Pitcher in half gallon with reed handle (F)
Pitcher in quart and half gallon with tapered bottoms and applied handle (E)
Stemware with large and small goblet, and 3/4 ounce cordial (B)

See the next page with Loop Pattern 520 examples on top row.

Catalog Page with 520 Loop Pattern

Pattern 520, Loop, Ball and Chain, and Miscellaneous [No. 520 Loop, No. 651 Ball & Chain, No. 584 Spindle, No. 559 Panel, and No. 546 Optic Diamond Band] (left to right, top to bottom)
1. No. 520 Loop Bowls, 8" HF, Cover Showing Loop Pattern, 9" HF, 6" HF
2. No. 651 Ball & Chain Spoon Engraved 173, Butter, Spoon, Cream
3. No. 584 Spindle Pitcher 1/2 gal. Eng. 213, No. 559 Panel Bowl 6" HF, No. 546 Optic Diamond Band Cream, No. 584 Spindle Bowl 6-1/2" HF

Pattern 521 consists of Beer Mugs. They have plain cylindrical bowls with heavy bottoms and came in 14, 12, 10, 8, 5, and 3 ounce sizes. The 14 ounce mug has tall sides. See Barware photograph on page 39 on the bottom row the first mug.

Pattern 521, Beer Mugs

Pattern 523 consists of Weiss Beer Mugs. They hold 9 ounces and have a hourglass shape with flutes from below the rim to above the foot with heavy bowls and came with or without a handle. (C)

Pattern 523, Weiss Beer Mugs

Pattern 522 consists of Tumblers. They are plain and cylindrical. The thin walled tumbler holds 5 ounces and the sham with thick walls and heavy bottom holds 4 ounces They also came etched with Band 200.

Pattern 522, Tumblers

Pattern 524 is a Cocktail. It holds 4-1/2 ounces and has a plain conical bowl. The paneled stem is narrow below the bowl and flares out then tapers back in above the foot.

Pattern 524, Cocktail

Pattern 525 is a Cocktail. It holds 4-1/2 ounces and has a conical shaped fluted bowl on a paneled stem that flares out then tapers back in above foot.

Pattern 525, Cocktail

Pattern 531 is a Champagne. It holds 4 ounces and has a cup shaped fluted bowl with a paneled stem.

Pattern 531, Champagne

Pattern 526 is a Beer Mug. It holds 13 ounces and is tall with fluted bowl and heavy bottom.

Pattern 526, Beer Mug

Pattern 532 consists of Ales. They have trumpet shaped fluted bowls on a stem with round knop slightly under the bottom of the bowl. The 6-1/2 ounce ale has wider flutes and has a fluted stem from below the knop down to the foot. The 4-1/2 ounce pony ale has narrower flutes and has a plain stem (no flutes) below the knop. See Barware photograph on page 39 in the second row the fourth ale.

Pattern 532, Ales

Pattern 527 is a Champagne. It holds 3 ounce and has a cup bowl on hollow stem that tapers down to a round knop above the foot.

Pattern 527, Champagne

Pattern 533 is a Champagne. It has a cup shaped fluted bowl on a paneled stem that tapers down to the foot.

Pattern 533, Champagne

Pattern 528 consists of Beer Mugs. They were designed by John Oesterling. The mugs are tall and cylindrical with horizontal thumbprints in a band around the bowl where the handles are joined near the top and bottom. They came in a tall 13 ounce, 10 ounce medium, 8 ounce, and 5 ounce pony sizes. See Barware photograph on page 39 on the bottom row the fourth mug. (C)

Pattern 528, Beer Mug

Pattern 534 consists of Beer Mugs. They are cylindrical with heavy bottoms and tapered rims in a large 11 ounce, medium 9 ounces, and pony 5-1/2 ounce sizes

Pattern 534, Beer Mugs

Pattern 535 is a Tumbler. It holds 5 ounces and is fluted.

Pattern 535, Tumbler

Pattern 529 is a Beer Mug. It holds 11-1/2 ounces and has a barrel shape with fluted bowl and heavy bottom.

Pattern 529, Beer Mug

Pattern 536 is a Cocktail. It holds 3 ounces and has a cup bowl with fluted bottom joined to a straight stem.

Pattern 536, Cocktail

Pattern 530 is an Ale. It holds 7 ounces and has a tall trumpet shaped fluted bowl with heavy bottom that protrudes out on stocky stem.

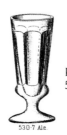

Pattern 530, Ale

Pattern 537 is a Finger Bowl. It is plain with a star design in the bottom. It came plain or etched with Band 30 or 40. (B)

Pattern 537, Finger Bowl

Patterns 538, 539, 540 and 541 are Tumblers. They all have fluted bowls. Pattern 538 holds 4 ounces, pattern 539 holds 3-1/2 ounces, pattern 540 holds 5 ounces, and pattern 541 holds 4 ounces.

Patterns 538, 539, 540, and 541, Tumblers

Pattern 542 is a Soda. It holds 12 ounces and is a plain tumbler with tall sides.

Pattern 542, Soda Tumbler

Pattern 543 is a Tumbler. It holds 12 ounces and is fluted.

Pattern 543, Tumbler

Pattern 544 consists of Solid Stem Salvers. They are plain and have a ridge around the top. The solid heavy stem has two protruding rings, one a fourth from the top and the other above the foot. The hollow foot flares out and has a narrow protruding ring in the middle. They came in 14, 12, 11, 10, 9, and 8 inches in diameter. (G & H)

Pattern 544, Solid Stem Salver

Pattern 545 is a Caster Set with extra bottles. It has a narrow rib design. The caster has five openings, and the front has two open salt holders on tiny feet, the middle is round and has a cover, the other two openings hold pouring bottles with stoppers. The bottles have plain necks on the top half above a protruding narrow ring with the rest of the neck ribbed onto the bowl and stopping a fourth way up with clear glass to fit in the caster. The finial and stoppers have a ring pattern. There is also a matching vinegar and pepper bottle with this set. See Casters, Urn Pattern and Miscellaneous photograph on page 119 in the center under the Urn pattern for the caster missing the bottles. (F)

Pattern 545, Caster Set

Pattern 546 is a Diamond Band pattern which I call "Optic Diamond Band". Kamm called it "Panel with Diamond-Point Band"[31]. This pattern had a diamond point band in the middle of fluted bowls. The sugar bowls were joined at the bottom of the bowl with a large protruding ring. The cream pitchers came in two sizes and are sometimes called a toy cream pitcher as they are under 5 inches tall. The open sugar bowls came in three sizes with either straight or flared rims. The flanged butter has a flat bottom and it has a knob finial. This butter is in the same style as pattern 473 with a different design. Other pieces in this pattern are unknown. See Loop 520, Ball and Chain, and Miscellaneous Patterns photograph on page 113 on the bottom row in the center for the cream pitcher. (D & E)

Pattern 546, Optic Diamond Band

Pattern 546, Optic Diamond Band Sugar and Cream

Pattern 547 consists of Ales. They have tall fluted bowls from below the rim to above the foot. They are the same size in height except one holds 12 ounces and the other holds 10 ounces and is a heavy bottomed sham.

Pattern 547, Ales

Pattern 548 consists of Ales. They have tall fluted bowls from below the rim tapering in above a large protruding ring below the bowl with a fluted stem above the foot. They are the same size in height except one holds 12 ounces and the other holds 10 ounces and is a heavy bottomed sham.

Pattern 548, Ales

Pattern 549 consists of Schoppens and a Plate. The schoppens are fluted from below the rim to above the foot and are similar in style to pattern 547. They came in 9, 7, 5-1/2, and 4 ounce sizes. The fluted plate is round with sides that come up and it looks like a saucer. If there are other pieces to this pattern is unknown.

Pattern 549, Pattern, Plate & Schoppen

Pattern 553 is a Weiss Beer and Champagne. The 16 ounce weiss beer is trumpet shaped and has tall flutes on a stocky stem and the 15 ounce sham is the same size in height but has a heavy bottom. The champagne holds 4 ounces and has a cup shaped fluted bowl with paneled stem.

Pattern 553, Weiss Beer & Champagne

Pattern 550 is a Beer Mug. It holds 16 ounces and is fluted and has a tapered rim. It is similar to pattern 529.

Pattern 550, Beer Mug

Pattern 554 is a Tumbler. It holds 4-1/2 ounces and has a cylindrical shape with fluted bowl.

Pattern 554, Tumbler

Pattern 551 consists of Beer Mugs. They are cylindrical with flutes that protrude out from below the wide clear rim to the bottom of the mug. The mugs are the same size in height except one holds 17-1/2 ounces and has a heavy bottom and the other holds 20-1/2 ounce half litter. Pattern 571 has a similar mug. (C)

Pattern 551, Beer Mug

Pattern 552 is a Weiss Beer. It holds 15 ounces and has a trumpet shape and fluted bowl with heavy bottom. The tall flutes are on the lower three-fourths of the bowl and stop above a protruding ring on a flared foot.

Pattern 552, Weiss Beer

Pattern 555 is the Nail City[32] pattern and was one of the patterns made for the San Francisco Exhibition in 1881. I think Kamm named this pattern as Wheeling used to be known as the "Nail City" due to its large production of nails and she thought the design on the handles of the pitchers resembled "nailheads". The pattern has panels in the upper half of the bowls with ribs below. The high foot bowls are on a fluted bulbous stem with a ring at the top. The finial is fluted with a round top. It was made in a complete line of table ware.

Sugar footed and covered (E)
Cream (D)
Spoon (C)
Butter on short foot covered or
    uncovered (E)
Celery (D)
Nappy 4" footed (C)
Bowls in 6, 7, 8, 9 inch high
    foot covered (E & F)
Pitcher 1/2 gallon (E)

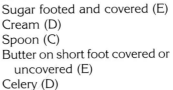
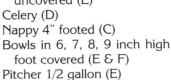

Pattern 555, Nail City

Catalog Page with No. 555 Nail City, No. 559 Panel, and No. 561 Patterns

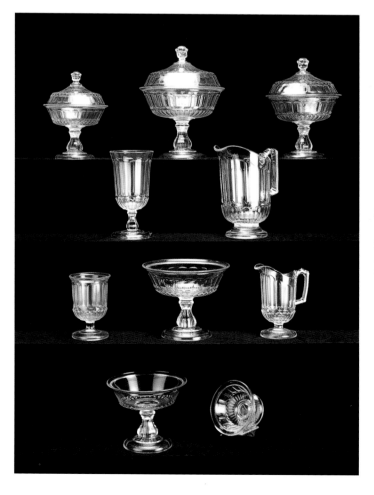

Nail City and Nail City Variant [No. 555 Nail City, No. 556 Nail City Variant] (left to right, top to bottom)
1. No. 555 Bowls 6" HF, 8" HF, 7" HF Deep Bowls Covered
2. No. 555 Celery, Pitcher Half Gallon
3. No. 555 Spoon, Bowl 8" HF Deep Bowl Open, Cream
4. No. 556 Bowl 6" HF Open, No. 555 Cover Showing Pattern

117

Pattern 556 is a Nail City Variant. It is similar to pattern 555 without the flutes in the middle of the bowl and has the same shape in bowls, stems covers and finials. It came in 7, 8, and 9 inch bowls. If there are more pieces to this pattern is unknown. See Nail City 555 Pattern with 556 Bowl photograph on the previous page on the bottom row the first pattern. (D & E)

Pattern 556, Pattern

This is a start of several patterns with a stem which resembles an explanation mark. The stem has a narrow elongated trumpet shape with knop or ring slightly above the foot (it looks like a baseball bat). This stem will be called "explanation mark" stem from here forth.

Pattern 557 consists of Cocktail. It holds 5 ounces and has a tapered cylindrical shaped bowl with a fluted bottom on the explanation mark stem.

Pattern 557, Cocktail

Pattern 558 consists of Cocktails. They had either a straight or flared top and are on the explanation mark stem. They came in a 4-1/2 ounce large cocktail and 3-1/2 ounce small cocktail.

Pattern 558, Cocktail

Pattern 559 consists of Footed Bowls called "Panels". They are fluted bowls with scalloped rims on a fluted hourglass shaped stem. They came in 5, 6, 7, 8, and 9 inch sizes and were open. They were on the catalog page with 555 and 561 bowls above. If there are other pieces to this pattern is unknown. See Loop 520, Ball and Chain, and Miscellaneous Patterns photograph on page 113 on the bottom row in the center above a cream pitcher. (D & E)

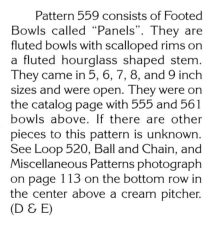

Pattern 559, Footed Bowls

Pattern 559, Panel Bowl

Pattern 560 was made for the San Francisco Exhibition of 1881. I call this pattern "Urn" as Kamm used that name for a similar unattributed pattern[33], However, she did not attribute that pattern to Central nor they did not make the one she had mentioned. Kamm described the 560 pattern in Book Three, page 16, number 19, and called it "Central, 560". This pattern has a complete line of table ware and came plain or etched with Band 40. It has the explanation mark stem. The bowls were wider at the top with narrower bottoms and had a cover that was flat on top then curved out and down with wider curves toward the bottom. The finial had a slightly rounded center then flares out and tapers down to a ring before flaring out again on a wide circle before attaching to the cover. The stemware had tapered cylindrical bowls with flat bottoms above the explanation mark stem. See Casters, Urn Pattern, and Miscellaneous photograph on the next page the top row.

Sugar (D)
Cream (C)
Spoon (C)
Butter (D)
Celery (D)
Nappy 4 inch heavy round (B)
Nappy 4 inch stocky foot (B)
Nappy 4-1/2 inch footed (B)
Bowls, 5, 6, 7, 8, and 9 inch covered or open (C & D)
Stemware in goblet 10 ounce, champagne 6 ounce., claret 3-1/2 ounce, wine 2 ounce, ale 7-1/2 ounces (prices unknown)

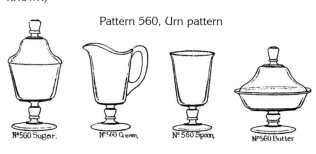

Pattern 560, Urn pattern

Casters, Urn Pattern [No. 560], and Miscellaneous (left to right, top to bottom)
1. No. 560 Urn Pattern Bowls 5" & 8" HF, Celery, Bowl 8" HF, Bowl 4" LF, Center
   No. 545 Caster (missing bottles)
2. No. 242 Cruets in Caster, No. 251 Cruet Bottles, No. 894 Revolving Caster
3. No. 579 Hand Salts (etched), No. 999 Revolving Caster (missing bottles), No. 579
   Hand Salt (crystal)

Pattern 561 is a Flute pattern. It does not have a name. It came on the explanation mark stem. It has a 5 and 6 inch plate with high walls which looked more like a saucer. The 6 inch plate had a flanged rim and a 7 inch nappy looks like the plate except there was more space under the rim before the flutes. There was a 8 inch oval with flanged rim and 5, 6, 7, 8, and 9 inch open footed bowls. There is an individual cream pitcher and a 8 inch cheese plate and cover. The cheese plate has a star design in the bottom, the flutes are high up on the cheese cover and it has a flame finial. There were probably more pieces to this pattern. (D)

Pattern 561, Bowl

Pattern 561, Pattern

Pattern 562 is a Cocktail. It holds 3-1/2 ounces. The bowl has a tapered cylindrical shape with a fluted bottom and is on the explanation mark stem. It came plain or engraved with Band 40 and is similar to pattern as 557.

Pattern 562, Cocktail

Pattern 563 is Stemware. It came in a 12 ounce goblet and 4 ounce wine with plain round bottomed bowls on spool stems.

Pattern 563, Stemware

Patterns 564 and 565 are Tumblers. They are plain with fluted bowls. Pattern 564 holds 4 ounces and pattern 565 holds 3 ounces.

Patterns 564 and 565, Tumblers

Pattern 566 is a Beer Goblet. It holds 10 ounces and has a tapered cylindrical bowl with flat bottom above the explanation mark stem. It is similar to pattern 560 stemware except the base of the bowl is a little wider.

Pattern 566, Beer Goblet

Pattern 567 is Stemware. They have plain conical bowls on straight stems and came plain or decorated with Bands 40 or 70 and engraved 179 or 185. They came in a 10 ounce heavy goblet, 9-1/2 ounce light goblet, 6 ounce champagne, 3-1/2 or 4 ounce claret, and 2 or 2-1/2 ounce wine.

Pattern 567, Stemware

Patterns 568, 569, and 570 are Cocktails. The bowls have a tapered cylindrical shape with a fluted bottom on the explanation mark stem. Pattern 568 holds 4 ounces, pattern 569 holds 2 ounces, and pattern 570 holds 1 ounce. They are similar to pattern 557 and came plain or engraved.

Pattern 568 to 570, Cocktails

Pattern 571 is a Beer Mug. It holds 13 ounces and is cylindrical with a fluted bowl and a heavy bottom. The flutes protrude out below the clear rim to the bottom of the mug. Pattern 551 has a similar mug.

Pattern 571, Beer Mug

Pattern 572 consists of Table Salts. They came in ribbed individual and table salts. They are square and the individual salt is slightly different from the table as it has ribs on the rim where the table has a flat surfaced rim. See Salts and Miscellaneous Ware photograph on page 69 on the bottom row on the right (the 10th pattern). (B)

Pattern 572, Individual & Table Salts

Pattern 573 is a Wine. It holds 1 ounce and is trumpet shaped with flutes from below the rim to where it joins a bulbous paneled stem.

Pattern 573, Wine

Pattern 574 is a Champagne. It holds 6-1/2 ounces and has a cup-shaped bowl and is on the explanation mark stem. It came plain or engraved.

Pattern 574, Champagne

Patterns 575 and 576 are Ales. They have tall tapered cylindrical bowls and are on the explanation mark stem. One catalog had pattern 575 illustrated as a "Champ." instead of an ale so there could be other stemware pieces in this pattern. Pattern 575 holds 5 ounces and pattern 576 holds 6 ounces. They are similar to pattern 560's stemware and to pattern 566 in a beer goblet.

Pattern 575 & 576, Ales

Pattern 577 is Stemware. It is cylindrical with a thumbprint band around the bottom of the bowl and is on a spool stem. It came in a tall 17 ounce weiss beer, in a 11 ounce large ale, 9 ounce medium, 8 ounce, and 5-1/2 ounce pony. It also came in a 4-1/2 ounce hot whiskey with straight or flared top. The flared top hot whiskey has a double ring knop in the stem.

Pattern 577, Stemware

Pattern 578 is a Tumbler. It holds 8 ounces and is fluted with a heavy bottom.

Pattern 578, Tumbler

Pattern 579 is the Hand Salt. It is a shaker salt with a hand reaching up around the bowl. The bowl has a fish scale pattern and came in crystal or etched. See Salts and Miscellaneous Ware photograph on page 69 in row five on the left and right (the first and eighth salts). Also see Casters, Urn Pattern, and Miscellaneous photograph on page 119 on the bottom row on the left and right. (E each)

Pattern 579, Salt

Pattern 580, Stand & Hand Lamps

Pattern 580 consists of Stand and Hand Lamps. They have a plain oval font with flat bottom and are on a hollow stem with cup foot. The stand lamps came is five sizes and the hand lamps in three. (D)

Pattern 581 consists of Stand and Hand Lamps. They have an oval font with wide band that tapers in at the middle (like a rubber band) and are on a hollow stem with cup foot. The stand lamps came in 5 sizes and the hand in three. The fonts came with a clear band or an etched band called "Banded". (D)

Pattern 581, Stand & Hand Lamps

Pattern 582 consists of Stand and Hand Lamps. Thuro called it "Fingerprints"[33], but I call it "Thumbprint Band". It has a roundish font with a clear round top joined in the middle by a narrow protruding ring with an elongated thumbprint pattern around the bottom. They came on the hollow stem and cup foot. (E)

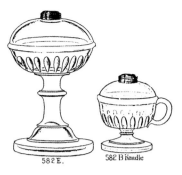

Pattern 582, Stand & Hand Lamps

Thumbprint Band Pattern 582 Hand and Stand Lamps. *From the Collection of Harry and Nancy Young*

Pattern 583 is a Hot Whiskey. It holds 4 ounces and has a fluted cylindrical shape and is on a spool stem.

Pattern 583, Hot Whiskey

121

Pattern 584 is a pattern I call "Spindle", it could also be called Spool as the stems resemble spindles or spools. This pattern has tapered cylindrical bowls with lower indentation that tapers in toward the stem. The stem is like two spools or two rings joining in the middle with a narrower piece of glass. The compotes are beautiful and very modern looking. The bowl on the compotes curve down to a lower indentation that tapers in toward the stem. The covers are a reverse of the bowls and they are on a finial that has a small round tip then a large ring with a smaller ring below it. The molasses can does not resemble the pattern as it is plain. The pattern came plain or engraved. See Loop 520, Ball and Chain and Miscellaneous Patterns photograph on page 113 on the bottom row the first pattern is the half gallon pitcher engraved 213 and the fourth pattern is a 6-1/2 inch bowl.

Sugar (D)
Cream (C)
Spoon (C)
Butter and cover (D)
Celery (D)
Bowls in 5, 6, 7, 8, and 9 inches high foot open (D)
Bowls in 6, 7, 8, and 9 inches high foot covered (E)
Goblet, champagne 5-1/2 ounces, wine 2-1/2 ounces, claret 3-1/2 ounces (B)
Molasses can (F)
Pitcher half gallon (D)

584 Sugar   584 Cream.

584 Butter & Cov   584 Spoon.

Pattern 584, Spindle

7 in 584 Bowl H.F. & Cov.

584 Spoon.

NO 584 PATTERN.

584 Sugar.

584, Cream.

8 in 584 Bowl, H.F & Cov.

7 in 584 Bowl H.F. & Cov.

584 Butter & Cov.

9 in 584 Bowl H.F. & Cov.

8 in 584 Bowl H.F. &

9 in 584 B. H.F &

Catalog page with Spindle Pattern, No. 584

Pattern 585 was called "Leaflets"[34] by Kamm and I will keep that name. Another name used was Near Garland. The name was given from the leaf like pattern under the rim on most of the pieces, however, it resembles a fleur-de-lis more than a leaf. This pattern had samples sent to the San Francisco Exposition in 1881. The molasses can and bread plate have only the Greek key variation pattern that is near the bottom of the bowls. This pattern has a wonderful finial of a reclining dog. The dog has pointed ears and when found they usually have been ground off. There are four pieces with a beautiful bird pattern. The large bread plate has a tree limb in the middle with two birds on branches above a nest with eggs on each side. The pickle with handles and 7 and 8 inch ovals have one bird on each side of the tree with the nest only on the left and a small round 4 inch nappy has only one bird with the nest. The shape of the bowls is similar to pattern 584 except the cover has a much higher top and are joined at the stem with a ring on a short wide foot. The molasses can has an elongated thumbprint band on the bowl and horizontal ovals below the neck with the Greek key design in the middle.

Sugar (E)

Cream (D)
Spoon (D)
Butter and cover (F)
Celery (D)
Oval 7 and 8 inch with bird pattern center (C & D)
Nappy 4 inch round (B)
Nappy 4 inch footed (B)
Bowls 7, 8, low foot covered (F)
Molasses can (See Pitchers, Molasses Cans & Miscellaneous photograph on page 65 on the bottom row the third pitcher) (E)
Bread plate oval with handles and Greek key variation with star design in the bottom 13 inches (E)
Bread tray large hourglass shape with bird pattern center 14-1/2 inches with handles (E)
Pickle a small version of the above bread plate 9 inches (D)
Horse Radish footed with handles and cover (E)
Pickle jar cylindrical with flat bottom, handles, and cover (F)
Stemware in a goblet (C)
Pitcher (E)

Pattern 585, Leaflets

585 Sugar   585 Spoon   585 Butter & Cov.   585 Cream.

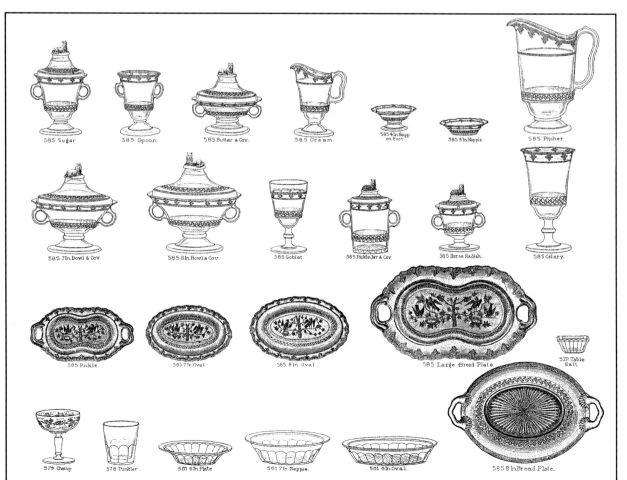

585 Sugar   585 Spoon.   585 Butter & Cov.   585 Cream.   585 4 In. Napp. on Foot   585 4 In. Nappie   585 Pitcher.

585 7 In. Bowl & Cov   585 8 In. Bowl & Cov.   585 Goblet   585 Pickle Jar & Cov.   585 Horse Radish.   585 Celery.

585 Pickle   585 7 In. Oval.   585 8 In. Oval.   585 Large Bread Plate   572 Table Salt

574 Champ.   578 Tumbler   561 6 In. Plate   561 7 In. Nappie.   561 6 In. Oval.   585 8 In. Bread Plate.

Catalog page with Leaflets Pattern, No. 585 and other No. 500 patterns

123

Pattern No. 585, Leaflets (left to right, top to bottom)
1. Bread Plate 13-1/2", Large Bread Tray with Bird Design 14-1/4"
2. Horse Radish, Molasses Can, Cream
3. Pickle 9" and Oval 8" with Bird Design in Bottom
4. Nappy 4", Butter, Goblet

Pattern 586 consists of Ales. They have cylindrical bowls with an elongated thumbprint band on the bottom of the bowls. The tall 17-1/2 ounce weiss beer is on a stocky stem and the 11 ounce large, 9 ounce medium, and 5-1/2 ounce pony ale are on spool stems.

Pattern 586, Ales

Patterns 588 and 589 are plain Tumblers. Pattern 588 is a 4-1/2 ounce light tumbler. Pattern 589 is a 3-1/2 ounce sham and 3 ounce heavy bottom with thick walls "Ex. Sham".

Pattern 588 and 589, Tumblers

Pattern 587 consists of Beer Mugs. They are cylindrical with heavy bottoms and have an elongated thumbprint band around the bottom of the mugs. They came in a 11 ounce large, 9 ounce medium, and 5-1/2 ounce pony.

Pattern 587, Beer Mugs

Pattern 590 consists of Ales. They have a tall cylindrical shape with a thumbprint band around the bottom of the bowls and are on the explanation mark stem. They came plain or engraved in a 6-1/2 ounce ale and 4-1/2 ounce pony ale.

Pattern 590, Ales

124

Pattern 591 is an Egg. It holds 5 ounces and has a plain rounded bowl on short stem and foot.

Pattern 591, Egg.

Patterns 592 and 593 are Ales. The bowls have a fancy bottom of flutes with either round or oval notches inside. They are on a stem joined with three rings. Pattern 592 is a 10 ounce ale and pattern 593 holds 8-1/2 ounces.

Pattern 592 and 593, Ales

Pattern 594 consists of Beer Mugs. They are cylindrical with fluted bowls and heavy bottoms. They hold 14, 12, 10, 8, 5 or 3 ounces. See Barware photograph on page 39 the in the second row the first mug.

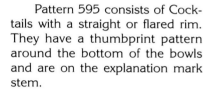

Pattern 594, Beer Mugs

Pattern 595 consists of Cocktails with a straight or flared rim. They have a thumbprint pattern around the bottom of the bowls and are on the explanation mark stem.

Pattern 595, Cocktails

Pattern 596 is a Tumbler. It is in the Huber pattern.

Pattern 596, Tumbler

Pattern 597 is an individual Salt. It has an octagon shape with flat bottom. (A)

Pattern 597, Individual Salt

Pattern 598 is a Tumbler. It holds 3-1/2 ounces and is plain.

Pattern 598, Tumbler

Pattern 599 is Stemware. They have a flared top in a tapered cylindrical shape with a flat bottom. The stem has a round knop slightly below the bowls. They came plain or engraved Band 40 in a 10 ounce large ale, 7 ounce medium ale, 4 ounce pony ale, 3-1/2 ounce claret, 2 ounce wine, 1 ounce cordial, and a hot whiskey.

Pattern 599, Stemware

Pattern 600 is a Beer Mug. It holds 17 ounces and has tall flutes from below the rim to bottom of the bowl with a heavy bottom.

Pattern 600, Beer Mug

The next three stand lamps have the same stem and foot. The font is joined to a stem with narrow ribs in the middle of two hourglass shapes. The hourglass shape below the font protrudes above the ribs. At the bottom of the ribs is a protruding ring and below the ribs is the other hourglass shape above the foot. I call this stem a "column stem" as it resembles a column. The lamps are on a cup foot.

Pattern 601 consists of Stand and Hand Lamps. The font has a pattern that looks like woven ribbon in the middle with a narrow protruding band above and below. It came on the column stem with cup foot. The stand lamp came in six sizes and the hand lamp in three. (F)

Pattern 601, Hand & Stand Lamps

Pattern 602 consists of Stand and Hand Lamps. The font has a pattern that looks like chains near the top and bottom sections linked together with vertical bands with a protruding narrow band in the middle that makes the font look like it is being squeezed in on the sides. It is on the column stem with cup foot. The stand lamp came in six sizes and the hand lamp in three. (F)

Pattern 602, Stand & Hand Lamps

Pattern 603 is a Stand Lamp. The font has a wide plain flat top that tapers in toward the bottom and is similar to the font in pattern 467. It came either plain or engraved and is on the column stem with cup foot and came in five sizes. (F)

Pattern 603, Stand Lamp

125

Pattern 604 is a Beer Mug. It holds 17 ounces and is cylindrical. It has a flute band with a thin notched line in the middle between a protruding narrow ring where the handles join the bowl near the top and bottom. The bottom of the bowl has a short flute band with thin notched lines.

Pattern 604, Beer Mug

Pattern 605 is a flared Hot Whiskey. It holds 3-1/2 ounces and has a flared rim and fluted bowl and it is on the stem with a round knop near the top.

Pattern 605, Hot Whiskey

Patterns 606 and 607 are Tumblers. They are fluted with tapered cylindrical bowls and came plain or engraved with Band 40. Pattern 606 holds 3 ounces and pattern 607 holds 3-1/2 ounces.

Pattern 606 and 607, Tumblers

Pattern 608 is a Pickle and Cracker Jar. The pickle is cylindrical and has ribs from top to bottom with a clear protruding band about a quarter of the way down. This band was probably for identification of the contents. It has a clear flat cover and the finial has a rounded top with two rows of teardrops joined at the points with a narrow middle. The cracker jar is barrel shaped and had a wide clear band in the middle. It had a rounded ribbed cover but the finial was missing from the catalog page so it cannot be identified. (pickle D)

Pattern 608, Pickle & Cracker Jar

Pattern 609 is a Hot Whiskey. It holds 5 ounces and is plain with a flared rim and is on the stem has a round knop near the top.

Pattern 609, Hot Whiskey

Pattern 610 is the Thumbprint Band. It has elongated oval thumbprints and is a large pattern with many pieces. The thumbprint band is around the bottom of the bowls, covers, and on the top of the foot. The stem is ribbed and the low foot pieces have a ribbed stem and plain foot. The finial has a rounded top with two rows of teardrops joined at the points with a narrow middle. The handles are round at the top and bottom and curve in at the middle.

Sugar (D)
Cream without cover (C)
Cream covered with metal top (D)
Cream individual (often mistaken for a toy creamer) (C)
Spoon (C)
Butter and cover (D)
Celery (C)
Oval bowls in 6, 7, 8, and 9 inches (C)
Comport in 4 inch footed (low foot) (B)
Comport in 7, 8, 9, and 10 inch shallow bowl high foot (D)
Bowls and covers in 6, 7, 8, and 9 inch deep bowls covered (E)
Plates in 5, 6, 7, 8, 9, and 10 inches with star design centers (unknown)
Pitcher in quart and half gallon with reed handles (E)
Nappy round bowls in 5, 6, 7, 8, and 9 inches (C)
Stemware on three different stems, ribbed, bulbous, or spool (9-1/2 ounce goblet was on the ribbed stem, goblet A was on a bulbous stem, and B was on a spool stem) (unknown)

Pattern 610, Thumbprint Band

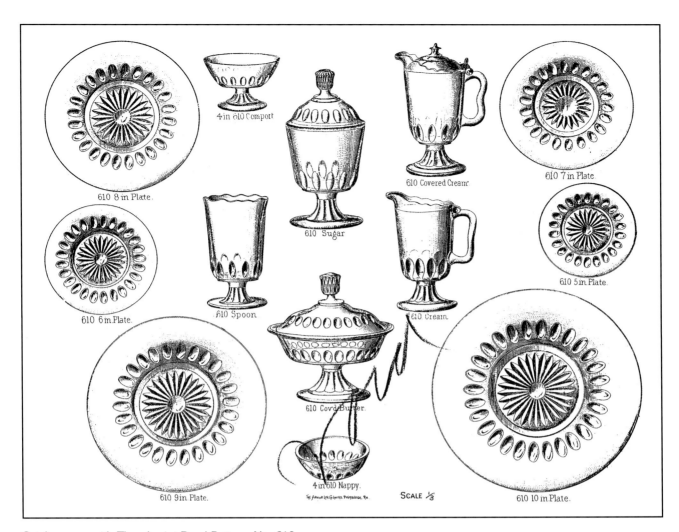

Catalog page with Thumbprint Band Pattern, No. 610

Thumbprint Band patterns [No. 610 Thumbprint Band, No. 577 Stemware, No. 622 Ale] (left to right, top to bottom)
1. No. 610 Celery, Bowl 7" HF, No. 577 Goblet, No. 610 Pitcher Eng. 148, No. 610 Goblet
2. No. 610 Bowls High Foot Open, 6", 7", 8" Deep Bowls
3. No. 610 Bowls High Foot Open, 9", 8", 7" Shallow Bowls
4. No. 577 Hot Whiskey Flared Top, No. 610 Cream, No. 622 Ale, No. 610 Cream with Metal Top, No. 610 Individual Cream 4-3/8" high

Pattern 611 is a Huber Beer Mug. It holds 17 ounces and has a tall cylindrical bowl with heavy bottom.

Pattern 611, Beer Mug

Pattern 612 consists of Beer Mugs. They were designed by John Oesterling. They are cylindrical and have tall arched ribs in a large 12 ounce, large 10 ounce, medium 8 ounce, and pony 5 ounce sizes.

Pattern 612, Beer Mugs

Pattern 613 is Stemware. They have tall tapered cylindrical bowls on stems with a round knop near the top. They came plain or engraved Band 40. Ales came in a large 10 ounce, medium 7 ounce and pony 4 ounce. Other stemware included a 3-1/2 ounce claret, 2 ounce wine, and 1 ounce cordial.

Pattern 613, Stemware

Pattern 614 is a Tumbler. It holds 2 ounces and is plain with a heavy bottom.

Pattern 614, Tumbler

Pattern 615 is a Cocktail. It holds 3 ounces and has a thumbprint band around the bottom of the bowl. The bowls are cup shaped with either straight or flared rims and it is on a cut paneled stem. This pattern is in the same style as pattern 620.

Pattern 615, Cocktail, Flared or Straight

Pattern 616 is a Tumbler. No picture is available as it was on a shipping order list in a Central catalog from the 1880s.

Patterns 617 and 618 are Tumblers. Pattern 617 is a 3-1/2 ounce Huber tumbler and pattern 618 is a 4 ounce plain tumbler with star bottom.

Patterns 617 and 618, Tumblers

Pattern 619 is an Ale. No picture is available as it was on a shipping order list in a Central catalog from the 1880s.

Pattern 620 is a Cocktail. It holds 4-1/2 ounces and has a thumbprint band around the bottom of the bowl. The bowls are cup shaped with either straight or flared rims and it is on a cut paneled stem. This pattern is in the same style as pattern 615.

Pattern 620, Cocktail

Pattern 621 is Stemware. It came in a 3-1/2 ounce wine and 4-1/2 ounce claret. They have plain tapered cylindrical bowls and are on a fluted stem that joins above the foot with two rings.

Pattern 621, Stemware

Pattern 622 consists of Ales. They have tall tapered cylindrical bowls with a thumbprint band around the bottom of the bowls. They are on a spool stem and came in a 6-1/2 ounce large, 6 or 5-1/2 ounce medium, and 4 ounce pony sizes.

Pattern 622, Ales

Pattern 623 is a Tumbler. It holds 3-1/2 ounces and is fluted.

Pattern 623, Tumbler

Pattern 624 is an Ale. It holds 10 ounces and has a tall tapered cylindrical shape with a thumbprint band around the bottom of the bowl and is on a stocky stem.

Pattern 624, Ale

Pattern 625 is a Tumbler. It holds 9 ounces and is plain.

Pattern 625, Tumbler

Pattern 626 is an Egg. It holds 5 ounces and is plain with a rounded bowl on stocky foot.

Pattern 626, Egg

Pattern 627 is a Stand Lamp. This pattern is called "Pride" by Thuro[36]. The font has a pattern that looks like large teardrops (or raindrops) with one right side up and the other upside down next to each other. The stem is joined below the font with a short section of clear glass above a ring followed by ribs down to a row of protruding teardrops above the foot. The cup foot has a scalloped design on it. The lamp came in five sizes. (G)

Pattern 627, Stand Lamp

Pattern 628 is a Stand Lamp. This pattern is called "Pride Plain" by Thuro[37]. It has a clear font in the same design as pattern 627 and is on the same stem and foot. It came in five sizes. (F)

Pattern 628, Stand Lamp

Pattern 629 is a Stand Lamp. Thuro named it "Merton"[38]. It has a plain rounded font that tapers down to a flat band at the bottom and is on the column stem with cup foot. See Oil Lamps and Whirlpool Colognes photograph on page 135 on the bottom row the third lamp. (E)

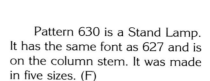

Pattern 629, Stand Lamp

Pattern 630 is a Stand Lamp. It has the same font as 627 and is on the column stem. It was made in five sizes. (F)

Pattern 630, Stand Lamp

Pattern 631 is a Stand Lamp. It has the same font as 628 and is on the column stem. It was made in five sizes. (F)

Pattern 631, Stand Lamp

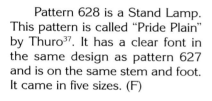

Catalog page with Patterns 629 and 630, Stand Lamps and Oregon Shade

Pattern 631, Stand Lamp

Pattern 637 is a Cordial. It holds 1 ounce with plain cylindrical bowl and is on a plain stem.

Pattern 637, Cordial

Pattern 638 is a Wine. It holds 3-1/2 ounces and has a flute band around the middle of a round bowl and is on a plain flared stem.

Pattern 638, Wine

Patterns 639, 640, and 641 are Tumblers. They have tapered cylindrical fluted bowls. Pattern 639 holds 9 ounces, pattern 640 holds 11 ounces, and pattern 641 holds 13-1/2 ounces.

Pattern 639 to 641, Tumblers

Pattern 632 is a Schoppen. It holds 6-1/2 ounces and is cylindrical with a fluted bowl (looks like a tumbler).

Pattern 632, Schoppen

Pattern 642 is a plain Plate.

Pattern 642, Plate

Pattern 633 consists of an Ale and a Bitter Bottle. They have fluted bowls. The tall ale holds 13 ounces and is cylindrical. The bitter bottle has a roll top and came with or without cork. (A & C)

Pattern 633, Ale & Bitter Bottle

Pattern 643 is a Cordial. It holds 1 ounce and has a plain round bowl on the cut paneled stem.

Pattern 643, Cordial

Patterns 634 and 635 are Schoppens. They have tapered cylindrical fluted bowls and a short stem. Pattern 634 holds 4 ounces and pattern 635 holds 6-1/2 ounces.

Pattern 634 and 635, Schoppen

Pattern 644 is Stemware. They have conical shaped bowls with fluted bottoms that join a straight paneled stem in a 4-1/2 ounce large cocktail, 2-1/2 ounce small cocktail, and 1 ounce cordial.

Pattern 644, Stemware

Pattern 636 is a Cordial. It holds 1 ounce and has a plain tapered cylindrical bowl with heavy bottom. The stem is a short version of the explanation mark stem.

Pattern 636, Cordial

Pattern 645 is Stemware. They have tapered cylindrical bowls on a cut paneled stem. They came in a 10 ounce goblet, 5-1/2 ounce champagne, 4 ounce claret, 2-1/2 ounce wine, and 1 ounce cordial.

Pattern 645, Stemware

Pattern 646 is unknown

Pattern 647 consists of Cocktails. They hold 3 ounces and the bowls are plain with either straight or flared rims on a cut paneled stem. They are similar to pattern 648.

Pattern 647, Cocktail

Pattern 648 consists of Cocktails. They hold 4-1/2 ounces and the bowls are plain with either straight or flared rims on a cut paneled stem. They are similar to pattern 647.

Pattern 648, Cocktail

Pattern 649 consists of Ales. They have plain tall trumpet shaped bowls with tapered flutes in the bottom of the bowl before joining the spool stem. They came in 7-1/2 ounces, 6 ounce medium, and 4-1/2 ounce pony sizes. See Barware photograph on page 39 in the third row the seventh ale (second from right).

Pattern 649, Ales

Pattern 650 is the Dot and Dash Pattern. This name came from Kamm[39] as she thought the pattern looked like diagonally placed dot-and-dash designs.

These were around the base of the body inside the band of diagonal boxes. When you look at the design closely they look more like a circle attached to an elongated oval with another circle on top of the oval, but we will keep the Dot and Dash name. The bowls have the dot and dash band pattern around the bottom, while the top of the bowls have a thin narrow bead band. The handles are ornate with a plain round area in the middle below a beaded ring design at the top and the bottom joins a rib design with another ring. The finial looks like a cross. The low foot bowls have a plain stocky stem while the high foot bowls have two rings, one near the top and the other above the foot. They came plain or engraved with 172, 174, and all over with Band 50.

Sugar (D)
Cream (D)
Spoon (C)
Butter and cover (E)
Celery (D)
Nappy 4 inch round (C)
Comport 4 inch footed and with handles (C)
Comport 7, 8, 9 and 10 inch shallow bowl (C)
Bowls 6, 7, and 8 inch low foot covered with handles (E)
Bowls 6, 7, 8, and 9 inch high foot and cover (E)
Pitcher half gallon (E)

Pattern 650, Dot and Dash

Catalog Page with Dot and Dash Pattern, No. 650

Dot & Dash Pattern, No. 650 (left to right, top to bottom)
1. Bowls High Foot, 8" Eng. 174, 6", 9", 7" Eng. 174 Deep Bowls
2. Nappy 7" LF with Handles, Butter, Sugar
3. Celery, Bowl 8" HF Shallow Bowl, 8" HF Deep Bowl Eng. 172
4. Spoon, Cream, Spoons Eng. 174 showing differences in same engravings

Pattern 651 is the Ball and Chain pattern, called Bead and Chain[40] by Kamm. This is a beautiful pattern but I have never seen a bowl (compote) in it and have listed below the only pieces found in catalogs. The pattern has a ball or bead band around the top and on the flanged handles. The foot is oval with a chain band that does not show where it meets the projecting feet. The bowls are six-sided and taper in toward the foot. The finial consists of a circle of rings with a larger ring on both sides of the top and is attached to the bottom by two large loops. This pattern was mentioned in *American Pottery and Glass Reporter* on March 13, 1889 as "No. 651, the low priced set....." I wonder if this was a numbering error as this pattern is eloquent and it does not appear to be cheap at all. It came plain or engraved 173. See Loop 520, Ball and Chain and Miscellaneous Patterns photograph on page 113 on the second row.

Sugar (D)
Cream (D)
Spoon (D)
Butter and cover (E)
Comport 4 inch (C)
Pitcher half gallon (F)

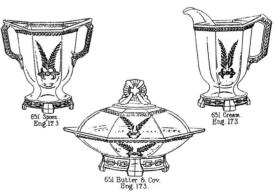

651 Spoon. Eng. 173

651 Cream. Eng. 173.

651 Butter & Cov. Eng. 173.

Pattern 651, Ball and Chain Pattern

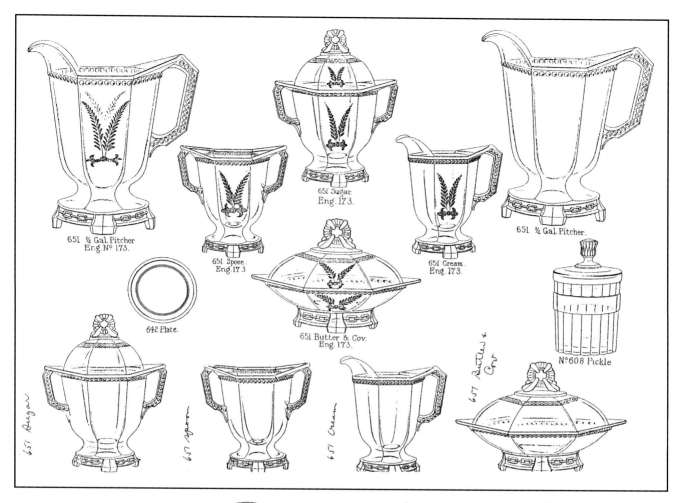

Catalog page with Ball and Chain Pattern, No. 651

Pattern 652 is a Wine. It holds 2 ounce in the Huber pattern and is on a spool stem.

Pattern 652, Wine

Pattern 653 consists of Beer Mugs. They are plain with cylindrical heavy bottomed bowls with a rim that tapers in slightly. They came in a 11 ounce, 9 ounce medium, and 5 ounce pony sizes.

Pattern 653, Beer Mugs

Patterns 654 to 660 are Tumblers. Patterns 654 and 655 both hold 3-1/2 ounces and are fluted. Pattern 656 holds 2 ounces and pattern 657 holds 3 ounces, they are plain with heavy bottoms. Pattern 658 holds 3-1/2 ounces and is plain. Pattern 659 holds 2 ounces and is fluted with heavy bottom and thick walls. Pattern 660 holds 5 ounces and is fluted with a heavy bottom.

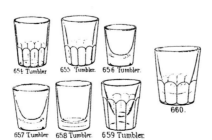

Patterns 654 to 660, Tumblers

Pattern 661 is a Beer Mug. It holds 32 ounces and is cylindrical with a fluted bowl. (D)

Pattern 661, Beer Mug

Pattern 662 is Stemware. It has a tapered cylindrical bowl with a flute bottom on a tapered paneled stem. They came in a 8-1/2 ounce goblet, 7 ounce champagne, 4 ounce claret, 3 ounce wine, and 1 ounce cordial.

Pattern 662, Stemware

133

Pattern 663 is a Straw Jar and Cover. It has a plain tall cylindrical shape with a protruding ring at the rim and is on a flanged foot. The cover has a flat top with mushroom shaped finial.

Pattern 663, Straw Jar

Pattern 664 is Stemware. They have cylindrical bowls that taper in with short flutes before joining a spool stem. They came in a 10 ounce large, 9 ounce medium, and 5-1/2 ounce pony ale, 2-1/2 ounce wine, and 1 ounce cordial.

Pattern 664, Stemware

Pattern 665 is a Bar Tumbler. It holds 10-1/2 ounces and has a plain tapered cylindrical bowl.

Pattern 665, Bar Tumbler

Pattern 666 is a Beer Mug with a Horseshoe base. It holds 7 ounces. The bowl is plain and the horseshoe pattern is on the foot. See pattern 672 for another beer mug with a horseshoe pattern. (R)

Pattern 666, Beer Mug with Horseshoe Base

Pattern 667 consists of Cocktails. They are plain and the cylindrical bowl has a flat bottom and it has a straight flared stem. They came in a large 4-1/2 ounce or small 3-1/2 ounce.

Pattern 667, Cocktails

Pattern 668 is a Bar Tumbler. It holds 9-1/2 ounces and has a plain tapered cylindrical bowl.

Pattern 668, Bar Tumbler

Pattern 669 is a Sherry. It holds 1-1/2 ounces and has a trumpet shaped bowl on a cut paneled stem.

Pattern 669, Sherry

Pattern 670 is an Ale. It holds 7 ounces and has a plain cylindrical bowl with flat bottom and is on the stem with a large round knop slightly under the bottom of the bowl.

Pattern 670, Ale

Pattern 671 consists of Bar Tumblers. They are fluted and came in a 3-1/2 ounce size and in a 2 ounce sham with heavy bottom.

Pattern 671, Bar Tumblers

Pattern 672 is a Beer Mug with a Horseshoe band. It holds 7 ounces and is cylindrical with a horseshoe band around the bottom of the bowl. The other horseshoe pattern is 666. (R)

Pattern 672, Beer Mug, Horseshoe Band

Patterns 673, 674, and 675 are Bar Tumblers. They are all fluted. Pattern 673 and 674 have tall flutes and very heavy bottoms they both hold 1-1/2 ounces. Pattern 675 holds 2-1/2 ounces with a heavy bottom and 3-1/2 ounces in a light tumbler.

Patterns 673 to 675, Bar Tumblers

134

Pattern 676 is a Cocktail. It holds 3-1/2 ounces and has a cylindrical shape with a narrow flute band on the flat bottom and is on a straight flared stem.

Pattern 676, Cocktail

Patterns 677, 678, and 679 are Tumblers. Pattern 677 holds 12-1/2 ounces and has a plain tapered cylindrical bowl with heavy bottom. Pattern 678 holds 12 ounces and has a heavy bottom with a rim that tapers in. Pattern 679 holds 8 ounces and has a plain tapered cylindrical bowl.

Patterns 667 to 679, Tumblers

Pattern 680 is a Cocktail. It holds 2-1/2 ounces and has a trumpet shaped bowl on a long straight stem.

Pattern 680, Cocktail

Pattern 681 is an Egg. It has a plain rounded bowl and is attached to a saucer foot. See pattern 435 for a similar egg.

Pattern 681, Egg.

Pattern 682 is an Ale. It holds 9 ounces and has a honeycomb pattern with indented sides in the honeycomb pattern. It is on a bulbous fluted stem.

Pattern 682, Ale

Oil Lamps and Whirlpool Colognes (left to right, top to bottom)
1. No. 725 Barrel Stand Lamp, No number Columbian Coin Stand Lamp, No. 311 Mountain Laurel Stand Lamp, No. 792 Coin Blank Stand Lamp, No. 877 Flute Band Stand Lamp
2. No. 950 Whirlpool Cologne, No. 877 Flute Band Stand Lamp, No. 950 Whirlpool Stand Lamp, No. 950 Whirlpool Cologne, No. 821 Dewdrop Night Lamp
3. No. 488 Stand Lamp, No. 857 Clear Panels and Ribs Stand Lamp, No. 683 Stand Lamp, No. 467 Stand Lamp
4. No. 870 Brick Window Stand Lamp, No. 821 Dewdrop Stand Lamp, No. 629 Stand Lamp

"Block stem." The next three stand lamps have the same stem and foot. The stem is joined to the font with a glass ring then tapers down in hourglass shape onto a rectangle shape with round corners with a protruding ring underneath it before joining the cup foot. I will refer to this stem as the block stem. For an example see pattern 683 of this photograph.

Pattern 683 consists of Stand Lamps. The font has a clear band around the top of the flared bowl which tapers down to a flat bottom and is on the block stem. They came in five sizes. See Oil Lamps and Whirlpool Colognes photograph above in row three the third lamp. (E)

Pattern 683, Stand Lamps

Pattern 684 consists of Stand Lamps. The font is oval in shape with a wide clear band around the middle that could be engraved. It is on the block stem and came in five sizes. (E)

Pattern 684, Stand Lamp

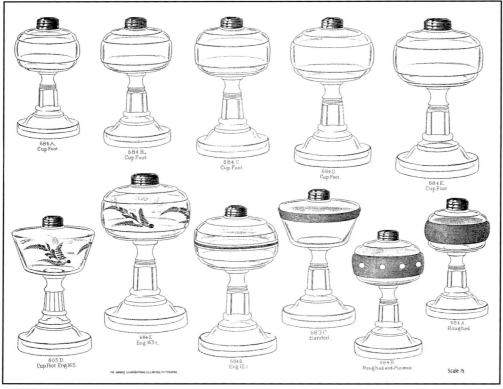

Catalog page with Pattern 684 Stand Lamps showing different "cuts"

Pattern 685 consists of Stand Lamps. The font is oval in shape and has a design of large rings held together with three small rungs with five rungs in the middle of the rings. The design has been referred to as a basket weave design. It is on the block stem and came in five sizes. It has the same style font as pattern 684. (F)

Pattern 686 consists of Beer Mugs. They are plain cylindrical mugs with heavy bottoms and a curved handle that resembles a twig. They hold 13, 10, 8, and 5 ounces. See Barware photograph on page 39 on the bottom row the second mug which holds five ounces.

Pattern 685, Stand Lamp

Pattern 686, Beer Mugs

Pattern 687 is Stemware. They have tapered cylindrical bowls and are on a plain flared stem. They came in a 9-1/2 ounce goblet, 4 ounce claret, and 3-1/2 ounce wine.

Patterns 688 and 689 are Oyster Plates. They both have six sections for holding oysters with a clear rib in between and a scalloped rim. Pattern 688 has plain clear glass and bottom. Pattern 689 has a round design like tiny beads on the bottom of the oyster cups and on the bottom of the plate in the middle. (R)

Pattern 687, Stemware

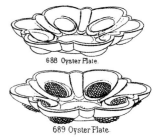

Patterns 688 and 689, Oyster Plates

Pattern 690 is a Claret. It holds 3-1/2 ounces and has a plain round bowl on a plain flared stem.

Pattern 690, Claret

Pattern 691 is a Candlestick. It is 10-3/8 inches high with a wonderful etched pattern of a draped child with his right arm reaching across his chest to the drape and his left arm up as if he was holding up the candle. The clear holder for candle has a scalloped rim and it is on a clear wide foot. This same design is still being made by Baccarat and the candelabra is called "Enfant." See Novelties photograph on page 143 on the top row the first and fifth patterns (on the left and right). (F each)

Pattern 691, Candlestick

Pattern 692 is unknown.

Pattern 693 is Claret. It holds 3-1/2 ounces and has a plain tall round bowl that tapers down to a plain stem.

Pattern 693, Claret

Pattern 694 is a Whiskey. It holds 4-1/2 ounces and has a cylindrical bowl with short narrow stem and wide foot. It came with or without a handle.

Pattern 694, Whiskey

Pattern 695 is unknown

Patterns 696 and 697 are Tumblers. They are plain with thin cylindrical bowls. Pattern 696 holds 2-1/2 ounces and pattern 697 holds 2-3/4 ounces.

Pattern 698 is a Tumbler. It holds 13 ounces and is fluted with heavy bottom.

Patterns 696 to 698, Tumblers

Pattern 699 is a Claret. It holds 3-1/2 ounces and has a round bowl and long plain flared stem. Note: there was also a 4-1/2 ounce wine illustrated in the 1900 Central Glass Works catalog.

Pattern 699, Claret

With the 700 patterns come the start of colors although articles regarding the use of color was not mentioned in research until 1885. The patterns were made in the 1880s and the colors were amber, blue, and canary. Some variations of the colors have been used with names like honey amber, root beer amber, and electric blue, but since Central used amber, blue and canary that is what will be used.

Pattern 700 is a Recumbent Horse Ink Stand. It has a reclining horse in the back and a shell design in the front with ink holders on both sides. "PAT APLD FOR" is in the glass in front of the horse. It came in crystal (plain) with the horse etched and in colors. One horse ink had "Pat Applied for Made for 1888 World's Fair in Philadelphia"[41]. See Colored Novelties photograph on page 166 in the third row in the middle. (R)

Pattern 700, Recumbent Horse Ink Stand

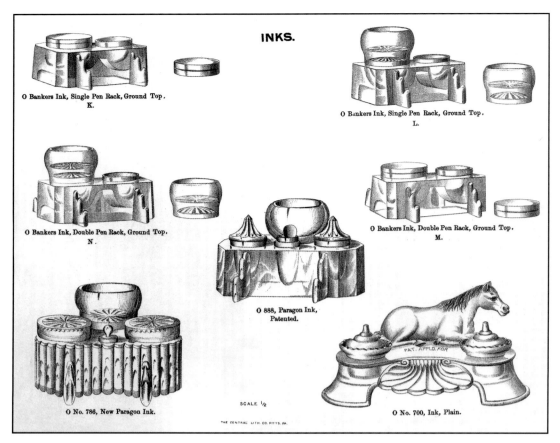

Catalog Page of Inks Showing Pattern 700, Reclining Horse. *Courtesy The Metropolitan Museum of Art, The Elisha Whittelsey Collection, The Elisha Whittelsey Fund, 1955 (55.643.2)*

Recumbent Horse, Pattern 700, Ink Stand

Pattern 701 is a Cocktail. It holds 5 ounces and has a cylindrical bowl that tapers in at the bottom with short flutes that join a paneled stem with a knop slightly under the bowl.

Pattern 701, Cocktail

Pattern 702 is a Rabbit Mug. On the left side of the mug (this is the side the catalog page shows as they were printed in reverse) there is a rabbit running on grass with his feet outstretched and behind him is a tree with a branch cut off in the background. The right side has the rabbit lying down with another tree behind him in the background and a log cabin. There are a couple of rabbit mugs that do not match the Central catalog drawing. A. This mug is beautifully detailed showing the leaves on the trees and tall grass in front and behind the rabbit on the left with leaves in the grass beneath the rabbit. The right side has wheat stalks in front of the rabbit with various plants in the grass under him. The log cabin has a window in the attic and one on the second floor, the roof has shingles and is very articulate. This mug has a lamb in the bottom. The handle has a little knob where it attaches to the bottom of the mug. This may be the Challinor, Taylor and Company rabbit mug reissued by the U.S. Glass Company[42]. B. This mug looks like a poor copy of the previous mug. It does not have all the extra leaves and plants in the grass, the trees look like puffs of cotton and there is no tall grass in front of the rabbit on the left side. The right side has only one stalk of wheat and the log cabin is more like a stick drawing. This mug has a clear bottom. C. This mug is heavier than the other two and the rabbit seems more defined than the previous one but there are other differences. The trees are different and do not have the cut branch on them and the leaves are also different, there is no tall grass in front of the rabbit, and instead of wheat there is one cattail reed in front of the rabbit on the right side. The rabbis front feet are tucked underneath him where the other two mugs have the front feet out. The log cabin is crude and the chimney is barely visible. Placement of the rabbits tail is also different. This mug has a rayed bottom. I do not think any of the above mugs were made by Central. This pattern was reissued by the U.S. Glass Company under Toy Mugs. See Novelties photograph on page 143 in the third row on the right (sixth pattern) which is not Centrals rabbit mug. (E)

Pattern 702, Rabbit Mug

Catalog page of Novelties showing Rabbit Mug, Pattern 702

Patterns 703 and 704 are Tumblers. They are fluted and pattern 703 holds 2-1/2 ounces and pattern 704 holds 2 ounces.

Patters 703 and 704,
Tumblers

Pattern 705 is called Simplicity. This is a plain pattern with large handles that resemble "ears" and that is how I found some of the patterns. They are on a bulbous stem with two rings on the high foot, one slightly under the bowl and the other above the foot with only the ring above the foot on low foot bowls. The foot is hollow and flat and has a flat edge. The finial is a tapered rectangle that goes up to a tiny point. It came plain or engraved with three different engravings of number 173, 174, and 189 and probably others. There is a written notation on a catalog page with 705 ware of 5, 6, 7, 8, and 9 inch nappies and was probably written in by a Central employee. The bowls are identical to pattern 769.

Sugar (D)
Cream (C)
Spoon (C)
Butter and cover (E)
Celery (the rim is slightly flared) (C)
Comport 4-1/2 inch stocky stem with handles (C)
Comport 7, 8, 9, and 10 inch shallow bowls (C & D)
Bowls 6, 7, 8, 9 inch high foot covered (D)
Stemware in a 10 ounce goblet, 4 ounce claret, and 2-1/2 ounce wine. Engraving 205 was used on the goblets (unknown)

705 Cream
Eng. 189

705 Spoon
Eng. 189

705 Cov'd Butter
Eng. 189

Pattern 705,
Simplicity

705 Sugar & Cov
Eng. 189

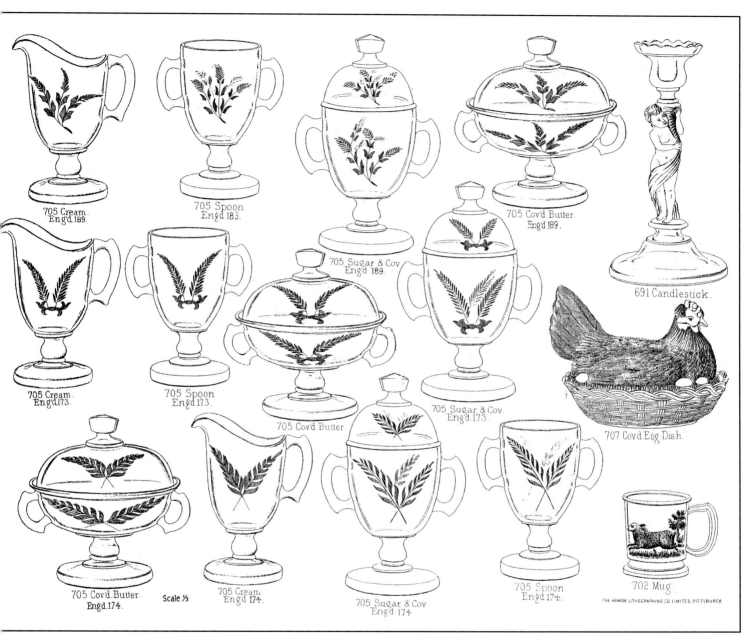

705 Cream.
Eng'd 189.

705 Spoon
Eng'd 189.

705 Sugar & Cov
Eng'd 189.

705 Cov'd. Butter.
Eng'd 189.

691 Candlestick.

705 Cream.
Eng'd 173.

705 Spoon
Eng'd 173.

705 Cov'd. Butter.

705 Sugar & Cov.
Eng'd 173.

707 Cov'd. Egg Dish.

705 Cov'd. Butter.
Eng'd 174.

Scale ⅓

705 Cream.
Eng'd 174.

705 Sugar & Cov
Eng'd 174.

705 Spoon
Eng'd 174.

702 Mug

THE ARMOR LITHOGRAPHING CO. LIMITED, PITTSBURGH.

Catalog Page with Simplicity, Pattern 705, and other 700 Patterns No.
691 Candlestick, No. 707 Covered Egg Dish, and No. 702 Rabbit Mug)

141

Simplicity and Acorn Top Patterns (No. 705 Simplicity & No. 769 Acorn Top). Bowls have Same Stem and Foot. (Left to right, top to bottom)
1. No. 705 Bowl 8" HF Eng. Band 50, No. 769 6" HF, No. 769 7" HF Eng. 219, No. 705 8" HF Eng. 189
2. No. 705 or No. 769 HF Shallow Bowls, No. 769 Cream Eng. 219, No. 705 or No. 769 Bowl 6" HF Deep Bowl
3. No. 705 Butter, Sugar (2 missing covers) Eng. 189, Butter Base
4. No. 705 Spoon Eng. 713, Cream Eng. 189, Goblet Eng. Band 50, Goblet Eng. 189

Pattern 706 is a Cocktail. It holds 3-1/2 ounces and has a cup bowl and is on a cut paneled stem.

706 Cocktail
3½ oz.

Pattern 706, Cocktail

Pattern 707 consists of Covered Egg Dishes with a Hen on Nest. An article in Josephine Jefferson's book, *Wheeling Glass*, mentioned: "The manufacture of chickens at the factory was an idea of Mr. Oesterling's. He had seen such a mold in Germany, and when the company began their production the response was astonishing. Whether Central was one of the first glass houses to manufacture chickens, it is impossible to determine, but orders for fifty barrels from single concerns were a daily occurrence." The egg dishes came etched and are beautifully detailed with every feather visible. The hen has three eggs, two in the front and one in the back, and is sitting in a wicker basket. The dishes came in large, medium, and individual sizes. The sizes I have are large 8 inch, medium 7 inch, and individual 5 inch. The hen has a flared tail and when the hen is lifted off the basket there is an outline of straw around the bottom. The bottom of the bowl also has a basket pattern. These are being reproduced and were also made by other glass companies. For the three sizes see Novelties photograph on this page on the top row in the middle. (D & E)

707 Cov'd Egg Dish

Pattern 707, Hen on Nest Cov'd Egg Dish

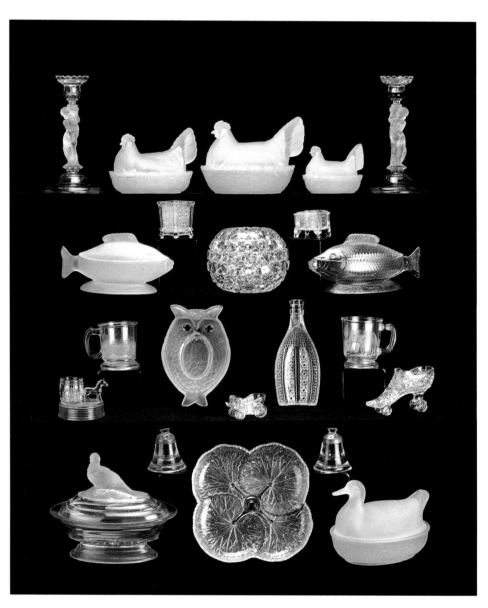

Novelties (left to right, top to bottom)
1. No. 691 Candlestick, No. 707 Covered. Egg Dishes Med., Lge., Ind., No. 691 Candlestick
2. No. 747 Fish Dish (Etched), No. 782 Coal Bin Match, No. 893 Rose Bowl, No. 822 Stove Salt, No. 747 Fish Dish (Crystal)
3. No. 865 Horse Pulling Barrel Match, No. 728 Elephant Mug, No. 732 Owl Pickle, No. 16 Carriage Salt, No. 823 Half Bottle Pickle, No. 702 Rabbit Mug, No. 831 Slipper Skate
4. No. 758 Pheasant Covered. Dish, No Number Liberty Bell Salt, No. 763 Lily Pad Comport, No Number Liberty Bell Salt, No. 727 Duck Dish (Etched)

Patterns 708 and 709 are Tumblers. They are fluted and pattern 708 holds 3 ounces and pattern 709 holds 2-1/2 ounces.

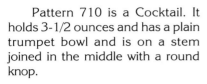

Patterns 708 and 709, Tumblers

Pattern 710 is a Cocktail. It holds 3-1/2 ounces and has a plain trumpet bowl and is on a stem joined in the middle with a round knop.

Pattern 710, Cocktail

Pattern 711 is a Cocktail. It holds 5 ounces and has a plain tapered cylindrical bowl and is on a bulbous stem.

Pattern 711, Cocktail

Patterns 712, 713, and 714 are Tumblers. Pattern 712 is a plain 4-1/2 ounce tumbler, pattern 713 is a 3-1/2 ounce fluted tumbler, and pattern 714 is a 14 ounce plain tumbler.

Patterns 712 to 714, Tumblers

Pattern 715 is an Ale. It holds 7-1/2 ounces and has a plain trumpet shape bowl on stocky stem.

Pattern 715, Ale

Pattern 716 is an Ale. It holds 9 ounces and has a fluted tapered cylindrical bowl. It tapers in below the flutes with a heavy bottom and is on a stocky stem.

Pattern 716, Ale

Pattern 717 is unknown

Pattern 718 consists of Blown Beers. They have a hourglass shape and are on a flared foot. An article in *Crockery and Glass Journal* in May of 1883 mentioned: "a novelty in the shape of a beer glass has lately been turned out which is attracting general attention. The glass is made of very light and firm ware and strongly resembles an old-fashioned hour glass. The new style of bar goods is rapidly supplanting the old and cumbersome beer mug". They were made in a 10, 8, and 5 ounce size.

Pattern 718, Blown Beer

Pattern 719 is a Tumbler. It holds 5 ounces and is plain.

Pattern 719, Tumbler

Pattern 720 is Corner Medallion. An article on page 30 from *Crockery and Glass Journal* dated June 21, 1883 mentioned: "The East End Works are running night and day in order to fill all the orders…. A new set bearing a strong resemblance to the Riverside "Jersey Lily", has had an immense run for some weeks, and the orders are much in excess of present ability to fill." The pieces have round bowls with notched edges with square stems on rectangular feet. The pattern is ornate and resembles an oriental rug (or shawl) with fringe. The finial is flat and round

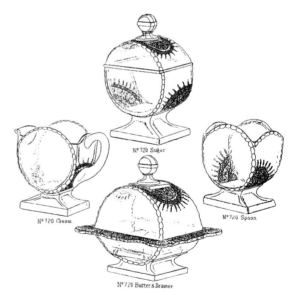

Pattern 720, Corner Medallion

with a protruding flat band in the middle. This pattern had pieces that did not come with the "fringe" on them and they included stand and hand lamps, shaker salt, molasses can, cruet set, and pressed bar bottle. The bar bottle has a square bottom. The finial was a notched rectangle shape with pointed top on the cruet and a flat top on the bar bottle. The pieces came plain or engraved No. 189, or 194. The stand and hand lamps have a round font with notches around the parameter. The sides have bar ridges on the lower half down to the stem. The stem is flared and the foot is oval and comes to a tip in the front and back with a cup foot. The stand lamps came in five sizes and the hand lamps in three. The lamps are very rare.

Sugar and cover (with flat rim) (E)

Cream (E)

Spoon (D)

Butter came with drainer (F)

Celery (D)

Oval 7 and 8 inch with handles (these are more rectangular than oval) (D)

Comport 4 inch with four feet (C)

Casserole 7 and 8 inch covered with handles on four feet (F)

Bowls 7, 8, high foot and cover (F)

Molasses Can (see Pitchers, Molasses Cans and Miscellaneous photograph on page 65 on the bottom row the second pattern) (F)

Pitcher (E)

Stand and Hand lamps, (stand lamps 5 sizes, hand lamp 3 sizes) (H & I)

Patterns 720, Barber Bottle and Molasses Can

Corner Medallion and Corner Medallion Variant [720 and 782] (left to right, top to bottom)

1. No. 720 Bowl 6-1/2" HF Covered, Butter, Bowl 8" HF Open
2. No. 720 Sugar Eng. Calla Lily (missing cover), Spoon, Sugar, Cream, Eng. 189
3. No. 720 Spoon, Sugar, Comport 4", Cream
4. No. 782 Corner Medallion Variant Honey Dish

Catalog page with Corner Medallion, Pattern 720

Corner Medallion, Pattern 720, Hand & Stand Lamps

Pattern 721 is an Ale. It holds 10-1/2 ounces and has a tapered cylindrical bowl and is on a fluted bulbous stem.

Pattern 721, Ale

Pattern 722 is a Tumbler. It holds 7-1/2 ounces and has a Swirl pattern three-fourths way up. See pattern 772 Swirl Pattern for similar tumbler.

Pattern 723 consists of Stand and Hand Lamps. They are a variant of pattern 720 Corner Medallion lamps. The font is more like a rounded triangle than oval with notches around the parameter. The stem is flared and the foot is oval coming to a tip in the front and back with a cup foot like the 720 lamps. It came plain or engraved 195. The stand lamps came in five sizes and the hand in three sizes. (H)

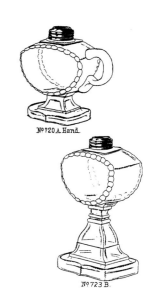

Pattern 723, Stand & Hand Lamps

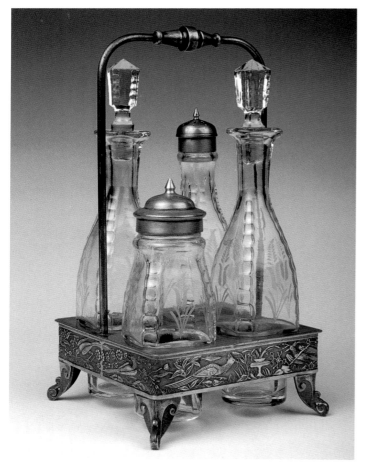

Corner Medallion, Pattern 720, Caster in silver holder

Pattern 723, Stand Lamp

Pattern 724 is a Bitter Bottle. It is a plain bottle with roll top, long neck and bulbous shape. (C)

Pattern 724, Bitter Bottle

Pattern 726 is a Tumbler. It holds 2-1/2 ounces and is fluted with thick walls.

Pattern 726, Tumbler

There are two patterns for 725. One is a Bitter Bottle with long fluted neck and bulbous shape. (C)

Pattern 725, Bitter Bottle

The other pattern 725 is the Barrel or Keg Stand Lamp. The font has a design of a barrel or keg on its side. The stem is flared and the foot is oval and comes to a tip in the front and back with a cup foot. They have the same stem and foot as patterns 720 and 723. The stand lamps came in five sizes. See Oil Lamps and Whirlpool Colognes photograph on page 135 on the top row the first lamp. (R)

Pattern 725, Barrel Stand Lamp

Barrel or Keg Lamps, Pattern 725. *From the Collection of Wayne Laucius, Mt. Bethel, PA*

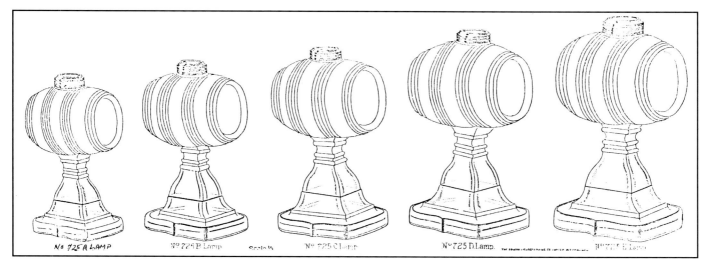

Pattern 725, Barrel Lamps

147

Pattern 727 is the Duck Dish and came etched. This is a beautiful dish with a duck sitting in a pond. The cover is the duck with wonderful feather detail and there is a tiny upturned wing tip feather before the tail. The oval bowl has cattails and other aquatic plants between wavy lines representing water. There is a cord band around the rim of the bowl and underneath it are lines for grass around the pond. The base has a pebbled bottom with a crawfish, frog, and fish with open mouth. It is seven inches long. There is a similar duck dish in blue milk glass[43]. I am not aware of Central making blue milk glass and it could have been made by the U.S. Glass Company after Central joined them and they took over Centrals molds. See Novelties photograph on page 143 on the bottom row on the right. (F)

Pattern 727, Duck Dish

N° 727 Etched Duck.

Pattern 728 is the Elephant Mug. This "Jumbo" mug appeared early in the fall of 1882 and was made in crystal and colors. Jumbo was with the P.T. Barnum Circus in the 1880s and billed as the "Worlds Largest Elephant". He was a huge elephant and was a favorite attraction as he toured all over. He was matched up with a baby elephant and they were displayed together to the excitement of audiences. Unfortunately, Jumbo had a tragic death as he was hit by a train and killed in 1885. Novelties were produced in honor of Jumbo and are highly collected today. The Central elephant mug has Jumbo on one side and the baby elephant on the other. On the front side of the mug there is tall grass and a palm tree in front of Jumbo and tall grasses behind him. On the backside the baby elephant has his trunk out, there are tall plants behind him and a palm tree above his lower back, and there are tall plants in front of him and another palm tree. The handle has three rings near the top and toward the bottom. It was made in colors and they are rare. This mug was also reissued by the U.S. Glass Company. See Novelties photograph on page 143 in the third row the second pattern. (G)

Pattern 728, Jumbo Elephant Mug

N° 728 Mug.

Pattern 729 consists of Ales. They have tall cylindrical fluted bowls with flat bottoms and are on spool stems. The medium ale held 6 ounces, and the pony ale held 4-1/2 ounces.

Pattern 729, Ales

N° 729 Med Ale 6 oz.   N° 729 Pony Ale 4½ oz.

Pattern 730 is the Paneled Ribbed Shell Pattern which is the name I use. It was called "Panel, Rib and Shell" by Kamm[44], however, the shell looks more like a fan. This is a complete pattern with lots of pieces including oil lamps. The shape is six sided and the front and back are wider and have a large oval panel with a shell design in each corner, the narrower sides are ribbed from rim to bottom of the bowl. The handles are very decorative with round protruding top and bottom with a wavy design. The stems are either stocky or stocky with a ring in the middle on low foot pieces, or with a panel and rib pattern on the high foot. The feet are plain six sided to match the bowls. It came plain or engraved number 204. This pattern also is found with a daisy and button panel instead of the plain panel. Whether Central made it or U.S. Glass did when they reissued the pattern is unknown. The Paneled Ribbed Shell with Daisy and Button pattern was made in a pitcher in crystal and colors, other patterns are unknown. See Colored Novelties photograph on page 166 on the top row the first two patterns for the colored pitchers with daisy and button panels.

Sugar (E)
Cream (D)
Spoon (D)
Butter (E)
Celery (D)
Salt, table salt master and individual (See Salts and Miscellaneous Ware photograph on page 69 on row six the first two salts.) (C)
Salt , shaker (C)
Horse radish covered and footed (E)
Pickle jar and cover with flat base (E)
Oval 7 and 8 inch (with pointed ends) (C)
Nappy 4 inch (flat bottom) (C)
Comport 4 inch footed (C)
Bowls 6, 7, and 8 inch low foot covered (E)
Bowls 6, 7, and 8 inch high foot covered (F)
Stemware in a Goblet (C)
Tumbler (C)
Pitcher quart and half gallon (F)
Stand lamp in 5 sizes (H)

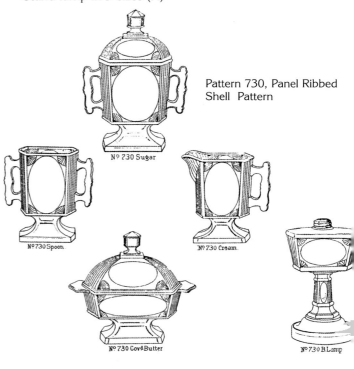

Pattern 730, Panel Ribbed Shell Pattern

N° 730 Sugar
N° 730 Spoon
N° 730 Cream
N° 730 Cov'd Butter
N° 730 B Lamp

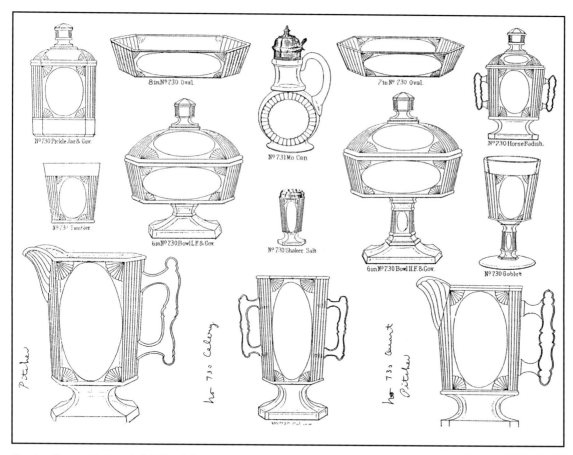

Catalog Page with Paneled Ribbed Shell, Pattern 730 (and 731 Pilgrim Molasses Can)

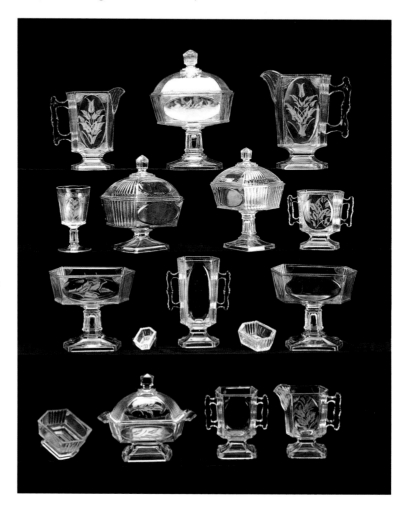

Paneled Ribbed Shell Pattern 730 [All Engraved 204]
(left to right, top to bottom)
1. Pitcher quart, Bowl 9" HF, Pitcher 1/2 gallon
2. Goblet, Bowl 7-1/2" LF, Bowl 6-1/2" HF, Sugar
   (missing cover)
3. Bowl 7-1/2" HF, Individual Salt, Celery, Master Salt,
   Bowl
   7-1/2"
4. Nappy 4-1/2" footed, Butter, Spoon, Cream

Pattern 731 is a Pilgrim Molasses Can. It is bulbous shaped with a round bowl with ribs around the parameter. The neck is plain with a protruding ring under the screw top followed by a hourglass shape on top of a protruding ring before joining the bowl. The foot is round. It came plain or engraved 204 and was made in colors. This style molasses can was also made by other companies. See Pitchers, Molasses Cans and Miscellaneous photograph on page 65 on the second row on the right (fifth pattern). (E)

Pattern 731, Pilgrim Molasses Can

Pattern 732 is the etched Owl Pickle. This has been reproduced. On the left side the Central owl is 8 inches from tip of the ear to the bottom of the tail and the right side measures a little under 8 inches, and the width is 5-1/4 inches wide (outside to outside) where the reproduction is longer, wider, and in colors as well as etched. The reproduction is also heavier than the original owl. The Central owl is usually found etched and colors are rare. See Novelties photograph on page 143 in the third row the third pattern. (E)

Pattern 732, Owl Pickle

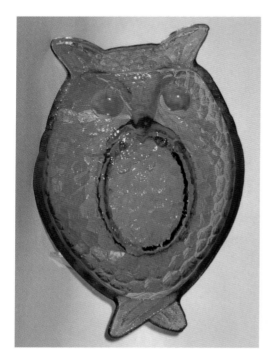

Pattern 732, Owl Pickle in rare blue. *Courtesy of Bob and Jo Sanford.*

Pattern 733 consists of Beer Mugs. They were designed by John Oesterling. The mugs have tall rounded bowls and are on a flat rimmed foot. They came in 10, 8, and 5 ounces. See Barware photograph on page 39 in the third row the fifth mug.

Pattern 733, Beer Mugs

Pattern 734 is a Cordial. It holds 1-1/2 ounces and has a round bowl with a large oval thumbprint band and is on an upside-down bulbous stem.

Pattern 734, Cordial

Pattern 735 is Stemware. They have an oval thumbprint band on the bottom of the bowls and have either tall cylindrical or rounded bowls that taper down on straight flared stems. There were two 3-1/2 ounce champagnes, one with a straight top and the other with a tapered rim, a 2-1/2 ounce wine, and a 1 ounce cordial.

Pattern 735, Stemware

Pattern 736 is a Cocktail. It holds 3 ounces and has a fluted cup bowl and is on a fluted stem with knop near the top.

Pattern 736, Cocktail

Pattern 737 is a Champagne. It holds 4 ounces and has a thumbprint band on the bottom of a wide cup bowl and is on a paneled stem.

Pattern 737, Champagne

Patterns 738 and 739 are Tumblers. Pattern 738 has a tall cylindrical fluted bowl in a 5 ounce large and 3-1/2 ounce small size. Pattern 739 has a plain heavy bottomed bowl and holds 1-1/2 ounces.

Patterns 738 and 739, Tumblers

Pattern 740 is the Strawberry Diamond pattern sometimes called Fine Cut. The pattern is on the lower half of the bowls and the design has an inverted diamond point pattern with the center point of the diamond pushed back into the diamond. This makes it look like a fine cut pattern. It came in a beautiful water set that included tray, goblets, and ice bowl. There may be more pieces in this pattern but the only pieces the catalogs show were the water set, a 8 ounce tumbler, and an ice cream bowl with a single handle. The ice cream bowl sides have the strawberry diamond design on six round panels between a plain rib and the water tray has ten round panels between a plain rib, both have the design on the bottom. The water tray has handles. The goblets are on a spool stem. They were made in crystal and colors.

N° 740 Water Set

Pattern 740, Strawberry Diamond Pattern

Pattern 741 is an Ale. It holds 9 ounces and is referred to as a pilsner. It has a cylindrical bowl with four vertical thumbprints between tall narrow vertical bars on the stocky stem. (C)

N° 741 9 oz Ale

Pattern 741, Ale

Pattern 742 consists of Ales. They have a cylindrical fluted bowl and are on a bulbous stem with wide narrow ring near the top (looks like a pacifier). They came in a large 9 ounce and 5 ounce pony size.

742 Large Ale 9 oz

Pattern 742, Ale

Pattern 743 is an Ale. It holds 9 ounces and has a thumbprint band on the bottom of a tapered cylindrical bowl and is on a straight flared stem.

N° 743 9 oz Ale

Pattern 743, Ale

Strawberry Diamond, Pattern 740, Pitcher, Goblet, Water Tray, Pitcher 1/2 gallon

Pattern 744 is a Tumbler. It holds 3-1/2 ounces and is fluted.

Pattern 744, Tumbler

Pattern 745 is the Ring Stem Stemware. They have tall trumpet bowls with heavy bottoms and a hollow ring stem (foot). The stems have six rings, the top ring is underneath the bottom of the bowl then there is a slight space then five rings that flair out and get wider toward the bottom. They came in a 9 ounce beer and in 7, 5, 3-1/2, 2, and 1/2 ounce sizes. They were usually made in crystal but the ring foot was also made in color. See Barware photograph on page 39 on the second row the first ale. (C & D)

Pattern 745, Ring Stem stemware

Ring Stem Beer Glass, Pattern 745, with blue rings. Holds 9 ounces.

Catalog page with ales showing Ring Stem Ales, Pattern 745, on the bottom

Pattern 746 is a Tumbler. It holds 8 ounces and is plain with a heavy bottom.

Pattern 746, Tumbler

Pattern 747 is the Fish Dish. This dish came plain or etched. It is oval and the cover measures 7-3/4 inches and the bowl from the nose to tip of the top part of the tail measures 9-1/4 inches and it is 3-1/4 inches wide. The foot has a design of water with a seashell, flower, lobster, six leafed plant, and a fish on both sides. See Novelties photograph on page 143 in the third row on the left for the etched dish and on the right for the crystal dish. (F)

Pattern 747, Fish Dish

Pattern 748 is the Log Cabin pattern. This was a very popular set. An article in *Crockery and Glass Journal* dated October 02, 1884, mentioned: "Just now the greatest run is being made by the "Log Cabin", a rather unique set.... The goods are all made in imitation of a very old cabin, and as finished make very attractive table furniture. It came into prominence during the last year (1883)...."

The pieces are rectangular and most are on four stump feet or on a knot holed tree trunk stem for the high foot bowls. The covers are in the shape of a roof with shingles and the final is a chimney. The bottom of the bowls have a floor pattern of boards with knot holes. The logs are stacked meeting at the corners. There is stippling in between the logs representing mortar. The handle is made up of three tree branches with the top one curving up, the bottom one curving down, and the middle one straight. The colored pieces are extremely rare. Finding pieces in perfect shape is rare as the covers (roofs) usually have chips. There are reproductions in crystal and colors. The door on the Central pieces have a rope loop handle, if it does not, it is the reproduction. There are other differences but the door handle is the most obvious. The names given below are the names Central gave the pieces. A catalog from the Henry Ford Museum showed a high foot compote which also had the four low foot feet on it, this piece would be extremely rare. The sugar, spoon, and pickle jar have a door in the front with logs in the back and a window on each side. The high foot compotes have a door on the left and window in the front with two windows in the back and log sides. The pitchers have a door in the front and window in the back.

Sugar and cover 4-1/2 inches high and 4 inches long by 3 inches wide (F)

Cream (E)

Spoon (Note: the spooner and pickle jar have the same dimensions, 4-3/4" high by 3 inches long and 2-1/2 inches wide) (E)

Butter and cover 6 inches long with handles and no door or windows (F)

Pickle jar and cover (F)

Nappie 4 inch log only pattern (no handles, door or window, this measures 3-1/2 inches inside the handles) (D)

Comport 4 inch with handles – no door or windows (E)

Comport 6, 7, and 8 inch uncovered with handles, door and windows (F)

Comport 6, 7, and 8 inch covered with handles, door and windows (I)

Bowls 6, 7, and 8 inch high foot without cover (I)

Bowls 6, 7, and 8 inch high foot covered (R over $300)

Pitcher (I)

Known pieces in color are rare and can go into the thousands of dollars depending on color and condition and the Lutted's in color is extremely rare (R)

There is another log cabin pattern that has been attributed to Central, and it is the Lutted's Cough drop pattern. It was made 7 inches long and 5 inches wide (to the outside rim of rounded logs) and in larger sizes. These were made for store cough drop displays and usually were made in clear. Colors in amber, blue, and canary are rare. The covers had clear panels on both sides with "LUTTED'S S.P. COUGH DROPS GENUINE HAS 'J.L' STAMPED ON EACH DROP". "Each Drop" was on the lower part of the cover between the shingles and had the lettering on the inside of the cover. Another cover was different and had the lettering on the outside with "LUTTED'S S.P. COUGH DROPS". In the bottom of the bowls is 'JAS. LUTED BUFFALO. N.Y. U.S.A.". There are two windows in the front and back with a door on each end. These have also been reproduced and are very heavy, the lid has "Lutted's S.P. Cough Drops" only, the bottom of the bowls have the board floor pattern instead of writing, there are no doors on the ends, and the stippling is missing between the logs. A glass scoop with 'JAMES LUTTED BUFFALO. N.Y." was made to go with the cough drop bowl.

Nº 748 LOG CABIN PATTERN.

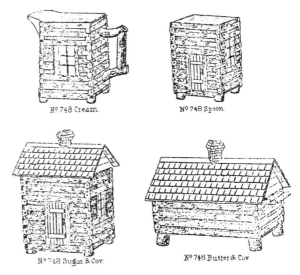

Nº 748 Cream.   Nº 748 Spoon.

Nº 748 Sugar & Cov.   Nº 748 Butter & Cov

Pattern 748, Log Cabin

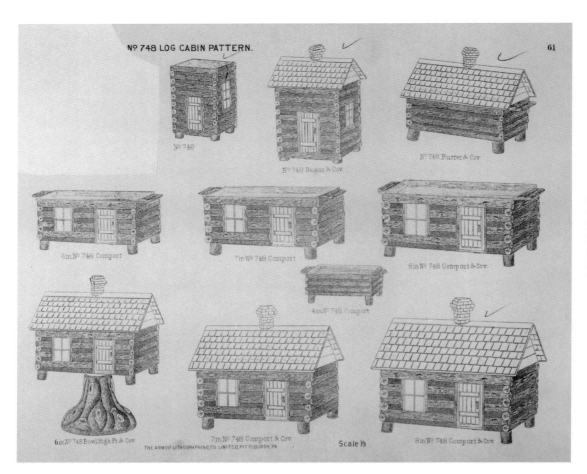

Catalog Page with Log Cabin Pattern 748 with Rare Low Footed Bowl on High Foot Stand. *From the Collections of Henry Ford Museum & Greenfield Village*

Log Cabin Pattern 748 (left to right, top to bottom)
1. Bowl 6" HF, Sugar, Bowl 8" HF, Cream, Bowl 7" HF
2. Butter, Pickle, Sugar
3. Bowl 6", Nappy 3-1/2" with Handles, Bowl 7", Nappy 4", Bowl 8"
4. Bowl 8" LF, Pitcher 1/2 gallon, Lutted's Cough Drops 7" LF

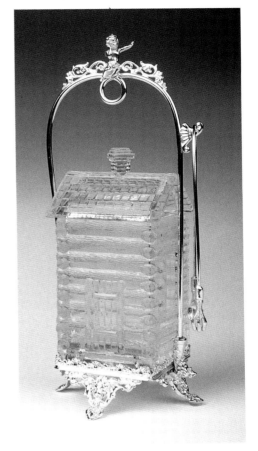

Colored Log Cabin Pattern 748 (left to right, top to bottom)
1. Sugars (two), Pickle in Caster, Sugar (missing cover), Ken Kercheval Showing his Log Cabin Collection
2. Lutted's Cough Drop Showing Engraving, Lutted's Cough Drop Bowl
3. Sugar (missing cover), Spoon, Pickle, Spoon, Spoon
4. Pickles (2), Spoon in Rare "Root Beer Amber"

Log Cabin, Pattern 748, Pickle in silver holder

Lutted's Pattern 748 in rare amber color

Bottom of Lutted's Pattern 748 bowl, showing wording in amber

Pattern 749 is a Tumbler. It holds 3 ounces and is fluted with a heavy bottom.

Pattern 749, Tumbler

Patterns 754 and 755 are Tumblers. They are fluted and pattern 754 holds 4-1/2 ounces and pattern 755 holds 9 ounces.

Patterns 754 and 755, Tumblers

Pattern 750 is a Stand Lamp. It has a plain oval font and the stem has the Paneled Ribbed Shell design (pattern 730) on a cup foot and came in five sizes. (G)

Nº 750 Lamp.

Pattern 750, Stand Lamp

Pattern 756 consists of Ales. They have trumpet shaped bowls on plain stems and hold 6 ounces or 4-1/2 ounces in a pony ale. Note: there were three ale sizes illustrated in the 1900 Central Glass Works catalog.

Pattern 756, Ales

Pattern 751 is unknown
Pattern 752 is a Wine. It held 3-1/2 ounces and has a cup shaped bowl. The stem has three narrow rings slightly below the bowl and a plain flared stem.

Pattern 752, Wine

Pattern 757 is a Cordial. It holds 1 ounce and has a tapered cylindrical shape with fluted bowl and is on a stem with a double ring slightly under the bowl with a plain flared stem above the foot.

Pattern 757, Cordial

Pattern 753 is the Leaf Pickle. It has a shallow bowl and is nine and a half inches long by six and three-eighths inches wide. It has a leaf shape showing the veins on the leaf with a small frog in the middle. There is a bee in the top half and a turtle on the lower half of the leaf. It came in crystal and colors. (F)

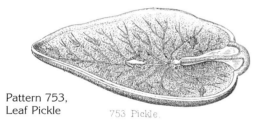

Pattern 753, Leaf Pickle

753 Pickle.

Leaf Pickle, Pattern 753

Pattern 758 is the Pheasant Oval dish. It is plain except the cover which measures 7-1/4 inches. It has a beautifully etched pheasant with long tail on top of grass and leaves in various shapes. The flanged bowl measures 8-1/2 inches instead of 8 and has a star design in the bottom. There are round bowls with the identical pheasant design but I am only aware of Central making the oval dish. See Novelties photograph on page 143 on the bottom row the first pattern on the left. (F)

8in.758 Ovals.

Pattern 758, Pheasant Oval

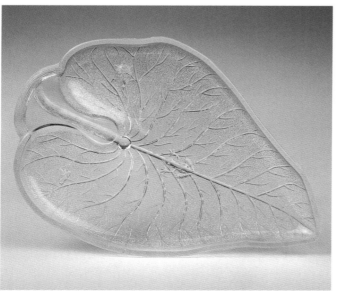

Pattern 759 is unknown
Pattern 760 is a Tea Nappy. It came in a 5 and 6 inch size and has a fluted bowl and plain flared rim with a star design in the bottom (it looks like a saucer).

760 Nappy.

Pattern 760, Tea Nappy

Pattern 761 is a Cocktail. It holds 3-1/2 ounces and has a cup shape bowl and is on a straight stem with round knop slightly under the bowl.

Pattern 761, Cocktail

Pattern 762 is a Tumbler. It holds 3-1/2 ounces and is plain.

Pattern 762, Tumbler

Pattern 763 is the Leaf Comport. It is 8 inches and has a pattern that looks like four cabbage leaves with veins. The bowl has a small plain round center with four narrow bars extending out to the leaves. The stem is plain and the wide round foot is tiered. It came in crystal and colors. See Colored Novelties photograph photo on page 166 on the top row on the right (patterns three and four) for canary and amber with the blue bowl underneath them. It is also shown in crystal in the Novelties photograph on page 143 on the bottom row in the middle. (F)

Pattern 763, Leaf Comport

Pattern 764 is the Flower Oval Bowl. It measures 8 inches and has a pattern of flowers above leaves with pointed tips. The flowers have large centers and resemble sunflowers. The rim of the bowl has twelve scallops above the flowers. The bottom has a star design. It came in crystal and colors. (R)

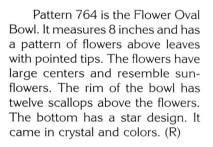

Pattern 764, Flower Oval Bowl

Pattern 765 is a Goblet. It holds 8 ounces and has a conical bowl with thin toothpick size ribs around the bottom half of the bowl and is on a plain flared stem.

Pattern 766 is a Tumbler. It holds 9-1/2 ounces and has a button and diamond pattern a fourth down from the rim. This design is similar to pattern 810 Tudor.

Pattern 767 is a Handled Tumbler. It holds 5 ounces and has a plain cylindrical bowl with a flat handle (the handle resembles like a pop-top on a can).

Pattern 768 is a Cream Pitcher. It is plain with a narrow neck with "lipped" pouring spout and round bowl in a bulbous shape with a reed handle. It was on a page with other small cream pitchers the same size so it would be under 5 inches tall. It came in crystal and colors. The cream pitcher is shown in the catalog page below. (D)

Pattern 765, Goblet

Pattern 766, Tumbler

Pattern 767, Handled Tumbler

Pattern 768, Cream Pitcher

Colored catalog page showing Pattern 768 Cream Pitcher and Miscellaneous Colored Ware. *From the Collections of Henry Ford Museum & Greenfield Village.*

Pattern 769 was called "769 WARE" and came with "Sett Plain" or "Sett Eng'd. No. 213". I call this pattern "Acorn Finial" pattern. It is a plain set with tapered cylindrical bowls in the sugar, cream and spoon. The handles are flat similar to pattern 767 with a circle opening except the cream pitcher which has two circle openings. The stems are bulbous with a narrow ring at the top and bottom and the foot is hollow and has a flat edge (like pattern 705). The finial is in the shape of an upside down acorn. See Simplicity and Acorn Top patterns photograph on page 142 on the second row the third pattern for the pitcher with double handle and on the top row in the middle for two bowls.

Sugar and cover (D)
Cream (D)
Spoon (C)
Butter and cover (D)
Comport 7, 8, 9 and 10 inch high foot shallow bowls (C)
Bowls in 6, 7, 8, and 9 inch high foot and cover (D)

Pattern 769, Acorn Finial pattern

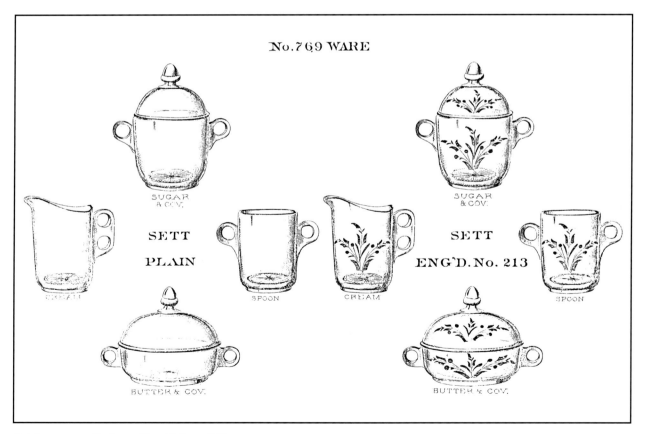

Catalog page with Acorn Top, Pattern 769

Pattern 770 is a Weiss Beer. It holds 16 ounces and has a plain tapered cylindrical bowl on a stocky stem.

Pattern 770, Weiss Beer

Pattern 771 consists of Beer Mugs. They are plain tall cylindrical bowls with heavy hollow bottoms. The came in 13, 10, 6, and 5 ounce sizes.

Pattern 771, Beer Mugs

Pattern 772 is a Swirl Pattern. This pattern had many pieces in stemware and barware including tumblers, beer mugs, and bar bottles as well as stand and hand lamps. If other table ware was made is not known. This swirl design was popular and used on several pieces with different pattern numbers. The stemware has tapered cylindrical bowls with the swirl design on the bottom three-fourths of the bowl and they are on a spindle stem. The beer mugs have the swirl design just under the lip to the bottom of the bowl and were designed by John Oesterling. They came in 13, 10, 8, and 5 ounces with a "twist" handle. The font on the stand lamps has the swirl design between the rounded top and bottom. The stem has the swirl design between a thin ring at the top and bottom with a flute band above the cup foot. The stand lamp came in five sizes and the hand in three sizes.

Tumbler 9-1/2 ounces with pattern in bottom half of the bowl (B)

Tumbler 7-1/2 small with pattern on bottom three-fourths of the bowl (B)

Beer Mugs (C)

Weiss Beers 16 and 14 ounce size with stocky stem (C)

Cologne large size (came in colors) (D)

Bitter bottle for cork (came in colors) (D)

Bar bottle (came in colors) (E)

Stemware 10 ounce goblet, 5 ounce champagne, claret, and wine (A & B)

Stand Lamps (See Colored Oil Lamps photograph on page 161 on the top row numbers three and five) (came in colors) (H)

Hand Lamps (came in colors) (G)

772 SWIRL PATTERN

NOTE: Tumbler No. 722

Pattern 772, Swirl Pattern

SWIRL PATTERNS [No. 772, No. 773, No. 774, and No. 884]) (left to right, top to bottom)
1. No. 884 Bar and Swirl Bowl 8" HF Covered
2. No. 772 Stand Lamp, No. 884 Tumbler, No. 884 Cologne, No. 884 Water Bottle
3. No. 772 Stand Lamp, No. 772 Bitter Bottle, No. 772 Beer Mugs 5 and 8 ounces
4. No. 772 Tumbler 9-1/2 oz., No. 774 Ale 5-1/2 oz., No. 774 Ale 4 oz., No. 773 Ale 9 ounce

Swirl patterns with Pattern 772, Cologne and Bitter Bottle, in Amber, and Pattern 884, Cologne, in Crystal

Patterns 773 and 774 are Ales. They have a swirl pattern and are on a stem with a large ball shaped knop slightly under the bottom of the bowl on a plain flared stem. Pattern 773 has tapered cylindrical bowls with the swirl design on the bottom three-fourths of the bowl in a large 10, medium 9, and pony 5 ounce sizes. Pattern 774 has tall tapered cylindrical bowls with the swirl design on the bottom three-fourths of the bowl in medium 5-1/2 and pony 3-1/2 ounce sizes. See Swirl Patterns photograph above on the bottom row numbers two, three and four for Swirl Ales. Also see Barware photograph on page 39 in the third row the fourth pattern in the middle. (B)

No. 773 Med Ale 9 oz.

Pattern 773, Ale, Swirl pattern

No 774 Med Ale 5½ oz.

Pattern 774, Ale, Swirl pattern

In 1885 color is starting to be used. An article in *Crockery and Glass Journal* dated January 01, 1885 mentioned: "The Central is experimenting with colors, and it is likely that early in the coming year it will place a line of colored goods of all descriptions in its sample rooms."

Oil lamps in color became very popular. This is shown in the photograph below.

Colored Oil Lamps (left to right, top to bottom)
1. No. 950 Whirlpool Stand Lamp, No. 876 Star Stand Lamp, No. 772 Swirl Stand Lamp, No. 792 Coin Blank Stand Lamp, No. 772 Swirl Stand Lamp
2. No. 821 Dewdrop (3) Stand Lamps, No. 876 Star Stand Lamp
3. No. 469 Oesterling Stand Lamp with Cobalt Stem/Foot, No. 486 Stand Lamp with Cobalt Stem/Base, No. 811 Shell Hand Lamp, No. ? Has Centrals Pat'd. Stem/Foot in Cobalt, No. 311 Mountain Laurel Stand Lamp with Cobalt Stem/Foot
4. No. 821 Dewdrop Night Lamp, No. 310 Night Lamp, No. 300 Night Lamp, No. 310 Night Lamp, No. 821 Dewdrop Night Lamp

Pattern 775 is the Pressed Diamond pattern. It has also been called Zephyr and Button and Bows. It is a huge pattern with many pieces. The first mention of this pattern was in the *Crockery and Glass Journal* dated January 01, 1885. "The Central has ready for the market an entire new set of magnificent imitation cut glass which it calls "775". The berry dishes, sugars, creams, and other pieces are cylindrical, the crystals diamond shaped, the diamonds inserted in such an ingenious manner as to give them in certain exposures a fine iridescence". Some of the patterns given this number have a different design like the boat (canoe) which has a rectangular button pattern in the diamonds. The ice cream or berry set looks more like the "daisy" part of daisy and button but without the button. The bread tray is a daisy and button pattern and was later moved in with the daisy and button patterns under pattern number 782. The design has a row of buttons at the top under the rim and at the bottom of the bowl. There are similar patterns made by other companies but they do not have the row of buttons at the top and bottom. The rims of the bowls and plates are scalloped. The finial has a small round disc top with a narrow diamond pattern on the sides with a narrow ring at the bottom. The stems have a washer looking knop slightly under the bowl on flutes that get wider at the foot. The foot and the bottom of the bowls have the diamond pattern in it. The pattern was made in crystal and colors and there were some 47 pieces produced. It was reissued by the U.S. Glass Company. The sizes for bowls in this pattern are not accurate and can vary from a quarter of an inch to as much as a half an inch.

Sugar (D)
Cream (D)
Spoon (C)
Butter with flanged rim and cover (F)
Butter individual butter pat (B)

Celery (D)
Custard with handle (looks like a tea cup) (C)
Goblet 9 ounce (C)
Tumbler 7-1/2 ounce (C)
Salts individual and shaker (See Salts and Miscellaneous Ware photograph on page 69 on the fourth row numbers nine, ten, eleven, and twelve for shaker salts and on the bottom row the first four are individual salts. (B & C)
Salts individual and shaker in green, this is a color rarity (R)
Pitcher half gallon (E)
Water set shown with tray, pitcher, finger (or ice) bowl, tumblers (R)
Boat (canoe shape) in 7, 9, and 12 inch (C & D)
Ice Cream or Berry Set small bowls are 4-1/2 inch (R)
Nappy round no foot in 4, 4-1/2, 5, 6, 7, 8, 9, and 10 inch (C & D)
Comports shallow bowl high foot 7, 8, 9, and 10 inch (C & D)
Bowls 4 inch with plain stem and foot no cover (C)
Bowls 4 inch high foot no cover (C)
Bowls 6, 7, 8, 9, and 10 inch high foot deep bowls covered (F to I)
Plates 5, 6, 8, and 9 inch (E & F)
Oil bottle with cut diamond stopper (E)
Finger bowl (C)
Octagon bowl this is a rarity and not in any of the catalogs (R)
Bread Plate (this is a daisy and button pattern and was later moved to pattern 835) (See Salts and Miscellaneous Ware photograph on page 69 on the top row on the right for the bread plate) (D)
Salvers in 8, 9, 10, 11, and 12 inches (E to I)

Pattern 775, Pressed Diamond pattern

Pressed Diamond Pattern 775 (left to right, top to bottom)
1. Bowl 8-1/2" HF, Bowl 12" HF, Bowl 8-1/2" HF
2. Shallow Bowls 11" HF and 8" HF, Pitcher Celery
3. Spoon, Cream, Tumbler, Goblet, Oil Bottle
4. Salt Shakers, Plate 10-3/4", Plate 8"

BLUE Pressed Diamond Pattern 775 (left to right, top to bottom)
1. Pitcher 1/2 gallon, Bowl 6-1/2" HF, Bowl 8" HF, Bowl 9-1/2"
2. Bowl 9-1/2 ", Plate 9", Custard, Slaver 10"
3. Nappy footed 6-1/2", Butter, Celery, Salver 8"
4. Salt Shakers, Nappy 5", Finger Bowl, Nappy 4", Tumbler, Ind. Salt

Amber Pressed Diamond Pattern 775 (left to right, top to bottom)
1. Bowls High Foot in 8-1/2", 7-1/2", 8", 9-1/2"
2. Cream, Sugar, Salver 12", Nappy 8-1/2"
3. Tumbler, Ind. Salt, Tumbler, Plate 8", Butter, Finger Bowl, Salt Shakers
4. Oil Cruet, Spoon, Celery, Sugar (missing cover), Goblet

Canary Pressed Diamond Pattern 775 and No. 780 Bowls (left to right, top to bottom)
1. No. 775 Bowls HF 6-1/2", 9-1/2", 8-1/2", 7-1/2"
2. No. 775 Boats 12", 9", 7", Boat 7" in Caster
3. No. 780 Bowls 4" & 8", No. 775 Nappies 4-1/2" (2), Nappy 7-1/2", Ice Cream Bowls (2)
4. No. 775 Plate 8", Bread Tray (with Daisy & Button Pattern)

Canary Pressed Diamond Pattern 775 (left to right, top to bottom)
1. Nappy 8-1/2", Bowl 10" HF, Nappy 7-1/2"
2. Butter, Salver 8-1/2 ", Salver 10-1/2"
3. Goblet, Celery, Tumbler, Oil Bottle, Sugar
4. Spoon, Cream, Salt Shakers, Individual Salt, Custard, Finger Bowl

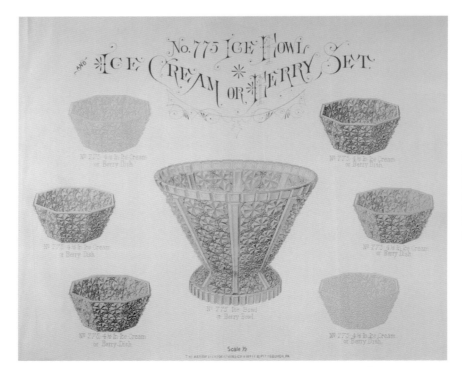

Catalog page with Pressed Diamond, Pattern 775, Ice Cream or Berry Set. *From the Collections of Henry Ford Museum & Greenfield Village*

Pressed Diamond Pattern 775 Salts in rare green

Pressed Diamond Pattern 775 Boat in silver holder

Pressed Diamond Pattern 775 Ice Cream or Berry Set of 775 pattern Octagon Bowl (amber) number 043

Pressed Diamond Pattern 775 Octagon Nappy

Patterns 776 and 777 are Tumblers. Pattern 776 is a tall 9 ounce plain tumbler. Pattern 777 is a 7 ounce plain tumbler that came with a "Lipped" rim (for pouring) as well as a plain rim.

Patterns 776 and 777, Tumblers & Lipped Tumbler

Pattern 779 is a Weiss Beer. It holds 17 ounces and is plain with a tapered cylindrical bowl and is on a plain flared stem.

Pattern 779, Weiss Beer

Pattern 778 is a Shaker Salt. It has a tall cylindrical bowl and tapers in at the neck before a screw top. It came in crystal and colors.

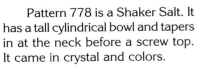

Pattern 778, Shaker Salt

Pattern 780 are the Pressed Diamond and Panel Nappies. They are a pattern 775 Pressed Diamond variant. They have square bowls with clear round panel corners with the pressed diamond design in between them. The rims are scalloped above the pressed diamond panels and are smooth above the clear panels. The bottoms of the bowls have the pressed diamond pattern. They were made in a 8 and 4-1/2 inch size and came in colors. See 775 Pattern and No. 780 Bowls in Canary photograph on page 164 in row three the first two patterns. (D & C)

Pattern 780, Pressed Diamond & Panel Nappies

Pattern 781 is a Goblet. It holds 10-1/2 ounces and has a trumpet shaped plain bowl and is on a plain flared stem.

Pattern 781, Goblet

Pressed Diamond Pattern 780, Square Nappy in silver holder

Pattern 782 is the Daisy and Button pattern. There are several designs given to this pattern but instead of putting all of the daisy and button patterns under this number Central gave different numbers to other designs, quite a few have a 800 pattern number. It seems that each time they made a new mold they gave that piece a new pattern number. Several of the daisy and button patterns were on a catalog page of Novelties. The designs with this pattern number are listed below. They were all made in crystal and colors.

Colored Novelties (left to right, top to bottom)
1. No. 730 Water Pitchers with D&B Panels (2), No. 763 Lily Pad Compote (2)
2. No. 831 Slipper Roller Skates (2), No. 822 Stove Caster, No. 838 Barrel Sugars (2), No. 859 High Top Roller Skate, No. 763 Lily Pad Compote
3. No. 822 Stove Salt, No. 782 Hourglass Salts (3), No. 866 Owl Match Box (2), No. 700 Horse Ink Stand, No. 840 Slipper Hanging Match, No. 823 Half Bottle Pickles (3)
4. No. 819 Swan Dish, No. 16 Carriage Salt, No. 782 Coal Bin Match (3), No. 865 Horse Pulling Barrel Match (2), No. 16 Carriage Candy

Salver in an octagon shape with a rib band around the rim and bottom of the foot on the paneled stem like pattern 775. The pattern looks like 'daisy' without the buttons like in the 775 ice cream set. (R)

Salt shaker in Hourglass shape. These measured from 3-1/2 to 3-3/4 inches high. The screw top rims are sometimes chipped. See Colored Novelties on page 166 in the third row the first three patterns. Also see Salts and Miscellaneous Ware photograph on page 69 in row four the first three salts. (D each)

Match Box in the shape of coal bin. This pattern is identical to one made by George Duncan and Sons of Pittsburgh, Pennsylvania. An article in the *Crockery and Glassware Journal*, May 28, 1885 mentioned: "The Central Glass Works of this city, and George Duncan & Sons, of Pittsburgh, have locked horns in a manner. The Pittsburgh firm, some time since, got out a new line of goods, and shortly afterwards a design the exact counterpart of that of Duncan & Sons was introduced by the Central, and the price materially cut. Whether this was by accident or otherwise Duncan & Sons took it up and at once commenced a cut on some of the special lines handled by the Central, and succeeded in bringing about an inquiry and propositions of adjustment." The pattern is to represent a coal bin and is square with round corners. It has the daisy and button design on two sides and is stippled on two sides (for the match striker) and is on four rounded feet that resemble a match. The bottom is ribbed. It is 3 inches high and the top is 2 inches by 2 inches. See Colored Novelties photograph on page 166 on the bottom row the third, fourth, and fifth patterns. Also see Novelties photograph on page 143 on the second row the second pattern for crystal. (D)

Butter and Honey dish. These are a Corner Medallion pattern 720 variant. The daisy and button pattern is on the bottom of the bowl and the "buttons" are square instead of hexagonal. The covers have a stippled decorative pattern with tassels, the sides are clear. The flanged bowls have a thin zig-zag line above a decorative band with a flower in an oval next to a diamond with a bead inside on a stippled background. The flanged bowl is scalloped and has four ribbed feet that get narrower at the bottom. The finial is the same as on 720 patterns. The butter measures 5-1/2 inches high (to top of finial) and is 7 inches long and 5 inches wide. The honey dish measures 4-1/2 inches high and is 6 inches long and 4 inches wide. See 720 Corner Medallion Pattern photograph on page 145 in the bottom for the honey dish. (F Butter, E Honey)

Corner Medallion Variant, Pattern 782, Butter & Honey Dishes. Butter Dish in Crystal, Honey Dishes in Blue, Canary, and Amber

Patterns 783 and 784 are Tumblers in the Swirl pattern. Pattern 783 is a 12 ounce soda with the pattern in the bottom three-fourths of the bowl. Pattern 784 holds 2 ounces and the pattern is slightly below the middle.

Patterns 783 and 784, Swirl pattern Soda & Tumbler

Pattern 785 is an Ale. It holds 8 ounces and has a tapered cylindrical bowl with long flutes from the rim to slightly above the flat bottom. It is on a straight stem with a large ring shaped knop slightly below the bottom of the bowl.

Pattern 785, Ale

Pattern 786 is the New Paragon Ink. It is kidney shaped with round ribs around the stand. It had two openings for ink with a cup for sponge in the back. There was also a small opening in the front to hold nibs. There are hooks in the front for holding pens. See catalog illustration of the New Paragon Ink under pattern 700 with other ink stand on page 138.

Pattern 786, New Paragon Ink Stand

Pattern 787 is a Weiss Beer. It has a trumpet shaped bowl on a wide foot.

Pattern 787, Weiss Beer

Pattern 788 is an Ale. It holds 8 ounces and has a tapered cylindrical bowl with flutes from rim to bottom and is on a spool stem.

Pattern 788, Ale

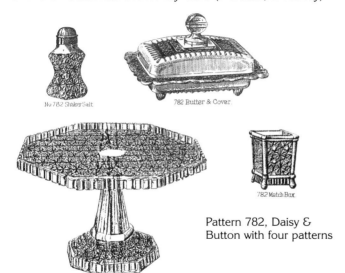

No. 782 Shaker Salt

782 Butter & Cover.

782 Match Box

Pattern 782, Daisy & Button with four patterns

On No. 782 Salver

Pattern 789 is an Ale. It holds 8 ounces and has a plain tapered cylindrical bowl and is on a spool stem.

Pattern 789, Ale

Pattern 791 consists of Stand and Hand Lamps. This lamp was named "Owen" by Thuro[45]. The font has a plain oval bowl with a protruding ring near the top for catching oil drips. The stand lamp is on the swirl stem like pattern 772. The hand lamp has a fluted stem and both lamps are on the cup foot. The stand lamps came in six sizes with the smallest size being "1/2 A" which would be used for a night lamp. The hand lamps came in three sizes. (F)

Pattern 790 is the "Hive" Stand and Hand Lamps. The font resembles a hive and has four wide horizontal rings that get narrower at the bottom. The stand lamp is on a hollow stem with cup foot. The hand lamps have a fluted stem and cup foot. The stand lamps came in five sizes and the hand lamps in three sizes. They were made in crystal and colors. See Oil Lamps photograph page 73 on row two in the middle. (H)

Pattern 790, Hand & Stand Lamps

Pattern 791, Stand & Hand Lamps

Pattern 792 are the Coin Blank Stand and Hand Lamps. This lamp was named "Coin Blank with Owen Base" by Thuro[46]. The "Coin Blank" name can stay as it is the same font that was used in the coin lamps. Since the stem has a swirl design I call it a "swirl stem" instead of Owen Base. The stand lamp is on the swirl stem like pattern 772 and the above pattern. The hand lamp has a fluted stem and both lamps are on the cup foot. They came plain or engraved 214 and in crystal and colors. The stand lamps came in five sizes and the hand in three sizes. See Colored Oil Lamps photograph on page 161 on the top row the fourth lamp. Also see Oil Lamps and Whirlpool Colognes photograph on page 135 on the top row the fourth lamp. (G)

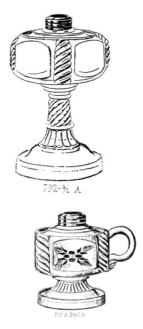

Pattern 792, Stand and Hand Lamps

Catalog page with Coin Blank, Pattern 792, Stand and Hand Lamps, and Hive Lamp, Pattern 790, in crystal and colors. *From the Collections of Henry Ford Museum & Greenfield Village*

Pattern 793 is a Spice Caster. It has a four leaf clover shape with four ribbed cup shaped bowls joined together. The ribs protrude out from the flat top and taper down to the bottom of the cups. It has a ribbed handle with button top. (R)

Pattern 793, Spice Caster

The next three patterns have a rope or lattice pattern on them. They were originally called "rope" by Albert Christian Revi[47]. Most of the pieces have a rope-like design around the rim and bottom of the low foot bowls with the illusion of twisted rope. As this name has been used for over thirty years I will not change it. These patterns were all patented. They were full sets with many pieces and came in crystal and colors. The shape of some of the pieces is bulbous. The bowls have flanged rims and round protruding sides that taper in to the rope pattern foot. The majority of compotes made have the bottom of the bowls smooth without a design in them, but the high foot bowls have a design both inside and outside the bowl. In the bottom of the bowls the inside has ribs that go in one direction and on the outside the ribs go in the opposite direction, giving the appearance of squares. The high foot bowls are on a plain hollow bulbous stem with a smooth tiered foot on the outside and ribs on the inside giving a design of blocks or bricks. All three patterns had the same number of pieces.

Pattern 794 is the Plain Rope pattern and came plain or engraved with Eng. 215.

Pattern 794, Plain Rope pattern

Pattern 795 is the Ribbed Rope which has ribs from top of bowl to the bottom. It also came in a 8 ounce goblet.

Pattern 795, Ribbed Rope pattern

Pattern 796 is the Rope and Thumbprint pattern which has rows of thumbprints staggered from the top of the bowl to the bottom. It also came in a stand lamp on a column stem and in a 8 ounce goblet on a bulbous stem and in tumblers.

Pattern 796, Rope and Thumbprint pattern

The rope pattern pieces are listed below.
Sugar in two sizes (C & D)
Cream in two sizes 4-1/2 and 5 inch sizes (C)
Spoon (C)
Butter in two sizes, 4-3/4 inches and 5-1/4 inches (E & F)
Celery (D)
Goblet (Thumbprints only) 8 ounce on bulbous stem (C)
Nappy 4-1/2 inch plain bowl scalloped top no rope pattern for 795 (C)
Nappy 4-1/2 inch ribbed bowl scalloped top no rope pattern for 795 (C)
Nappy 4-1/2 inch thumbprint bowl scalloped top no rope pattern for 796 (C)
Comport 4-1/2 inch scalloped top plain bowl (pattern on foot only for 794) (C)
Comport 4-1/2 inch scalloped top ribbed bowl (pattern on foot only for 795) (C)
Comport 4-1/2 inch scalloped top thumbprint bowl (pattern on foot only for 796) (C)
Comport 6, 7, 8 inch low foot (rope foot no stem) (C & D)
Comport 6, 7, 8 inch low foot covered (rope foot no stem) (E)
Comport 7, 8, 9, and 10 inch high foot (open) (D & E)
Bowls 6, 7, 8 inch high foot covered (E & F)
Finger bowl (B)
Molasses with metal tops 5-1/2 inches high (See Pitchers, Molasses Cans and Miscellaneous photograph on page 65 on the bottom row the first pattern for the Rope and Thumbprint molasses can.) (E)
Molasses with pouring spout 6-1/2 inches high (F)
Shaker salt (See Salts and Miscellaneous Ware photograph on page 69 on row four numbers six, seven and eight for Rope and Thumbprint salts) (C)
Sugar sifter (H)
Pitcher quart and half gallon with different handles (D & E)
Salver 8, 9, 10 inch (E & F)
Stand Lamps – Thumbprint font on column stem in 5 sizes (H)

Rope Patterns (left to right, top to bottom)
1. No. 794 Bowl 7" HF Eng. 215, No. 795 Salver 11", No. 794 Bowl 7" HF
2. No. 796 Bowls, 7" HF Deep Bowl, 9" HF Shallow Bowl, 9" HF Deep Bowl
3. No. 796 Sugar, Spoon, Molasses Can, Spoon, Cream 5"
4. No. 794 Spoon Eng. 215, Celery, Nappy, No. 796 Butter

Rope and Scalloped Diamond Point Patterns [No. 795 and No. 439] (left to right, top to bottom)
1. No. 795 Salver 10-1/2", Bowl 7" HF, Butter
2. No. 796 Bowl 9" Shallow Bowl, Salver 10", Spoon, Cream
   4-1/2"
3. No. 796 Sugar Sifter, Molasses Can, Butter (missing cover), Salt Shaker
4. No. 439 Toothpick, Pickle, Wines (3)

Blue Rope Patterns (left to right, top to bottom)
1. No. 796 Pitcher 1/2 gallon, Bowl 7" HF, Bowl 8" HF
2. No. 796 Mol. Pitcher 6-1/2", Cream, Salt Shakers, Sugar Sifter, Molasses Can
3. No. 796 Goblet, Butter, Cream, Sugar (missing cover)
4. No. 795 Butter, Bowl 7" HF

Amber Rope Patterns (left to right, top to bottom)
1. No. 796 Celery, Bowl 6" HF, Salver 9-1/2", Pitcher 1/2 gallon
2. No. 796 Sugar (missing cover), Cream, Goblet, Molasses Can, Butter, Sugar
3. No. 795 Pitcher and Spoon, No. 796 Lge. Sugar (missing cover), Mol. Pitcher
4. No. 794 Bowl 7" HF, No. 795 Bowls 9" and 8" HF

Pattern 797 is Stemware. They have plain tapered cylindrical bowls and are on straight flared stems in a 10 ounce goblet and 6 ounce hot whiskey.

Pattern 797, Stemware Goblet & Hot Whiskey

Pattern 798 is unknown

Pattern 799 is a "All Over Diamond" pattern. It was made in a 9-1/2 ounce tumbler and in a quart and half gallon pitcher. It has a smooth flat diamond pattern with ridges on the inside. The bottom has inverted diamonds. The pitchers came with a plain handle on the quart and a reed handle on the half gallon. The neck of the half gallon pitcher is longer than the quart pitcher. This pattern was made in crystal and colors. If there are more pieces to this pattern is unknown. Perhaps the pitcher and tumbler were part of a water set with a tray. See Pitchers, Molasses Cans and Miscellaneous photograph on page 65 on the top row for the pitcher.

All Over Diamond Pattern 799, Half Gallon Pitcher

Pattern 799, All Over Diamond Pattern

Pattern 800 is the "Leaf and Rib" pattern or Vertical Leaf and Rib. This design has a tall stippled vertical leaf between a plain thin rib around the bowl. The rims flare out and are scalloped with more scallops on the leave tips and rounded at the end of the ribs. The high foot stem has a ring near the top then is plain before joining three rings in the middle with more plain glass below on top of the foot which has the leaf and rib design. The finial is round and has a flower center with a bead band around it. This is a full set and came in crystal and colors. Some of the colors like blue and canary are so brilliant that they look new, however, I do not think they were reproduced. See Salts and Miscellaneous Ware photograph on page 69 in row four pattern number five for the master and individual salts.

Sugar (E)
Cream (E)
Spoon (D)
Butter (F)
Celery (E)
Salt individual (B)
Salt shaker (D)
Nappy 4-1/2 inch without foot (C)

Nappy 4-1/2 inch with foot (C)
Comport 7, 8, low foot covered (no stem) (F)
Comport 7, 8, 9 inch high foot (open shallow bowls) (E)
Bowls 6, 7, 8 inch high foot covered (F)
Pitcher 1/2 gallon (E)
Tumbler (C)
Salvers 8, 9, 10 inch (R)

Pattern 800, Leaf and Rib pattern

175

Vertical Leaf & Rib Pattern 800 (left to right, top to bottom)
1. Celery, Tumbler, Pitcher, Salt Shaker, Bowl 7-1/2" HF Shallow Bowl
2. Bowl 7-1/2" LF, Bowl 7" HF Deep Bowl, Sugar (missing cover)

Pattern 801 consists of Beer Mugs. They are plain with cylindrical bowls and heavy bottoms and came in 13, 10, 8, and 5 ounce sizes.

Pattern 802 consists of Beer Mugs. They are cylindrical with heavy bottoms. They have a design of two thumbprints in arched ribs around the lower half of the mug and the handle resembles a twig.

Patterns 801 and 802, Beer Mugs

Pattern 803 is a Goblet. This pattern was in the 1900 Central Glass Works catalog and holds 12 ounces.

Pattern 804 is a Goblet. It holds 10 ounces and has a plain round bowl and is on a plain stem. This pattern came in six sizes in the 1900 Central Glass Works catalog.

Pattern 804, Goblet

Pattern 805 is an Ale. It holds 8 ounces and has a honeycomb band. It has a conical shape with the honeycomb band in the middle of the bowl with flutes below it that taper down to join a short stem with a ring slightly above the foot. (C)

Pattern 806 is a Weiss Beer. It holds 29-1/2 ounces. It has a tall plain tapered cylindrical bowl and is on a spool stem. See Barware photograph on page 39 on the top row on the right (the seventh pattern).

Pattern 805, Honeycomb Band Ale

Pattern 806, Weiss Beer

Pattern 807 is a Double Castor. It has two ribbed barrel shaped shaker bottles in a caster. The bottles have a ring at the neck under the screw top and at the bottom. The handle and ring that hold the bottles is metal. The base has a scalloped rim and is on tiny feet, I am not sure if it is glass or metal.

Pattern 807, Double Castor

Pattern 808 is a Wine. It holds 3 ounces and has a plain trumpet bowl on a plain stem that tapers in before it joins the foot.

Pattern 808, Wine

Pattern 809 is a Wine. It holds 4 ounces and has a plain round bowl and is on a stem with a ring knop slightly below the bowl and a plain flared stem above the foot.

Pattern 809, Wine

Pattern 810 is the Tudor Pattern. It was given the name by Albert Christian Revi[48]. The pattern consists of bands of octagonal buttons in squares alternating with diamond point squares. The design is on the lower part of the bowls. It came in a complete set including Stand and Hand lamps. The bottoms on low foot bowls are flat. The high foot bowls have a plain stem with five protruding rings slightly below the bowl with the middle ring larger between two smaller ones. The foot is has three tiers with the Tudor design on the first and last tier. They came plain or engraved 219. The finial looks like a cross. The stand lamp is on the block stem similar to patterns 683, 684, and 685. The foot of the stand lamp is a cup foot with the Tudor design. The stand lamps came in five sizes and the hand lamps in three sizes. The hand lamp has the ribbed cup foot. This pattern was made in crystal and was unknown in color until I found the blue pitcher. Whether Central made it or it was reissued in color by the U.S. Glass Company is unknown.

Sugar (E)
Cream (D)
Spoon (D)
Butter (E)
Celery (D)
Salt individual (B)
Salt shaker (B)
Tumbler (C)
Toothpick (C)
Bone plate (C)
Pickle oval with flanged scalloped rim like pattern 439 (C)
Nappy 4-1/2 and 5 inch with one row of pattern (C)
Nappy 6, 7, 8 inch with two rows of pattern (D)
Pitcher with reed handle (F)
Comport with shallow flared bowls 6, 7, 8, and 9 inch (E)
Bowl and cover 5, 6, 7, and 8 inch (F & G)
Ice cream without cover (has saucer attached) (D)
Ice cream covered (has saucer attached) (E)
Stand and Hand Lamps (Stand G & Hand F)

Pattern 810, Tudor pattern

Tudor Pattern 810 [Engraved 219] (left to right, top to bottom)
1. Bowl 8" HF, Bowl 7" HF, Bowl 8" HF with Flared Top
2. Celery Eng., Celery, Sugar (missing cover), Spoon Eng.
3. Pitcher Eng., Sugar Eng., Cream Eng.
4. Ice Cream Dish, Pickle, Bone Plate

Tudor Pattern 810, Half Gallon Pitcher in rare blue color

Tudor Pattern 810, Stand Lamp

Pattern 811 consists of Stand and Hand Lamps. I named this pattern "Shell" as the font has a ribbed pattern resembling a shell. It is on the block stem and cup foot like pattern 810. The hand lamp is on the ribbed cup foot. The stand lamps came in five sizes and the hand lamps in three and they were made in crystal and colors. See Colored Oil Lamps photograph on page 161 on row three in the middle for the hand lamp. (H & I)

Pattern 811, Stand and Hand Lamps

Pattern 812 is a Tumbler. It holds 8 ounces and is cylindrical with a rounded bottom. This is an imitation cut glass pattern. The design is on the bottom three-fourths of the tumbler and consists of a star design within a square with a frame of double bars around the square. The tumbler has two rows of the star design. If there are other pieces to this pattern is unknown.

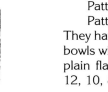

Pattern 812, Tumbler

Pattern 813 is a Pony Ale. It holds 7-1/2 ounces and has a tapered cylindrical bowl with an oval thumbprint band and is on a plain flared stem.

Pattern 813, Pony Ale

Pattern 814 is a Beer Mug. It holds 18 ounces and is a tall fluted cylindrical mug with a heavy bottom.

Pattern 814, Beer Mug

Pattern 815 is unknown
Pattern 816 consists of Ales. They have plain tapered cylindrical bowls with flat bottoms and are on plain flared stems. They came in 12, 10, 8-1/2, and 5 ounce sizes.

Pattern 816, Ale

Pattern 817 is a Molasses Can. It has three rings under the screw top then has long panels that get wider toward the round protruding bottom. (E)

Pattern 817, Molasses Can

Pattern 818 is unknown
Pattern 819 is the Swan Dish. It is oval and I think it is supposed to be a 'Swan Boat'. The head is attached to the body with a knop. The area behind the feathers looks like wood boards as does the bottom of the dish. The tail area has a decorative design instead of tail and the bottom has a round protruding ring. It measures 9-1/2 inches from head to tail. It was made in crystal, etched and colors. See Colored Novelties photograph on page 166 on the bottom row on the left (the first pattern). (H)

Pattern 819, Swan Dish

Pattern 820 is a Goblet. It holds 9-1/2 ounces and came plain or engraved number 205 and has a conical bowl on a bulbous stem.

Pattern 820, Goblets

A article from *American Pottery and Glassware Reporter* dated June 23, 1887 mentions new lamps with descriptions. "A first class line of lamps is ready for the fall trade which will certainly sell well. The new line consists of five different styles, six sizes each. No. 821, a dew drop in the different colors; No. 856, plain acorn; No. 857, panel groove top and bottom; No. 858, dew drop plain panel, and No. 870, which matches their latest table set. No. 856 is also in colors. All of these lamps have the drip foot on which the company has a patent." Please note that this article called the cup foot a drip foot where the catalogs referred to it as "cup foot". The lamps in the catalogs were A, B, C, D, and E sizes and lamp number six must have been a night light. If lamp six was a night lamp only a few are known as the catalogs illustrated only a few of the night lights and they are noted in the appropriate patterns. An article in *Pottery and Glass Reporter* in July 1889 mentioned that Central was having a great run on lamps which meant that lamps had been selling well for two years. Many of these lamps were reissued by the U.S. Glass Company.

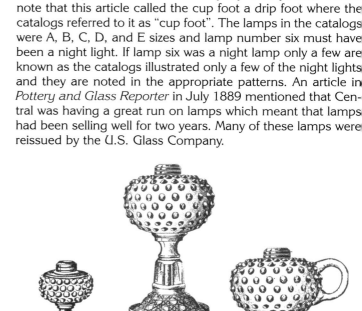

Pattern 821, Dewdrop Pattern

Pattern 821 is the Dewdrop Pattern. Central spelled dewdrop "Dew Drop" but I have combined the words. This pattern was called Central Hobnail by Thuro. The font on the lamps is round and has a round protruding circle pattern in alternating bands from top to bottom. The stand lamps are on the block stem and cup foot like pattern 810 (Tudor pattern). The hand lamp is on the ribbed cup foot. The night lamp has a plain stem. The catalogs show a rib band above the cup foot but on the majority of lamps it does not show. This pattern also came in a shade with a six scalloped rim which fits the night lamp. This pattern was made in crystal and colors. See Oil Lamps and Whirlpool Colognes photograph on page 135 on row two the fifth lamp for the night lamp and on the bottom row in the middle for the stand lamp in crystal. Also see Colored Oil Lamps photograph on page 161 on the second row the first three lamps and on the bottom row the first and last night lamps. (F – I)

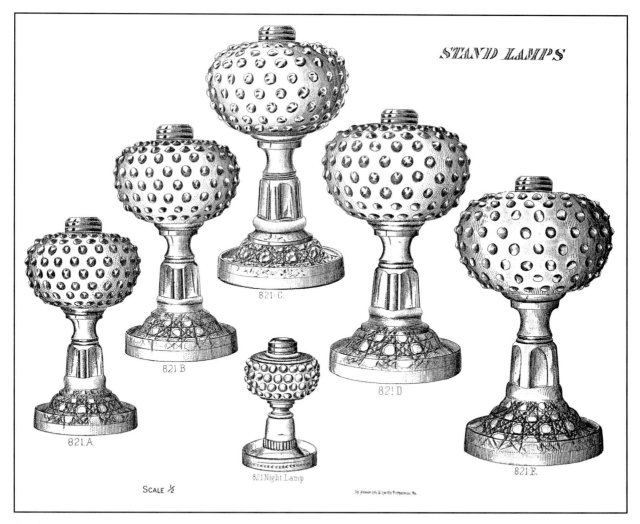

821 C.

821 B.

821 A.

821 Night Lamp

SCALE ½

821 D.

821 E.

Catalog page with Dewdrop, Pattern 821, Stand Lamps and Night Lamp

Pattern 822 is the Stove pattern. It came with a Caster Set and Salt in the shape of a stove. The salt has the Central Glass Company logo on the back and is the only pattern known to have the logo. The pieces have square centers and are on four curved feet. The stove has more detail than the salt. The caster and salt were probably made to be used together on the table. The caster has a metal handle and the bottles have a daisy and button pattern from below the neck down to the square bottoms. The bottoms measure 1-1/2 by 1-1/2 inches. The bottoms of the stove caster and salt also have a daisy and button pattern. The stove measures 5-1/2 inches from end to flanged front and is 4-1/2 inches wide. It is almost 3 inches long from end to flanged front and is 2-1/8 inches wide. See Colored Novelties photograph on page 166 the caster is on the second row the third pattern and the salt is on the third row the first pattern. Also see Novelties photograph on page 143 on the second row the fourth pattern for the salt in crystal. (Caster R, Salt G)

Carriage Salt, Pattern 822, with Central Glass logo

822 Salt
Crystal and Colors

Pattern 822, Stove Pattern Caster and Salt

822 Caster.
Crystal & Colors

Pattern 823 is the Half Bottle Pickle. This pattern is 8 inches long and is in the shape of a bottle cut in half. The bottom three-fourths has a pattern of four rows of "daisy" with the buttons in the center between three plain ribs. The end the bottle would stand on is ribbed. The neck and lower fourth of the bottle has a diamond point design with the pattern getting smaller toward the top. The top has a thin band that looks like wire for holding a cork on the bottle. It came in crystal and colors. See Colored Novelties photograph on page 166 on row three on the right (numbers 9, 10 and 11). See also Novelties photograph on page 143 in the third row the fifth pattern in crystal. (E)

Pattern 823, Half Bottle Pickle

Pattern 824 is the Fish Cream Pitcher. The pitcher is in the shape of a fish with open mouth for the pour spout. It is oval and 6-1/2 inches long. It has lovely detail in the scales and fins in the lower part of the bowl while the upper part sweeps up with round ribs. The handle is a curved tail and splits where it attaches to the bowl. It came in crystal and colors. (R)

Pattern 824, Fish Cream pitcher

Fish Cream Pitcher, Pattern 824

Pattern 825 is a Hot Whiskey. It holds 4-1/2 ounces and has a flared rim with slightly tapered bowl with a narrow fluted design on the lower fourth of the bowl. The stem has a hexagon knop slightly below the bowl followed by flutes down to the foot.

Pattern 825, Hot Whiskey

Patterns 826 and 827 are Ink Stands. They are square with flat edges and the covers have rounded edges. The top of the flat cover and the bottom of the ink stands have a tiny block pattern. See a catalog illustration of these inks under pattern 889 with other ink stands on page 201.

Patterns 826 and 827, Ink Stands

Pattern 828 is unknown

Pattern 829 is the "Oesterling" pattern. This pattern was named by Revi[49] in honor of John Oesterling, the first president of Central Glass Company. This pattern was mentioned as a new pattern in a March 17, 1887 article in *Pottery and Glassware Reporter*. It came in a complete line with many pieces. The bowls are round on the low foot pieces and oval on the high foot ones. They have tall wide ribbed rims with rounded ends and the same ribbed design is also on the foot only smaller. The stem has narrow ribs. The ribbed pattern on the rim and foot has a wide rib between three very narrow ones giving the rims a slightly scalloped edge. The handles are rounded with the top part coming straight out from just below the rim then curving out with higher top before attaching to the side of the bowl. The finial has a ribbed top above a protruding oval ring. It came plain or engraved with number 219. The foot of this pattern is very similar to pattern 310 night lamps outside edge of the foot. See Open Plaid and Oesterling patterns photograph on page 190 with the Oesterling pattern on the two bottom rows.

Sugar (E)
Cream (E)
Spoon (E)
Butter (F)
Celery (E)
Ovals 7, 8, and 9 inch with rib pattern only and tapered out rims (C)
Comport 4-1/2 inch (C)
Comport 7, 8, 9, and 10 inch high foot shallow bowls with rib pattern only (E)
Bowls 6, 7, and 8 inch high foot covered (F)
Shaker salt or pepper (C)
Molasses Can (F)
Pitcher half gallon (F)
Salvers 8, 9, and 10 inch with rib pattern only (F)

Pattern 829, Oesterling Pattern

Oesterling Water Pitcher

Catalog Page with Oesterling, Pattern 829, Engraved 219. Some early salesperson wrote the word "void" across this page.

Pattern 830 is the Flower Daisy and Button Pattern. The bottom half of the bowl has a daisy and button pattern with a flower design with six rounded petals on the top half of a "daisy" in the daisy and button pattern. It came in a complete line of table ware which was mentioned in *Pottery and Glassware Reporter*, on March 17, 1887, as a new ware being made and shipped. The catalogs illustrated only an individual salt, shober (shaker salt), and a 8 ounce tumbler. The salt has a scalloped rim and the bottom tapers in and only the top part of the flower is visible. The shober is footed with a narrow ring before the foot. The pitcher has a scalloped flanged rim with a narrow ring before the foot and the foot has a pattern of six rounded petals cascading down. The handle come straight out near the top of the bowl and the top part looks like it goes through the lower half before it curves back into the bowl. It came plain and engraved and in crystal and colors. It would have been made with sugar, cream, butter, etc., but I have only been able to find it in a pitcher. See Pitchers, Molasses Cans and Miscellaneous photograph on page 65 the third row on the right (fifth pattern).

Pattern 830, Flower Daisy and Button

Pattern 831 is the Slipper Roller Skate. It has a daisy and button pattern and was a new novelty in 1887. The rim is plain and curves up in the front. The toe is plain and there is a flat band in the back of the skate. The front has a flat band with tiny circles (for eyelets) in front of a tiny scalloped band before the daisy and button pattern.. It is 5-1/2 inches long and came in crystal and colors. See Colored Novelties photograph on page 166 in row two the first two patterns in blue and canary. Also see Novelties photograph on page 143 in row three on the right in crystal (7th pattern). (F)

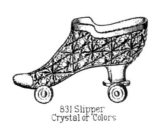

Pattern 831, Slipper Roller Skate

Patterns 832, 833, and 834 are Tumblers. They are barrel shaped with fluted bottoms. Pattern 832 holds two ounces, pattern 833 holds 4 ounces, and pattern 834 holds 9 ounces.

Patterns 832 to 834, Tumblers

Pattern 835 is a Daisy and Button Pattern Water Bottle and Tumbler. The water bottle has a bulbous shape with a fluted neck with a protruding ring at the bottom above the daisy and button pattern. The tumbler holds 9-1/2 ounces. See Salts and Miscellaneous Ware photograph on page 69 on the top row the second pattern for the water bottle and the second row patterns two, three, four, and five for tumblers. (E)

835 Water Bottle.

Pattern 835, Daisy & Button Pattern Water Bottle & Tumbler

835 ~9½

Pattern 836 is a Fairy Lamp. It has an open dome top with vertical ribs. The rim flares out and is 3-3/4 inches in diameter and has a flat ringed area a quarter inch inside for the top to fit on. The rim has narrow vertical flutes while the body has horizontal rings. The foot flares out and has a rib band with a wide rib between two narrow ones. The bottom has a flower with diamond point around it. The lamp is referred to as the "Central Glass Lamp", and the flower in the bottom was called "chrysanthemum"[50]. (R)

836 Lamp. Crystal, Etched & Colors.

Pattern 836, Fairy Lamp

Fairy Lamp, Pattern 836, showing lamp without and with chimney, with the oil burner inside the base, and the oil burner only. The oil font fits snugly into the base. *Courtesy of Lloyd and Nan Graham.*

Pattern 837 is a Wine. It holds 4 ounce and has a plain round bowl and the stem has a very narrow ring near the top below the bowl then the stem is slightly bulbous before the foot.

Pattern 837, Wine

Pattern 838 is the Barrel Pattern. It was made in a spoon, pickle and cover, and cream in crystal and colors. The pickle and cover could have been used for a sugar, however the catalogs called it a pickle. The design is of a wood barrel or keg with ribs representing the wood and narrow rings to represent staves near the top and bottom. There is an oval in the middle to represent where a cork or pour spout would have been used. The flared rim and foot have a curved notched design with the rims being scalloped. The cover also has the curved notched design and the font is a horizontal barrel. They are five inches tall with the cream pitcher being the same height at it tallest point. The only difference between the spoon and the pickle is the cover so if you do not have a cover you have a spoon. The

canary sugar has "838 Sugar" engraved in the bottom which makes me wonder if it could have been a salesman's sample. See Colored Novelties photograph on page 166 in the second row in the middle (the fourth and fifth patterns). (F each one)

Pattern 838, Barrel Pattern

Barrel Set, Pattern 838, with Canary Sugar (missing cover), Amber Spooner and Cream Pitcher

Pattern 839 is a Water Bottle. It holds 36 ounces and is plain with a bulbous shape. The rim has a wide narrow ring and tapers in on a long neck to the bulbous body.

Pattern 839, Water Bottle

Pattern 840 is the Match Slipper. This is a daisy and button pattern and was a new novelty in 1887. It is 6-1/8 inches long. The heel part of the slipper has a hole for hanging and there is a double row of beads around the heel. The front of the slipper has a stippled panel and the toe area is plain. The bottom has a diamond design like fine mesh. There is a clear space between the toe and heel area with a tiny line and dot design to represent the stitching in the sole of the slipper. It was made in crystal and colors. See Colored Novelties photograph on page 166 in the third row in the middle (eighth pattern) for the canary slipper. (G)

Pattern 840, Match Slipper

Pattern 841 is the Train Engine Clock. This pattern shows the front of a locomotive and came in crystal and colors. (R)

Pattern 841, Train Engine Clock

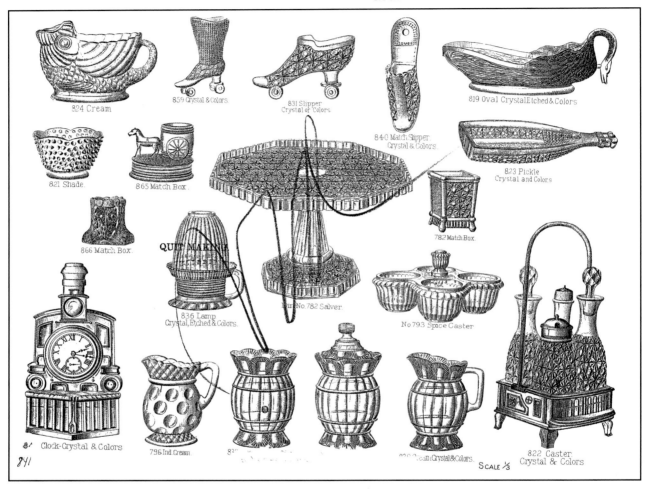

Catalog page of novelties showing Train Clock, Pattern 841, and other novelties

Pattern 842 consists of Beer Mugs. They have plain tall cylindrical bowls with heavy bottoms and came in 13, 10, 8, and 5 ounce sizes.

Pattern 842, Beer Mug

Pattern 844 consists of Beer Mugs. The have tall cylindrical fluted bowls with heavy bottoms and came in a 13, 10, 8, and 5 ounce size.

Pattern 844, Beer Mug

Pattern 843 is a Block Tumbler. It holds 7-1/2 ounces and is cylindrical. It has a square block pattern three-fourths up on the bowl with pointed notches extending up into the rim. This was a popular pattern and made by other glass companies. If there are other pieces in this pattern is unknown.

Pattern 843, Block Tumbler

Pattern 845 is a Goblet. It holds 9-1/2 ounces and has a tapered cylindrical bowl with tall thin ribs on the bottom three-fourths of the bowl and is on a plain flared stem.

Pattern 845, Goblet

Pattern 846 is Stemware. The tapered cylindrical bowls have wide flutes and the rim tapers in slightly. They have a hexagon knop slightly below the bowl and are on a flared stem.

Pattern 846, Stemware

Patterns 847 and 848 are Custard cups (they look like coffee cups). They both hold 4-1/4 ounces. Pattern 847 has a cylindrical shape and the rim tapers in slightly. Pattern 848 has a conical shape with flat bottom.

Patterns 847 and 848, Custards

Pattern 849 is Stemware with a Thumbprint Band. They have cylindrical bowls with either a straight top or flared top. The stem has a hexagon knop slightly below the bowl followed by flutes down to the foot. They came in a 9 ounce medium size and 7 ounce pony size.

Pattern 849, Stemware

Pattern 850 is unknown

Pattern 851 is a Syrup. It is a plain bottle with long narrow neck with a thin ring a fourth way down and is on a cylindrical body. In the Central Glass Works catalog this same pattern was called "Syrup and Cap" which might mean the cap was also made of glass

Pattern 851, Syrup

Pattern 852 is a Brick Pattern Bottle and came with and without Handle. It holds 24 ounces and is 8 inches high. It may have been a forerunner of the Brick Window pattern 870. It has a large square shaped clear panel in front and back between a pattern of bricks. The bottle is oval and has a fluted neck with a rolled rim that flares out. The stopper is diamond cut. See Brick Window Pattern 870 photograph on page 193 on the second row numbers three and four in crystal and amber. (E)

Pattern 852, Brick Pattern Bottle

Pattern 853 is a Tumbler. It holds 2 ounces and is fluted with heavy bottom.

Pattern 853, Tumbler

Pattern 854 is a Bottle and came with or without Handle. It holds 27 ounces and has a rectangular shape with rounded corners. On the front and back there is a plain panel in the shape of a shield with a wide notched band around the parameter. The neck is flared with a rolled rim that flares out. The stopper is diamond cut. The notched design is similar to pattern 720 Corner Medallion. (D)

Pattern 854, Bottle

Pattern 855 is a Block Pattern Bottle and came with or without Handles. It holds 32 ounces. The top part of the bottle has a plain round top and joins in the middle with a protruding block pattern with tapered flat bottom. The neck is straight with rolled rim that flares out. The stopper is diamond cut. (E)

Pattern 855, Block Bottle

The next three lamps (patterns 856, 857, and 858) were new in the fall of 1887.

Pattern 856 is an "Acorn" Stand Lamp. It has a plain font that resembles an acorn. It is on a column stem and cup foot. It came in five sizes and was made in crystal and colors. If there is a hand lamp with this font is unknown. (F)

Pattern 856, Acorn Stand Lamp

Pattern 857 consists of Stand and Hand Lamps with "Clear Panels and Ribs". They were referred to as "panel groove top and bottom". They have a pattern of clear panels between four ribs with four narrow bands above and below. The stand lamps came in five sizes and are on a column stem and cup foot. The hand lamps came in three sizes and are on a clear cup foot. See photograph on the next page and Oil Lamps and Whirlpool Colognes photograph on page 135 in row three the second lamp. (G)

Pattern 857, Hand and Stand Lamps

Clear Panels and Ribs, Pattern 857, Stand Lamp

Pattern 858 consists of the "Dewdrop and Panel" Stand and Hand Lamps. The pattern was called "Central Beaded Panel" by Thuro[51]. The font has a dewdrop pattern between clear ribs. The stand lamps came in five sizes and are on a column stem and cup foot. The hand lamp came in three sizes and are on a clear cup foot. They were made in crystal, blue and amber. (H)

Pattern 858, Dewdrop and Panel Stand and Hand Lamps

Catalog page with Dewdrop and Panel, Pattern 858, Stand Lamps and Patterns 300 and 310 Night Lamps in blue, amber and crystal. *Courtesy of Bethany College, Bethany, WV*

188

very poor reproduction made in Taiwan in cobalt and other colors which is easy to identify as a reproduction. The skate was made in crystal and colors. See Colored Novelties photograph on page 166 in the second row the sixth pattern in amber. (E)

Pattern 859, High Top Roller Skate

Pattern 860 is the Dog Salt in a Block pattern. It is an individual salt and is 3-1/8 inches long. The pattern has a dog lying down in front of a 1-1/4 by 1-1/2 inch rectangle with two rows of a block pattern on the sides. The back and front do not have the block pattern. The bottom has six squares of tiny diamond points in the middle with a rayed pattern out from it. The dog has on a collar and the rounded piece of glass he is lying on has a flat bottom. It came in crystal and colors and I do not think it has been reproduced. See Salts and Miscellaneous Ware photograph on page 69 on the bottom row in the middle (numbers five, six, seven and eight). (E)

Pattern 860, Dog Salt in a Block pattern

Dewdrop and Rib, Pattern 858, Stand Lamp

Pattern 859 is the High Top Roller Skate. The pattern is a ladies shoe skate with a high top. The high top part of the skate has a tiny diamond point pattern with a flat top that dips on the sides. On the front and back is a row of bars (resembling a closed zipper, was this a match striker?). The shoe part of the skate has a stippled alligator design with a plain toe. Above the toe and on the heel area are double rows of beads to represent stitching. There are five laced loops in clear glass between scallops above the toe area. The bottom (sole) has a diamond mesh design from the toe back about three-fourths. This roller skate was reproduced and the most obvious way to determine if it is the Central skate or a reproduction is in the wheels. The Central skate has a flat area inside the wheels with very little glass where the reproductions have an extra glob of glass making the area look like an upside down "V". According to Yalom[52], a reproduction of the skate was introduced in 1961 by Degenhart. In 1975 they started to put their logo on the right side of the shoe. It was also made by Boyd in 1985 and they put their logo on the left side of the heel. I have a blue high top skate in which the mold is identical to Centrals with the main difference being the wheels and the high top diamond point design is not pointed but round. Another difference is the row of bars on the front and back of the high top are wavy where the Central skate has neat bars. There is a

Pattern 861 is the Open Plaid pattern. The pattern has a loosely woven basket weave design made up of notched lines weaving in and out on the lower three-fourths of the bowls. This pattern has been attributed to Central but the only catalog reference is a 7-1/2 ounce tumbler. The tumbler has a beveled block design instead of the plain flat squares that Open Plaid has between the woven design. Also near the rim of the tumbler the extended lines come to a peak instead of being flat. If this pattern was made by Central is unknown but for now it will be included in the text. The pattern came in a complete line with sugar, cream, spoon, butter, celery, nappies, compotes and water pitcher. The butter has a plain scalloped flanged rim and the bottom of the bowl has the woven design. The stem on high foot bowls is fluted down to the middle which has a protruding wide rib band with more flutes below it to the foot. The finial has a pointed conical top above a rib band.

Pattern 861, Open Plain Tumbler

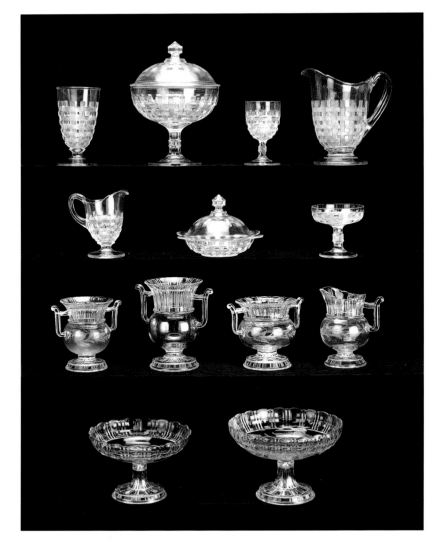

Open Plaid, No. 861, and Oesterling No. 829 Patterns (left to right, top to bottom)
1. No. 861 Celery, Bowl 8", Goblet, Pitcher
2. No. 861 Cream, Butter, Nappy footed 4-1/2"
3. No. 829 Spoon, Celery, Sugar (missing cover), Cream
4. No. 829 Bowls 7" HF and 8" HF Eng. 219

Patterns 862, 863, and 864 are Tumblers. Pattern 862 is a fluted 2 ounce tumbler, pattern 863 is a 2-1/2 ounce tumbler with narrow pointed flutes, and pattern 864 is a 2-1/2 ounce fluted tumbler.

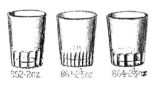

Patterns 862 to 864, Tumblers

Pattern 865 is the Horse Pulling Barrel Match Box. It is not a toothpick holder. It has a horse harnessed to a large barrel on wheels and is on a round ringed base (which resembles a jar lid). The diameter of the base is 3-1/4 inches and the top of the base has fine lines for striking matches. It measures 2-7/8 inches high. It came in crystal and colors. See Colored Novelties photograph on page 166 on the bottom row the sixth and seventh patterns in blue and amber. Also see Novelties photograph on page 143 on the third row the first pattern in crystal. (F)

Pattern 866 is the Owl Match Box. It is not a toothpick holder. It has been called Owl and Stump and has been reproduced. It has an owl peeking out through jagged bark in a triangular shaped hole in a tree stump. The tree stump has a jagged rim that is lower in the back. The bark on the stump is stippled. The base is triangular with the points cut off looking like sawed off tree branches. The bottom has an inverted diamond point pattern. It measures 2-1/2 inches at the tallest part. It was made in crystal and colors. The way you can tell the Central Owl from the reproduction is by the depth of the bowl. The Central owl is open all the way to the bottom and is a quarter inch above the 'V' area. The reproduction has a thick bottom that comes up just below the owls beak. The reproduction also has a concave bottom where the diamond point is and the Central owl has a flat bottom. See Colored Novelties photograph on page 166 on the third row numbers five and six in blue and amber. (E)

Pattern 865, Horse Pulling Barrel Match Box

865 Match Box.

Pattern 866, Owl Match Box

866 Match Box.

Pattern 867 is unknown.

Pattern 868 is a Double Caster. It has two vertical ribbed bottles (they look like a salt and pepper) in a horizontal ribbed stand joined in the middle with a pattern that looks like a leaf. The holders are cup shaped on short stems and wide feet.

Pattern 868, Caster

Pattern 869 is a Nappy. It came in 4-1/2 and 8 inch sizes. It is an imitation cut glass pattern and has a fan band around the top with a scalloped rim. Under the fans are diamonds with inverted diamond point between bars that look like X's that extend down with elongated diamonds meeting in the center of the bottom of the bowl. There is a rayed pattern in the elongated diamonds (it almost looks like a flower) and the center of the bowl has sunburst design. Underneath the bottom of the bowl in the very center is a very sharp protruding point. (D)

Pattern 869, Nappy

Pattern 869, Bowl top view

Pattern 869, Bowl (brilliant cut glass look)

Pattern 869, Bowl side view

Pattern 870 is the Brick Window Pattern. It was called Picture Window by Kamm[56] but I prefer to call it Brick Window. When it came out in 1887 it was said to be a cutting made to imitate a tower. It came in a complete line with stand and hand lamps and came plain or engraved with number 221. The pattern has a brick design circling around the bowls and covers with a clear panel opening between the bricks on two sides. However, some of the bowls have three clear panels instead of two. Most of the rims are flat except the shallow bowls with a wavy rim above the bricks. The bottoms of the bowls have a brick pattern with a rayed center while the small bowls have only a rayed center. The finial has two rows of small bricks, the high foot bowls have plain stem and the foot has a brick pattern. The stand lamps were made in five sizes and have a fluted stem with cup foot. The hand lamps were made in three sizes on a cup foot.

Sugar (E)
Cream (E)
Spoon (D)
Butter (F)
Celery (D)
Ovals (C)
Nappy 4-1/2 inch with no window pattern (C)
Nappy 7 inch covered (F)
Nappy 6, 7, and 8 inch open (D)
Comport 4-1/2 inch with no window pattern (C)
Comport 7, 8, and 9 inch shallow bowl (D)
Bowl and cover 7, 8, 9 inch (F)
Molasses Can (F)
Pitcher 1/2 gallon (F)
Salt or Pepper shaker (See Salts and Miscellaneous Ware photograph on page 69 in row four number four.) (C)
Salvers (F)

Stand lamp in 5 sizes (See Oil Lamps and Whirlpool Colognes photograph on page 135 on the bottom row the
   first lamp.) (G)
Hand lamp in 3 sizes (F)

Pattern 870, Brick Window

Catalog page with Brick Window, Pattern 870, Engraved 221

Brick Window Patterns [No. 870 and No. 852] (left to right, top to bottom)
1. Bowl 7" HF, Bowl 7" Showing Design, Pitcher 1/2 gallon, Stand Lamp 7-1/2"
2. Salver 8", Bowl 7 " HF, No. 852 Bottles holding 24 ounces
3. Celery, Spoon, Sugar, Nappy 4-1/2", Salt Shaker, Butter
4. Bowl 8" Flared Top, Nappy 8", Bowl 8" HF

Pattern 871 is the Lantern Salt or Pepper. It has a plain bulbous shape and came with a metal top with a round handle making it look like a lantern. The stem below the bowl has a clear section followed by four narrow rings on the flared foot. (E each)

871 Salt or Pepper

Pattern 871, Lantern Salt and Pepper

Pattern 872 is a Molasses Can. It has a plain bulbous shape with flat bottom. (C)

872 Mo Can

Pattern 872, Molasses Can

Patterns 873 and 874 are unknown

Pattern 875 consists of Cocktails. They hold 3-1/2 ounces and the cup bowls have either straight or flared rims. They have a narrow vertical notched band design around the bottom of the bowls and are on a bulbous fluted stem.

Pattern 875, Cocktails

Pattern 876 is the "Star" pattern. It has been called Effulgent Star, Star Galaxy, and All Over Stars, but an article from *Pottery and Glassware Reporter* dated June 14, 1888 referred to the new line of tableware as the "Star" pattern, No. 876, noting that it would be ready for the fall trade. The pattern has a six pointed star with sharp points. It came in a complete line of tableware including stand and hand lamps. The stems on the high foot bowls are fluted and the foot has three rows of stars. The finial has a star inside a hexagon. The goblet is on a plain bulbous stem. The stand and hand lamps were made in crystal, amber and blue. They came in five sizes on a fluted stem and cup foot. The hand lamp came in three sizes on a cup foot.

- Sugar (F)
- Cream (E)
- Spoon (E)
- Butter (F)
- Celery (E)
- Bread Plate (F)
- Salt master table salt, individual salt (See Salts and Miscellaneous Ware photograph on page 69 on the bottom row number four for the individual salt.) (C)
- Salt shaker (salt and pepper) (C)
- Goblet (E)
- Tumbler 9 ounce (D)
- Toy mug (E)
- Oval 6, 7, 8, 9 inch with ribbed sides (D)
- Nappy 4 (only two rows of stars), 5, 6, 7, 8 inch round (D)
- Comport 4-1/2 inch footed (rib foot) (D)
- Comport 7, 8, and 9 inch high foot shallow bowl (F)
- Bowls 6, 7, 8 inch high foot covered (G & H)
- Molasses Can (F)
- Water set with tray, pitcher tumblers, ice bowl with flared top (R)
- Tray for water set (R)
- Ice or orange bowl with scalloped rim (R)
- Pitcher 1/2 gallon (H)
- Salver 8, 9, and 10 inch (H)
- Stand Lamps (See Colored Oil Lamps photograph page 161 on the top row the second pattern and on the second row the fourth pattern.) (I)
- Hand Lamps (H)

Pattern 876,
Star pattern

No. 876-A-Hand-Lamp

No. 876-B-Lamp

Star Pattern No. #875 [Effulgent Star Pattern] (Left to right, top to bottom)
1. Stand Lamp, Bowl 9" & 8" HF, Salver 9-1/2", Bread Plate, Goblet, Celery
2. Toy Mugs (2), Stand Lamp, Toy Mug, Hand Lamp, Mol. Can, Bowl 7" HF
3. Cream, Individual Salt, Spoon, Butter, Nappy 5", Oval 9"

Catalog page with Star Pattern 876, Stand and Hand Lamps in color. *Courtesy The Museums of Oglebay Institute*

Pattern 877 is the Flute Band Pattern. It was called Shell by Revi[54], but it does not resemble a shell design. It came in a complete line of tableware including stand and hand lamps. The only pieces I have found in this pattern are a water pitcher and lamps. The pattern has a ribbed flute band pattern on the lower part of the bowls and on the foot. The goblet, high foot bowls, and salvers have a bulbous stem between thin ring bands. The low foot bowls have a short bulbous stem. The finial has a pointed center with ribbed flutes below. The handles are ribbed in a swirl design on the lower part coming out from the bowls. The pattern came in a complete line of tableware including stand and hand lamps. The stand lamp is on a whirlpool stem (see pattern 950) and cup foot and came plain or engraved. The hand lamp is on the cup foot.

Sugar (E)
Cream (D)
Spoon (D)
Butter (F)

Sugar individual covered (D)
Cream individual (C)
Celery (E)
Goblet (B)
Tumbler (B)
Salts, table, individual, and shaker salt and pepper (C)
Nappy 4-1/2 inch (C)
Comport 4-1/2 inch low foot with handles (D)
Comport 7, 8, and 9 inch high foot shallow bowl (D)
Bowls 5, 6, 7, and 8 inch high foot covered (E & F)
Salver 8, 9, and 10 inch (F & G)
Molasses can (F)
Pitcher 1/2 gallon (See Pitchers, Molasses Cans and Miscellaneous photograph on page 65 on the third row the first pitcher.) (E)
Stand lamps (See Oil Lamps and Whirlpool Colognes photograph on page 135 on the top row the fifth lamp and on the second row the second lamp.) (H)
Hand lamps (G)

Pattern 877, Flute Band pattern

Catalog page with Flute Band, Pattern 877

Flute Band, Pattern 877, Stand Lamp with Whirlpool Stem & Hand Lamp

Pattern 878 is a Weiss Beer. It holds 18 ounces and has a plain trumpet shaped bowl and is on a stocky stem.

Pattern 878, Weiss Beer

Pattern 881 is a Celery in a Block pattern. It is 12 inches long and has a block pattern with scalloped rim and has a rayed (or sunburst) pattern in the center of the bottom. (D)

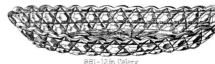

Pattern 881, Block Pattern Celery

Pattern 879 is a Bottle. It was made in 25 ounce and 30 ounce sizes. It is very plain and the tapered rim is followed by a thin ring on a long neck with a cylindrical body. It should be noted that this same bottle was made in eight different styles with different cuts in the Central Glass Works catalog of 1900.

Pattern 879, Bottle

Pattern 882 is an Ale. It holds 10 ounces and has a plain cylindrical bowl and is on the stem with a large round knop slightly under the bottom of the bowl.

Pattern 882, Ale

Pattern 880 consists of Ales. They came in 8 ounce and 4-1/2 ounce pony ale sizes and have cylindrical bowls with flared rims on plain flared stems.

Pattern 880, Ale

Pattern 883 consists of Ales. They are trumpet shaped with ribs on the lower fourth of the bowl and are on a spool stem. They came in 10 ounce, 6 ounce medium, and 4-1/2 ounce pony size.

Pattern 883, Ale

Pattern 884 is the Bar and Swirl pattern. This pattern has several pieces with swirl only as well as a complete line of tableware in the Bar and Swirl pattern. A reference to this pattern called "Twist" (instead of swirl) appeared in an article in *Pottery and Glassware Reporter* dated June 14, 1888. It also made reference to a perfect honey-color instead of amber. On the Swirl patterns the shape is bulbous with a swirl design on the lower half with straight ribbed necks on the caster bottles. There are two shaker bottles (probably a salt and pepper) and another bottle about the same size with a flared rim with a stopper with three rings on it. The oil bottle with long neck has a diamond design stopper. Some of the bottles have the pattern coming up to the rim and on others it's lower. Swirl only was made for castor sets in three or four bottle sets. It also came in a water bottle and bitter bottle. Bar and Swirl has a swirl design on the lower half of the bowls with an inverted rib band above. The stems have a swirl design and the foot has straight ribs (no swirl pattern) extending over the edge. The pressed handle pitcher and 4-1/2 inch comport have a swirl pattern foot. The finial has a flat top with round swirl knob. See Swirl Patterns, with 772, 773 and 884 Patterns photograph on page 160 for the Bar and Swirl compote on the top row and on the second row the Bar and Swirl tumbler next to 884 Cologne and Water Bottle.

Swirl patterns:
Caster Sets with 3 or 4 bottles (E & F)
Water bottle (D)
Bitter bottle (D)
Oil bottle (D)
Shaker salt and pepper (C)

Cologne (D)
Bar and Swirl patterns:
Sugar (E)
Cream (E)
Spoon (D)
Butter (F)
Celery (D)
Goblet (C)
Tumbler (C)
Salt shaker (C)
Oil individual bottle (E)
Pitcher 1/2 gallon with flat bottom and "stuck handle" (E)
Pitcher footed with pressed handle (F)
Molasses can (F)
Comport 4-1/2 inch footed (C)
Comport 8 9 inch high foot shallow bowl (D)
Nappy 4 inch round (bar pattern up to rim) (C)
Nappy 8-1/2 inch (C)
Bowls 6, 7, and 8 inch high foot covered (F)
Salvers 9 inch (F)

Pattern 884, Swirl Patterns, Bitter,
Water Bottle and Bar & Swirl patterns

Catalog page with Swirl and Bar and Swirl, Pattern 884

Pattern 885 is the Diamond Block pattern in caster sets and tumbler. The caster bottles and shaker bottles have a diamond block pattern on the bottom half of bulbous bottles. The necks are tapered with grooves extending up from the block pattern. The bottle has the diamond design stopper. The 8 ounce tumbler has a diamond block pattern three-fourth up on the bowl ending with pointed tips. An example of the pattern in an oil bottle is shown in the picture below. (E & F)

Pattern 885, Diamond Block pattern caster and tumbler

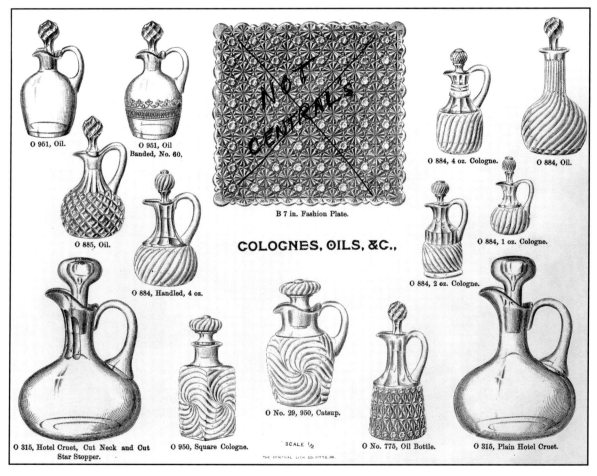

Catalog Page of Colognes, Oils, etc. from a U.S. Glass Company catalog Showing patterns made by Central as Factory O. *Courtesy The Metropolitan Museum of Art, The Elisha Whittelsey Collection, The Elisha Whittelsey Fund, 1955 (55.643.2)*

Pattern 886 is Stemware. It has a plain trumpet shaped bowl on a bulbous hourglass shape fluted stem. It came in a 9 ounce goblet, 5-1/2 ounce champagne, 4 ounce claret, 2-1/2 ounce wine, and 1 ounce cordial.

Pattern 886, Stemware

Pattern 887 is a Weiss Beer. It holds 36 ounces and has a plain round bowl and is on a spool stem. (C)

Pattern 887, Weiss Beer

Pattern 888 is the Paragon Ink Stand and was patented. On the top it has "PAT.D JAN 23.7? (1887?). It has a flat front with a double pen holder and flat panels on the corners and around the back and sides. It has thick glass and is very heavy. There are two round areas for ink (which would have had a metal or composition cover), a round area for sponge (which would have had an open glass insert), and a small opening for pen nibs (which would have had a metal or other top). It is 6 inches long and 5 inches wide from pen holder to the center point in back. See catalog illustration of the Paragon Ink under pattern 700 with other ink wells on page 138. (F)

Pattern 888, Paragon Ink

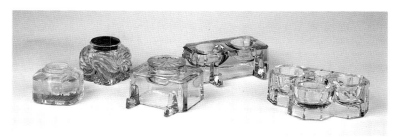

Ink Stands, some without pattern numbers (left to right) Pattern 890, Whirlpool Pattern 950, Single Bankers, Double Bankers, Paragon Ink Pattern 888

Number 889 is an Ink Stand. It is square with round corners with eight panels. The center panels on each side protrude out from the corner panels. This was a popular ink stand and was produced by Central and other companies. (C)

Pattern 889, Ink Stand

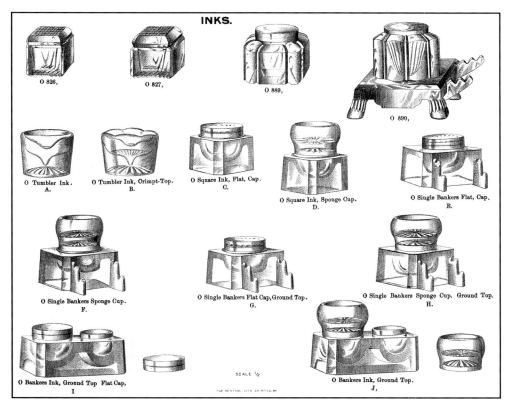

Catalog page of inks with No. 889 and No. 890 Ink Stands and others, from a U.S. Glass Company catalog showing patterns made by Central as Factory O. *Courtesy The Metropolitan Museum of Art, The Elisha Whittelsey Collection, The Elisha Whittelsey Fund, 1955 (55.643.2)*

Pattern 890 is an ink Stand. The ink bottle is similar to pattern 889 except the ink bowl tapers down in a conical shape. The stand has a flat top with double pen rack and is on four ribbed feet that resemble animal hoofs. See catalog illustration on the previous page with other inkstands. (F)

Pattern 891 is a Beer Mug. It came in a 13, 10, 8, and 5 ounce size. No illustration available.

Pattern 892 is the Drum Caster. It holds four bottles and is illustrated with pattern 517 caster bottles. It has a design of a snare drum with a metal handle attached on the sides. (R)

Pattern 893 consists of Rose Bowls and a Nappy in a Block Pattern. The rose bowls have a hexagon button and came in a large or small size with the button pattern all the way up to the top making the rim slightly scalloped. The nappy came in 8, 4, and 4-1/2 inches with only one row of buttons within point tips around the bottom of the bowl with a plain scalloped rim. See Novelties photograph on page 143 on the second row in the middle for the large rose bowl. It measures 5-1/2 inches high.

Pattern 894 is a Revolving Castor. It holds five bottles and and the castor came in two pieces with the section holding the bottles revolving. The castor and bottles have a band of round protruding circles outlined by a larger circle above a protruding oval outlined by a larger oval (resembling earrings). The stem is hollow three-fourths up, joined by a solid glass section with a split handle. The foot has the design on the inside with the "rings" on the upper part and a narrow rib pattern around the bottom. It is 11 inches high·and the revolving section is 7-1/4 inches wide at the widest part. See Casters, Urn Pattern and Miscellaneous photograph on page 119 in the middle row the third pattern. (I)

Pattern 890, Ink Stand

Pattern 892, Drum Castor

Pattern 893, Block Pattern

Pattern 894, Revolving Castor

Revolving Castor, Pattern 894

Pattern 895 is a Vertical Thumbprint Notched Ribs and Plain Panel Pattern. It is a full line of tableware and looks like a cut glass pattern. The pattern has a vertical oval thumbprint band between two narrow notched ribs between wide plain panels. The handles have a notched pattern on the outside edges and the finial has a hourglass shape of vertical thumbprints and notches and a narrow protruding flat disk on top. The rims are scalloped with the thumbprint band higher than the notched band. The stem has the same pattern and the foot is scalloped. See Pitchers, Molasses Cans and Miscellaneous on the bottom row number four for the molasses can. Prices are unknown.

Sugar
Cream
Spoon
Butter
Celery
Goblet
Tumbler
Nappy 4 inch no foot
Comport 4 inch footed
Bowls 5, 6, 7, and 8 inch high foot covered
Molasses can
Pitcher 1/2 gallon
Water bottle

Pattern 895, Vertical Thumbprint Notched Ribs & Plain Panel pattern

Catalog page with Vertical Thumbprint Notched Ribs and Plain Panel Pattern 895

Pattern 895, Vertical Thumbprint Notched Ribs and Plain Panel Molasses Can and Water Pitcher

Pattern 896 is a Double Salt. It has a shell design of two oval shells side by side each one on two tiny feet joined in the middle with a wire handle.

Pattern 896, Double Salt

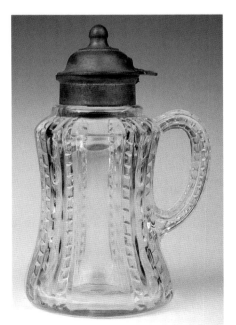

Vertical Thumbprint Notched Ribs & Plain Panel, Pattern 895, Molasses Can

Pattern 897 is a Tumbler. It holds 6-1/2 ounces and has a narrow peaked rib pattern around the bowl.

Pattern 897, Tumbler

Patterns 898 and 899 are Weiss Beers. They have trumpet shaped bowls on stocky stems. Pattern 898 holds 12-1/2 ounces and has a short flute band pattern on the bottom of the bowl. Pattern 899 holds 15 ounces and has an elongated thumbprint band pattern on the bottom fourth of the bowl.

Patterns 898 and 899, Weiss Beers

The next patterns with 900 and 1000 numbers are missing many of the catalog illustrations as these patterns were prior to joining the U.S. Glass Company and the Central catalogs from the museums had very few of these patterns illustrated. Some of them have been found in early U.S. Glass catalogs under "Factory O" for Central, but the other patterns are unknown at this time. The first thirty 900 patterns were blown tumblers. There were other blown tumblers listed with alphabetical letters A through Z instead of numbers.

Many of the 900 and 1000 patterns were listed in my 1900 Central Glass Works catalog with the majority of them being "lead blown" tumblers instead of blown tumblers. Because these are plain tumblers they will just be listed without showing illustrations. Several of these tumblers had more than one size in the Central Glass Works catalog where the earlier catalogs usually only had one or two sizes. There were a few 900 and 1000 patterns with illustrations that were found in the Central Glass Company catalogs before they joined the U.S. Glass Company and they are illustrated below. The cutoff pattern number when Central joined U.S. Glass is unknown but it must have been around pattern number 1030 as there are patterns listed up to that number from Central catalogs. After that pattern number advertisements have patterns listed for Central under "Factory O."

Patterns 900 to 909 are Blown Tumblers. They were cylindrical with different styles, heights, and hold different amounts. Pattern 900 holds 2-1/2 ounces, pattern 901 holds 3 ounces, pattern 902 holds 8 ounces, pattern 903 holds 3-1/2 ounces, pattern 904 holds 5-1/2 ounces, pattern 905 holds 11 ounces, pattern 906 holds 11 ounces, pattern 907 holds 7 ounces, pattern 908 holds 4-1/2 ounces, and pattern 909 holds 8-1/2 ounces.

Patterns 900 to 909, Blown Tumblers

Pattern 910 is a Blown Tumbler. It holds 4 ounces. This was called a Blown Whiskey in the 1900 Central Glass Works catalog.

Patterns 911 through 920 are Blown Tumblers. They have different styles, heights, and hold different amounts. Pattern 911 holds 6-1/2 ounces, pattern 912 holds 14 ounces, pattern 913 came in three sizes of 12, 11, and 10 ounces. Pattern 914 holds 14 ounces, pattern 915 holds 4 ounces, pattern 916 holds 20 ounces, pattern 917 holds 16 ounces. Pattern 918 was made in several sizes including 13, 10, 9, 7, 5, 3 ounces and a 2 ounce sham optic and 1-1/2 ounce sham. Pattern 919 holds 2 ounces and pattern 920 holds 2-1/2 ounces.

Patterns 911 to 916, Blown Tumblers

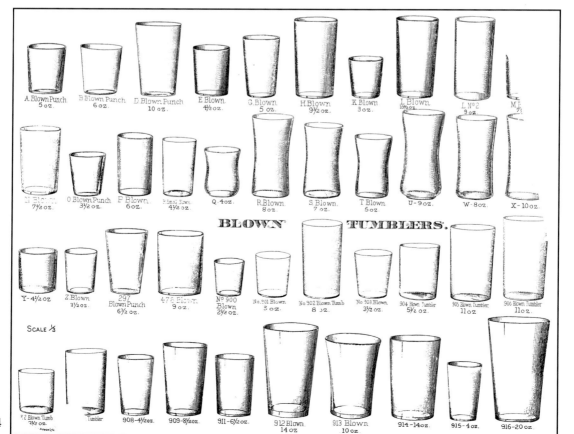

Catalog page showing Blown Tumblers

204

Patterns 921 through 927 are Blown Tumblers. Pattern 921 holds 4-1/2 ounces and is plain. Pattern 922 has a hourglass shape and holds 1-3/4 ounce or 1-1/4 ounce in a heavy bottom sham. Patterns 923, 924, and 925 have the same barrel or keg shape with pattern 923 holding 3 ounces, pattern 924 holding 5 ounces, and pattern 925 holding 9 ounces. Pattern 926 is plain and holds 10-1/2 ounces. Pattern 927 is plain and holds 6-1/2 ounces.

No.922 1¾oz No.922 sham 1¾oz. No.923-3oz. No.924-5oz. No.925-9oz. No.926 Blown 10½ oz. No.927 6½ oz.

Patterns 921 to 927, Blown Tumblers

Pattern 928 is a Blown Tumbler with Small Twist. It holds 3 ounces. There were quite a few of these tumblers produced with the small twist in different heights and holding different amounts. Some of them had an alphabetical listing instead of pattern numbers. One of the patterns with the small twist was number 476 in a 9 ounce tumbler. This pattern number was also made in plain tumbler.

928 Blown Small Twist 3 oz

Pattern 928, Blown Tumbler with Small Twist

Pattern 929 is a Blown Tumbler. It holds 7 ounces and has a hourglass shape. See Pitchers, Molasses Cans and Miscellaneous photograph on page 65 in the third row in the middle for this tumbler.

Pattern 930 is a Blown Tumbler. It holds 2-1/2 ounces and is plain.

No.929 Blown 7 oz 929 Blown 2½ oz

Patterns 929 and 930, Blown Tumblers

Pattern 931 is a Blown Tumbler. It holds 11 ounces.

Pattern 932 is a Blown Whiskey and holds 1-1/2 ounce with a thick bottom. Pattern 933 is a Blown Tumbler and holds 2-1/2 ounces. Pattern 934 is a Blown Whiskey and holds 3-1/2 ounces.

Patterns 935 and 936 are unknown.

Pattern 937 is a Blown Whiskey and holds 3 ounces. Pattern 938 is a Blown Sham Whiskey and holds 3-1/2 ounces. Pattern 939 is a Blown Tumbler and holds 9 ounces.

Patterns 940 to 948 are unknown

Pattern 949 is a plain lead blown Finger Bowl and a Pickle Jar with ground stopper. The pickle jar is cylindrical and has a flanged rim on short neck with rounded base and rayed bottom.

Pattern 949, Finger Bowl and Pickle Jar

949 Lead Blown Finger Bowl

949 Pickle Jar Ground Stopper

Pattern 950 is the Whirlpool Pattern. On October 10, 1889 an article regarding the Number 950 new ink stand was mentioned in the *Pottery and Glassware Reporter*. The pattern has swirls that extend out from a center point in the middle of the bowls. This same design is still made by Baccarat today. It was made in two sizes of ink stand. The large one measures 2-3/4 x 2-3/4 and is 2-1/2 inches high. The bottom of the ink also has a whirlpool design. The finial is a flattened circle with swirls and a small round dot in the center. The bottom corners are round not pointed. It also was made in a 2-1/2 ounce cordial, catsup bottle with spout, handle, and stopper, square cologne that is 5-5/8 inches high, and in stand and hand lamps. The stand lamps have a round font with the whirlpool design and the hollow flared stem also has the whirlpool design. The cup foot has a scalloped design around the top. The hand lamp has the whirlpool font and is on the ribbed cup foot. The stand lamps came in five sizes and hand lamps in three sizes in crystal, blue, and amber. The pattern was reissued by the U.S. Glass Company

See Whirlpool Ink Stand Pattern 950 on page 198. See Colored Oil Lamps photograph on page 161 on the top row the first lamp. Also see Oil Lamps and Whirlpool Colognes photograph on page 135 on the second row with the stand lamps in the middle and the cologne number one and four. Prices for Whirlpool patterns are, stand lamps (H), hand lamps (G), colognes (D), inks (E), and ketchup (E).

950 A Hand

No. 954, Small Ink and Cone

950 Catsup

Pattern 950, Whirlpool Pattern

Pattern 951 is an oil Bottle. It has a handle and plain long bowl that is round at the top with a flat bottom. It has a narrow neck and a pour spout and came with the cut diamond design stopper. It came plain or engraved with Band 60 and has the diamond stopper. It was reissued by the U.S. Glass Company. (C)

Pattern 951, Oil Bottle, Plain or Eng.

Pattern 952 is a Weiss Beer. It holds 20-1/2 ounces and is cylindrical with rounded sides and footed.

Pattern 953 is a Tumbler. It holds 6 ounces and is fluted.

Pattern 953, Tumbler

Pattern 954 is a 6 ounce Tumbler and a 1 ounce Cologne. There are no illustrations for these patterns.

Pattern 955 is a 1 ounce Cologne. It has a ball and rib pattern with a band of protruding circles in the middle of the bowl with rib band above and below. It has a fluted neck with a handle joined at the neck and top part of the bowl. The finial has ribbed sides with the ball pattern below the pointed top with ribs. This pattern was reissued by the U.S. Glass Company. (C)

Pattern 955, Cologne

Pattern 956 is a 12 ounce Tumbler.

Pattern 957 is unknown

Pattern 958 is a Blown Cocktail. It holds 3 ounces.

Pattern 959 is a Nappy. It came in a 8 and 4-1/2 inch size and is rectangular with round corners on the bottom. It has a fan design on the bottom center between protruding diamond shapes on each side. The sides are fluted and the ends are ribbed and have a scalloped rim.

Pattern 959, Nappy

Pattern 960 is a Nappy. It is an imitation cut glass pattern and round with a plain scalloped rim. The protruding design below the rim has a star in a circle with three pointed ribs on each side next to round panels with fine lines (or ribs).

Pattern 960, Nappy

The majority of the following patterns came from a U.S. Glass Company catalog for Central Glass as "Factory O" or from the 1900 Central Glass Works catalog. When known the U.S. Glass pattern numbers have been added and "USG" will be used when referring to the U.S. Glass Company.

Patterns 961 to 965 are unknown.

Pattern 966 is a Cordial and holds 3/4 ounce.

Pattern 967 is a Diamond Point Tumbler and holds 9 ounces. This pattern is the same style as number 439 Scalloped Diamond Point. It was reissued by the USG under number 997.

Pattern 968 is Lead Blown Stemware. It came in a 10 and 9 ounce goblet, 6 ounce champagne, 4 ounce claret, and 2-1/2 ounce wine.

Patterns 969 and 970 are unknown.

Pattern 971 is an Ale. It holds 9-1/2 ounces and was under "Factory O" with the USG number 1509. Central Glass Works had this pattern in a Sherry holding 2-1/4 ounces and a Sherry Wine holding 2-3/4 ounces as well as a small cocktail holding 3 ounces.

Patterns 972, 973, 974, and 975 are unknown.

Pattern 976 is a table Tumbler. It holds 9 ounces. It is a round thumbprint design from top to bottom and was under "Factory O" with the USG number 979.

Pattern 977 is a bar Tumbler. It holds 6-1/2 ounces and was under "Factory O" with the USG number 1889.

Pattern 978 is a Wine and holds 3-3/4 ounces.

Pattern 979 is a Tumbler and holds 7 ounces.

Pattern 980 consists of Decanters. These were shown in five styles with different cuts in the Central Glass Works catalog.

Pattern 981 is unknown

Pattern 982 is a Blown Tumbler. It came in four sizes of 20, 18, 15, and 13 ounces in the Central Glass Works catalog.

Pattern 983 is a Decanter and Bitter Bottle in the Central Glass Works catalog.

Pattern 984 is a Cocktail. It holds 3-1/4 ounces.

Patterns 985 through 990 are unknown.

Pattern 991 is a blown Sherry. It holds 2 ounces. Other lead blown stemware for this same number listed 12 pieces including the sherry, and a goblet, champagne and saucer champagne, hot whiskey, large and small claret, large and small wine, cordials in two sizes, and a rhine wine in the Central Glass Works catalog.

Pattern 992 is a Sauce Champagne from a mold at Island Mold in Wheeling, WV. The mold may have been a later 1900 pattern as in the early catalogs this pattern is a Tumbler. It is a bar Tumbler holding 4 ounces under "Factory O" with USG number 2179. It is also a Tumbler holding 5 ounces and fluted in the Central Glass Works catalog.

Pattern 993 is a Covered Dish. I am not sure if it is round or oval. It has a rib band design on the bottom of the cover and bowl. There are two handles with a small ring on the bottom part (making the handles look like ears with earrings). The finial has an oval center with a small ring on each side and two tiny protruding dots on the top.

Pattern 993, Covered Dish

Pattern 994 is unknown

Pattern 995 is a lead blown Finger Bowl and Finger Bowl Plate. The tapered cylindrical finger bowl is plain with straight rim. The finger bowl plate looks like a saucer and has a scalloped rim and rayed bottom.

Pattern 995, Lead Blown Finger Bowl and Finger Bowl Plate

Pattern 996 is unknown.

Pattern 997 is Lead Blown Stemware. It came in a 10-1/2 ounce goblet, 7 ounce champagne, and 6 ounce new claret in the Central Glass Works catalog.

Pattern 998 is Lead Blown Stemware. It came in nine sizes with large and small goblets, champagne, large and small claret, cordials in two sizes and large and small wine. These were in the Central Glass Works catalog.

Pattern 999 is the Thumbprint Panel and Swirl Rib pattern. An article in *China, Glass and Lamps* on February 04, 1891 mentioned that Centrals "No. 999 tableware is just out and is selling rapidly." The pattern has three rows of thumbprint band below a plain panel and the corners have wide swirled ribs. It has an unusual looking finial resembling a crescent moon with three thumbprints inside. This pattern was called "Swirl

and Dot"[55] by Ruth Webb Lee. She listed the number of pieces which I used below. She also said the pattern is rarely seen which means the U.S. Glass Company probably did not reissue it. See Casters. Urn Pattern 560 , and Miscellaneous photograph on page 119 on the bottom row in the middle. Prices are unknown.

Sugar
Cream
Spoon
Butter
Celery
Cake (Salver) 10 inch (there would have been smaller sizes too)
Caster revolving holding three bottles. The handle has a swirled neck with a round handle with thumbprints inside
Cruet with swirl stopper
Goblet
Salt and pepper shakers
Bowls 6 inch sweetmeat covered (there would have been more sizes)
Pitcher 1/2 gallon (Lee calls this a tankard pitcher and also listed a water pitcher)
Tumbler

Pattern 999, Thumbprint Panel & Swirl Rib pattern

New Line, No. 999.

CENTRAL GLASS COMPANY,
WHEELING, W. VA.

Advertisement from *Crockery and Glass Journal* in 1891, showing New Line Thumbprint Panel and Swirl Rib, Pattern 999

Coin Glass

One of the most important and highly collectible patterns that Central made is the U.S. Coin pattern. It does not have a known pattern number as it was acquired by the U.S. Glass Company when Central joined and became "Factory O". The pattern used a design of actual U.S. coins in the molds which were made for Central before they joined U.S. Glass and were probably designed in 1891 for 1892 production. Full credit for the pattern belongs to Central. This pattern is called Coin, U.S. Coin, and also referred to as Silver Age. According to Kamm[56] the name Central gave the pattern was "The Silver Age". She had seen an undated (1891) trade-catalog with several pages of coin illustrated before Central joined the combine. However, the catalog no long exists and if one did it could give us the pattern number Central used. She also mentioned that the pattern was supposed to have been in production for only five months.

The demand for the coin pattern was so great that Central "farmed" it out to nearby glass factories like Hobbs-Brockunier, Nickel Plate, and others when they could not turn out the patterns as quickly as the demand .

The coin glass was said to have been made to commemorate the Worlds' Columbian Exposition which was billed as the greatest world's fair to date. The idea of creating table glass with motifs of United States silver coins would also commemorate the 100th anniversary of the founding of the United States Mint 1792-1892.

The coins were dated 1892 featuring relief images of coins including silver dollars, half dollars, quarters, twenty cent pieces, dimes and half dimes. Both sides of the coins were used except for the half dime as only the 1892 dated side was shown on it. The coins used were the Morgan (Liberty) head half dollar and dollar and Seated Liberty coins. The Treasury department changed the designs of dimes, quarters, and half dollars in 1892 to the Barber Head design of Liberty.

The pattern came in a complete line of table ware including stand and hand lamps. The bowls are cylindrical and have a design of a band of coins between ribs with either plain or etched coins. The stems are hollow and the feet are ribbed. The finial is stacked coins. There are rare pieces with ruby or amber staining or gold paint. When the colored pieces are found the color is usually coming off. This pattern became number 15005 of the U.S. Glass Company after Central joined them.

The idea for the coin pattern was written in *Wheeling Glass*, by Josephine Jefferson, regarding Mr. Albert Maders return from a business trip out west. "Greatly impressed with the ingenious use of actual money as a decoration in the floor of a bar room, he wondered why impressions of money could not be used as a pattern on glass. He consulted Mr. Scott, who was delighted with the idea. The plan was taken to Mr. John Betz, the company's mold-maker, and he started to work. Weeks, then months went by, but finally the molds were ready. The first mold was struck and was a complete failure, the impression being indistinct and the money flush with the body of the glass. Mr. John Yaeger then suggested using a ribbed piece of glass instead of a smooth surface for the next attempt. A ribbed spooner was supplied and the mold struck again. This time the impression was clear and the money raised upon the sur-face of the spooner. Almost at once Central went into the production of coin glass on a large scale. Not only were individual pieces made, but the glass was turned out in full sets for the table. Goblets, cake stands, compotes, toothpick-holders, pitchers, spooners, sugars, pickles, relish dishes, celeries, bowls, punch-cups, mugs, and even lamps were made. Impressions of dollars, half-dollars, quarters, and dimes were used in clear and frosted glass. Although some coin glass with amber coins has been found, this was not the regular factory output but an indication of the originality of some workman who flashed the clear coins with amber glass.

Orders poured in and coin glass became the most popular pattern of the factory. Before many months passed, however, there arrived at the glass-house one day a government agent who told the Central officials that they were counterfeiting and that the production of the glass must stop. A complete count was made of all the coin glass in the factory. Permission was granted to the firm to complete all sets and all orders on hand. Then the molds were destroyed."

The following two articles from a Wheeling newspaper in May of 1892 tell about the molds being seized and destroyed.

Thursday, May 26, 1892, from *Wheeling Daily Intelligencer*

The Moulds Seized
By an United States Officer, who will Destroy them
Popular Glassware Condemned
As a Technical Violation of the Revised Statutes forbidding the Making of Anything in Imitation of U.S. Money – The Costly Experience of the U.S. Glass Company.

A set of glass moulds belonging to the U.S. Glass Company and used at the Central works and another set used at the Hobbs factory were seized yesterday by a special officer of the United States government and will be destroyed today under his supervision.

Several months ago the Central Glass Company, before it was merged in the U.S. company, brought out a novel series of sets of glassware, the distinguishing feature being the ornamentation of all the pieces with representations of silver coins, from dollars down to dimes, according to the sizes of the pieces of ware. The dies were very faithful representations of the coins, and the imitations on the glass were etched white. The effect was very novel and pretty, and the ware became popular at once, and has had a large sale.

The moulds cost several thousand dollars. When the two Wheeling factories sold out to the United States factories the moulds for lamps with similar ornamentation were taken to the Hobbs factory and the other ware continued to be manufactured at the Central.

On Tuesday a special agent of the treasury department who was at Pittsburgh, received a telegram telling him to look into the question whether this ware did not come within the prohibition of the law which forbids the making of any design or representation in imitation of United States coin. The officer called at the company's office in Pittsburgh, and from there came down here and examined the ware and the moulds. He said the ware could do no harm, and was not in itself illegal, but the existence of the moulds could not be allowed by law. He therefore took possession, and today the moulds will be destroyed under his superintendence. Possibly other designs will be substituted for the coin ornaments.

Manager Scott, of the Central factory, said last night that the company had about cleared enough to pay for the moulds. The only thing serious about the seizure was that it stopped the manufacture of a line of glass which was proving very profitable.

May 27, 1892 from *Wheeling Daily Register*, Page 5, Col. 2,

Patterns Destroyed:
The Coin Designs of the Hobbs and
Central Factories Demolished

On Wednesday, Mr. McSweeny, an agent of the United States Treasury Department seized a lot of molds in the United States Glass Company's factories "H" and "O" in this city. The molds were used for a novel design of lamp, with facsimile representations of United States coins of different denominations stamped upon them, which have been manufactured by the Central and Hobbs factories since they joined the United States Glass Company. The imitations were alleged to be in violation of the law. There was no objection to the lamp, but the authorities thought there was a possibility that the molds might be used for counterfeiting. Yesterday that part of the molds containing the coin design was destroyed, and the matter will be allowed to drop. The extreme penalty for the offense is a fine of $100.

Yesterday, under the direction of Mr. McSweeny, a workman took a chisel and cut off the design of the coins from the different molds. A Register reporter saw Manager Scott of factory "O", yesterday, and he stated that the loss will be merely nominal, as any other design can be substituted for the coin. He thought a figure of Columbus or Queen Isabella would be very appropriate. The coin idea was a novel one, and there was a strong demand for the lamps. The U.S. Glass Company will be allowed to dispose of all the lamps which it has in stock, and jobbers will be given the same privilege.

Coin glass is greatly sought after and probably brings the highest price. The majority of the patterns have a 1892 date but a couple have other dates. There were some reproductions made in the 1960s which are very difficult to tell from the originals. Reproduction glass appears whiter than the old glass and lacks some of the fine details. Toothpick holders seem to be the most reproduced item, yet compotes, bread trays were also made. As Coin glass is so rare it is impossible to put a price on the pieces. The best reference is with Tim Timmerman of Beaverton, Oregon who has written an excellent pattern guide on coin glass called *U.S. Coin Glass A Century of Mystery*. He has the current price listing on coin glass and is advertised in antique trade journals.

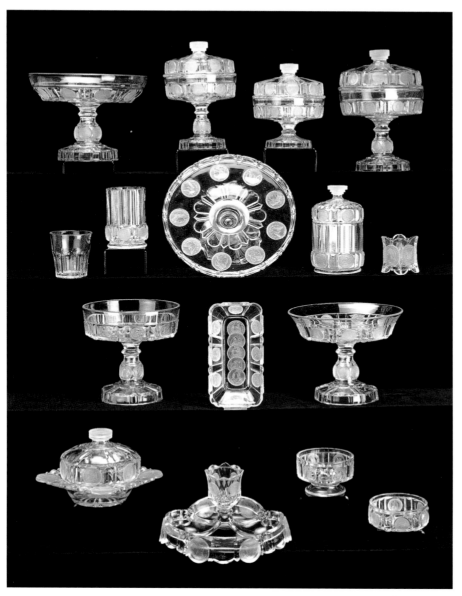

U.S. Coin Pattern (left to right, top to bottom)
1. Bowl 8" HF Flared Top, Bowl 5-1/2" HF, Bowl 5-1/2" LF, Bowl 7" HF
2. Tumbler, Spoon, Cake, Sugar, Toothpick
3. Bowl 6-3/4" HF, Pickle, Bowl 9-1/2" Flared Top
4. Butter, Epergne, Nappy 4" Footed, Nappy 4"

The molds for coin glass were said to have been made by the Hipkins Novelty Mold Shop in Martins Ferry, Ohio, as well as at the Central factory. However, while doing research and talking with John and Tom Weishar of Island Mould and Machine Company in Wheeling, West Virginia, they remember hearing that their "Great-great-grandpappy" rechipped the molds for the Columbian Coin pattern.

Columbian Coin Pattern

The coin molds were not destroyed and were rechipped with the pattern called Spanish Coin. As the Silver Age pattern may have been made in anticipation of the Columbian Exposition in 1892 to commemorate the 400th year anniversary of the discov-ery of America and the New World by Christopher Columbus a new design for the coin pattern with Spanish coins was created to commemorate it. The new molds had a design of Columbus, Amerigo Vespucci, the Spanish Coat-of-Arms, an eagle and shield and a crown and shield which protrude out from the glass. This pattern became known as Columbian Coin. Most of the pieces of this pattern were made in the same number of pieces as Coin with the exception of some of the open compotes and ones with scalloped tops. The stand lamps with round fonts were made in milk glass. The Columbian Coin pattern does not have the value of Coin glass. This was pattern number 15005-1/2 of the U.S. Glass Company and some of it was produced at the Nickel Plate Glass Company in Fostoria, Ohio.

Columbian Coin Pattern (left to right, top to bottom)
1. Stand Lamp 11-3/4", Bowl 8" HF, Stand Lamp Milk Glass 8-1/2", Tumbler and Pitcher (Gold Coins)
2. Celery, Toothpick (Gold Coins), Sugar (missing cover), Molasses Can
3. Nappy 4" Footed, Oil Bottle, Berry Bowl (Gold Flashed), Salt Shaker, Wines 4 ounce (Gold Coins) and 2 ounce
4. Beer Mug, Butter, Spoon, Cream

Some of the following patterns are from a 1892 U.S. Glass Company catalog with Central Glass as "Factory O", and from my 1900 Central Glass Works catalog. Both references are listed for comparison. Central Glass Works will be abbreviated to "CGW".

Patterns 1000 to 1005 are Tumblers. Pattern 1000 is a 3-3/4 ounce tumbler under USG number 2075 and is a 4 ounce fluted tumbler in CGW. Pattern 1001 is a 2-1/2 ounce tumbler under USG number 2149 and is a 2-1/4 ounce fluted tumbler in CGW. Pattern 1002 is a 3 ounce tumbler under USG number 2172 and is a 2-1/2 ounce fluted tumbler in CGW. Number 1003 is a 3-1/2 ounce tumbler under USG number 2184 and a 3 ounce fluted tumbler in CGW. Number 1004 holds 4 ounces under USG number 2304 and also holds 4 ounces in CGW and is fluted. Pattern 1005 is a 3 ounce tumbler in USG number 2010 and a 2-1/2 ounce tumbler in CGW.

Pattern 1006 is an Ale holding 5-1/4 ounces in USG number 1542 and is a 6-1/2 ounce Tumbler in CGW. Pattern 1007 is an ale holding 7 ounces in USG number 1513 and a 7-1/2 ounce Tumbler in CGW.

Patterns 1008 to 1011 are Tumblers. Pattern 1008 is a tumbler holding 12-1/2 ounces in USG number 2365 and also a 13 ounce handled tumbler under USG number 2484. Pattern 1009 is a 5-3/4 ounce tumbler under USG number 1844 and a 6 ounce tumbler in CGW. Pattern 1010 is a 2-1/2 ounce bar tumbler under USG number 1874 and a 2 ounce tumbler in CGW. Pattern 1011 is a heavy bar tumbler holding 2-1/2 ounces in USG number 1915 and a 3 ounce tumbler in CGW.

Pattern 1012 is a Cocktail and holds 3 ounces in CGW.

Pattern 1013 is a Nappy in 8 and 4 inches with a scalloped rim.

Pattern 1014 consists of Oyster Cocktails in one and two pieces in CGW.

Pattern 1015 is unknown.

Pattern 1016 consists of a lead blown Custard with handle and a Punch Bowl without handle. They have a conical bowl with flat bottom and the punch bowl is etched with number 35.

Pattern 1016, Custard Cup & Punch Bowl

Pattern 1017 is a Goblet holding 8 ounces from CGW.

Pattern 1018 is a Nappy. It is 8 inches and has a band of wide curved ribs between three narrower ones that get narrower at the bottom. The rim has wide scallops following the design of the ribs. The shape resembles a shell.

Pattern 1018, Nappy

Pattern 1019 is a Spice Tray. It is 8 inch and is serrated with three inserts. It is an imitation cut glass pattern and the pattern resembles a starburst design cut in half with only the bottom half on the bowl. Each side has two starbust designs and there is one on each end.

Pattern 1019, Spice Tray

Pattern 1020 is a lead blown Egg. It holds 4-1/2 ounces and has a plain round bottomed bowl and is on a bulbous stem.

Pattern 1020, Egg

Pattern 1021 is unknown.

Pattern 1022 is a Tumbler. It holds 8 ounces and was USG number 630 and holds the same amount in CGW.

Pattern 1023 is a Cocktail holding 3 ounces and Pattern 1024 is a Cocktail holding 3-3/4 ounces. They are from CGW.

Pattern 1025 is a lead blown Custard Cup with handle.

The next two lamp patterns were mentioned in an April 23, 1891 article in the *American Pottery and Glassware Reporter*. "Two new lamps have been introduced by the Central Glass Co., one figured and one plain, with a catch top, and they will doubtless sell well."

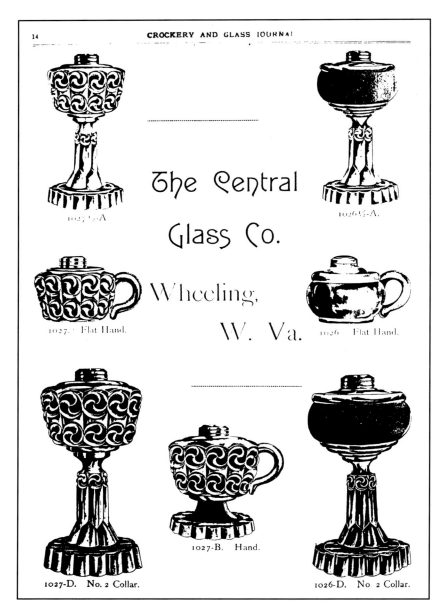

Advertisement from *Crockery and Glass Journal*, May 14, 1891, showing Patterns 1026 and 1027, Stand and Hand Lamps

Pattern 1026 consists of Stand and Hand Lamps with Oil Drip Font and Pinwheel Stem. Another article in the *American Pottery and Glassware Reporter* from July 23, 1891, mentioned the Central Glass lamps and a new line: "In all glass lamps with pressed figure feet and blown bowls and their new line of No. 1026 that hand, table and sewing lamps, and their stand lamp furnished with No. 1 or 2 collar, are among the strongest and solidest lamps shown this season." The plain fonts have a thick round ring on the top edge for the catch top (see pattern 791 font for similarity) followed by a bulbous bowl with three narrow tapering rings on the bottom before joining the stem. The stem has a pinwheel band at the top then is paneled down to protruding ribs. The foot is heavily scalloped. The flat hand lamp (no foot) has a flat ring base. The stand lamps came in five sizes including an "1/2 A" size which would be small for a table or sewing lamp.

Pattern 1027 is the Pinwheel Stand and Hand Lamp. The font has a band of two rows of pinwheels in panels. It came in the stand lamp, flat (no foot) hand lamp, and footed hand lamp with the scalloped foot. The stem has a pinwheel band at the top then is paneled down to protruding ribs. The foot is heavily scalloped like pattern 1026 and it came in the same sizes.

Pattern 1027, Stand and Hand lamp

Pattern 1026, Stand and Hand lamp

Pattern 1028 is a Spice Tray. It is square with a thin rib band design. It has a flanged rim and four circular openings for spices.

Pattern 1028, Spice Tray

Pattern 1029 is a Finger Bowl. It is plain and was in the CGW catalog.

Pattern 1030 is a Sherry. It held 1-3/4 ounces and was in the CGW catalog.

Pattern 1031 is unknown.

Pattern 1032 is a Bar Tumbler. It holds 1-1/2 ounces and was USG number 2008.

The last pattern illustrated is Pattern 1033 from the Central Glass Works catalog. It was in with the patterns using the same numbers up until they joined U.S. Glass. This is a pressed Beer Mug and holds 10 and 8 ounces. This beer mug was typical of the many mugs Central produced as they were famous for their barware.

There are two patterns advertised for "Factory O" of the U.S. Glass Company that need mentioned.

Pattern 1045 is lead blown Stemware with a Spiral Stem from a 1892 advertisement for "Factory O" of the U.S. Glass Company.

Pattern 1033, Beer Mug

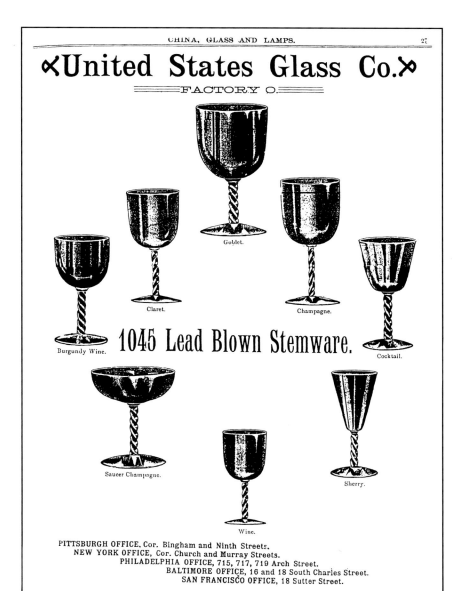

Advertisement from *China, Glass and Lamps*, September 28, 1892, showing 1045 Lead Blown Stemware from "Factory O" of the U.S. Glass Company

Patterns 1046 through 1060 are unknown. Pattern 1061 was the last advertisement found for "Factory O" of the U.S. Glass Company in *China, Glass and Lamps*, dated October 12, 1892. The pattern was lead blown stemware in wine, claret, goblet, champagne, cocktail, sherry, saucer champagne, and cordial.

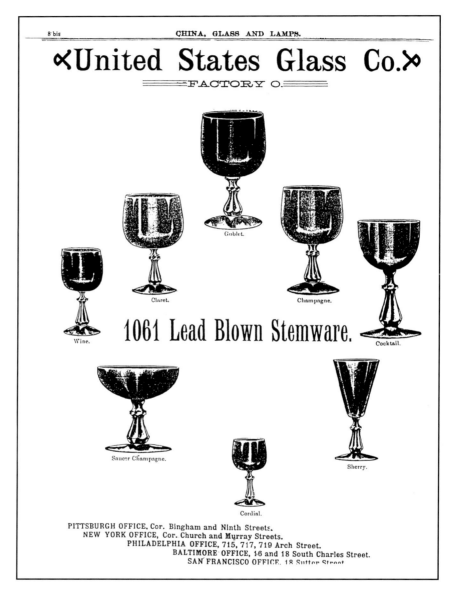

Advertisement from *China, Glass and Lamps*, October 12, 1892, showing No. 1061, Lead Blown Stemware, from "Factory O" of the United States Glass Company

Patterns Missing Numbers
and Mystery Patterns

Some patterns in the Central catalogs did not have a number. A couple of these patterns have already been mentioned in the text. They are Cord and Tassel, U.S. Coin, and Columbian Coin. Also missing pattern numbers were the Grant bitter and bar bottle, and Weiss beers. Central called the weiss beers, Punty beers, and today they are called pilsners.

A couple of patterns that have been attributed to Central but were not found in the catalogs are the Knights of Labor beer mug and ale and the Centennial Shield beer mug. The Knights of Labor mug has a knight and laborer shaking hands and was made for the labor union which started in 1869. The mug was made in three sizes. The Centennial Shield beer mug is plain except for the shield with 1876 written on it and was to have been made for the Centennial Exhibition in 1876. They both have Central beer mug styles but illustrations are missing from the catalogs. The Knights of Labor beer mug can be seen in the third row, the second mug of the Barware photograph on page 39. There is no illustration for the Centennial Shield beer mug.

A ale that should be attributed to Central is one with the Reymann Brewing Company advertising. It has same style bowl and stem as other ales made by Central and the brewing company was across the creek from the Central factory.

Knights of Labor Beer Mug and Ale

Reymann Brewing Co. Ale

Candlesticks in the shape of towers should be attributed to Central Glass.. The shape of the candlesticks resemble the support towers of the Wheeling Suspension Bridge and the brick style is very similar to the Brick Window patterns.

Tower Candlestick and Pattern 870, Brick Window Celery. *Courtesy West Virginia Museum of American Glass, Ltd. Weston, WV.*

Other patterns missing numbers include a light goblet called "Wreath". This pattern has been called Stippled Star Flower and there are several varieties of it made by other companies. The wreath pattern is stippled with a narrow band under the top followed by a flower design in the middle with stems and leaves curving out to buds made up of three circles. The bottom of the bowl is clear. This goblet was found in the Central Catalog from Island Mould. Also found in the same catalog were gas shades in the same design but called "Vine" instead of wreath.

Light Wreath Goblet

Vine Pattern Gas Shades

A Molasses Can without a pattern number was in the Island Mould catalog and was not found in the catalogs. It is called "Taylor" and is in the style of a Star and Punty syrup. It is cylindrical with tapered neck and the bowl has a design of a plain protruding octagon shape next to a star design. There was no pattern number for it .

At the right is the "Taylor" molasses can from the Island Mould catalog.

A font called "Mammoth Fount" was missing a pattern number as well as Octagon Pegs that came plain or "roughed". These were also made by other glass companies.

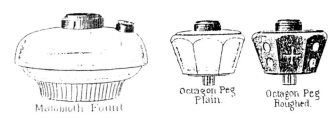

Mammouth Fount and Octagon Pegs

Oregon shades were missing pattern numbers and were in the catalogs as well as in the catalog from Island Mould. They were made plain or "roughed" and etched (called plain cut) in two sizes of 4 and 3-1/2 inches. These were also made by other glass companies so they are difficult to attribute.

The Liberty Bell Salt was illustrated in the catalogs without a pattern number. It is in the shape of the Liberty Bell with "1776 LIBERTY 1876" on the bottom. The salt can be seen in the Salts and Miscellaneous Ware photograph in the third row, the third salt on page 69.

Oregon Shade

Liberty Bell Salt

A Caster in the catalogs as "No. 1 & No. 2 Caster" with three or four bottles was missing a catalog number. The sets included a salt and pepper, bottle with stopper, and bottle with screw top in a metal holder (if the base is glass or metal is unknown). They were made in blue, amber, and crystal.

Squat Jars were also missing pattern numbers and came in half pint, pint, quart, half gallon, three quart, and one gallon sizes. Specia Jars were also missing numbers and came in the same sizes. The jars were cylindrical and the Squat jars had wide bases and were squatty and the Specia jars were tall.

No. 1 & 2 Caster

½ Pint

Pint

Quart

½ Gallon

SQUAT JARS.

3 Quart

1 Gallon

1 Gallon.

3 Quart

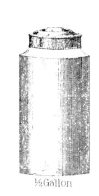
½ Gallon

Squat Jar

Quart.

Pint

½ Pint.

SPECIA JARS

Squat and Specia Jars without pattern numbers

A whole page of Ink Stands was without pattern numbers. There were two tumbler inks and the rest of the ink stands were square or rectangular with flat edges. They came with or without pen racks and the bankers inks came in several styles. An example of single and double bankers ink stands are in the Ink Stands photograph on page 201.

217

A. Tumbler Ink

B. Tumbler Ink, Crimpt. Top

C. Square Ink, Flat Cap

D. Square Ink, Sponge Cup

E. Single Bankers Flat Cap

F. Single Bankers Sponge Cup

G. Single Bankers Flat Cap, Ground Top

H. Single Bankers Sponge Cup, Ground Top

I. Bankers Ink, Flat Cap, Ground Top

J. Bankers Ink, Sponge Cup, Ground Top

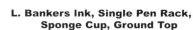

K. Bankers Ink, Single Pen Rack, Flat Cap, Ground Top

L. Bankers Ink, Single Pen Rack, Sponge Cup, Ground Top

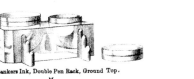

M. Bankers Ink, Double Pen Rack, Flat Cap, Ground Top

N. Bankers Ink, Double Pen Rack, Sponge Cup, Ground Top

Ink Stands without numbers

There are a few mystery patterns that I hope to locate someday. They were mentioned in the Research section and include the turkey dish, the lantern in the shape of a castle or house top, and night lamps or lanterns made in red, white, blue and amber. There was a novelty made to order in the shape of the electrical nose and ears used by a Mr. Evans in "A Parlor Match" and there are all the missing pattern numbers. Perhaps a reader can help.

When Central Glass Company reformed and became Central Glass Works in 1896 they picked up the pattern numbers from where they left off before joining the U.S. Glass conglomerate and kept and used some of the original patterns and numbers.

Easy Pattern
Identification Guide

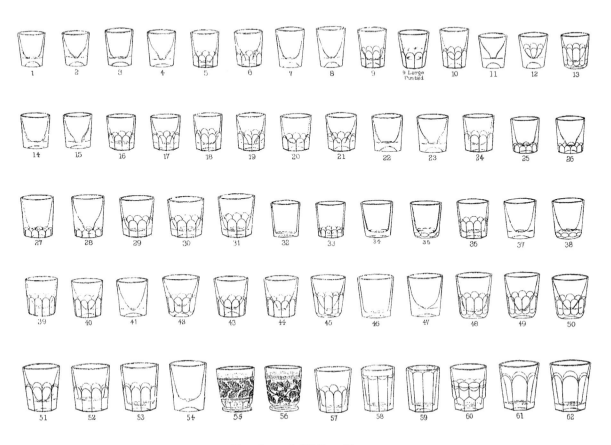

Numbers 1-62 Tumblers

**NOTE: 55 OAK LEAF Pattern
56 ROSE Pattern**

N° 16 Ind Salts

14 Cordial-1¾ oz

**NOTE: 14 is also
a Cordial**

**16 is also CARRIAGE
Individual Salts &
Candy Tray**

No 16 Candy Tray

Numbers 63-75 Tumblers

69 Tumbler Band 200

Numbers 76-83 Ales

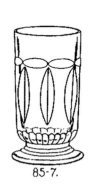

84 HUBER Handled Mug   **85 Ale**   **86 Weiss Beer & Sham**

87, 88 Unknown

Numbers 89-104 Handled Mugs   **105 Egg**

NOTE: 99 OAK LEAF Pattern,
100 ROSE (Cabbage Rose) Pattern   **106, 107 Unknown**

Numbers 108-134 Beer Mugs

108-6.

109-9½

110-10.

111-8.

112-9½

113-7

114-9.

115-10

116-8.

118-5.

119-9.

120-9½

122-5.

123-8.

126-7½

121-3½.

124-4½

125-8.

126 Block Handle.
8 oz.

117.
Good Templars Pony

127-10 old

127 Block Handle

128-4½.

129-8.

**117 GOOD TEMPLARS PONY
32 oz**

130-5.

131-7½

132-8.

133-9.

134-9½

135 Champ.
6 oz.

135
Cincinnati Tea Cup.

136 Goblet.
10 oz.

137
Goblet, large.
10 oz.

138 Claret
4 oz.

Note: Two Number 135:
ARGUS Stemware
(Thumbprint)
and
CINCINNATI TEA CUP
56 oz Beer Mug
HONEYCOMB Pattern

136 HONEYCOMB
Stemware

137 JANUS Pattern
(Stemware only shown)

138 HUBER
Stemware

Sugar.

139 Champ.
6 oz.

Cream.

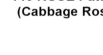

6 in. Covered.

Spoon.

141 -2½ oz.

142 Cordial.
1 oz.

142 HUBER
Cordial

143 unknown

139 HUBER
Stemware

140 ROSE Pattern
(Cabbage Rose)

141 ROYAL Pattern
(Honeycomb Band)
(Stemware only shown)

144
Goblet Small.   144
Goblet
Lge.

145
Small Goblet

146 Small Goblet.

147
Goblet.

144 OAK LEAF
Goblets

145 O'HARA
Stemware

146 HONEYCOMB
(New York)
Stemware

147 FLOWER & DIAMOND
Goblet
(Panelled Diamonds
and Flower)

148 Egg

149 Egg

**150 Pattern and
Heavy Plain Salvers**

151 unknown

152 OAK LEAF Pattern

153 HONEYCOMB Pitcher

**154 Plain Pitcher, Quart
155 Plain Pitcher, 1/2 Gallon**

**156 OAK LEAF
Celery**

**157 JANUS
Celery**

158 JANUS Pickle

159 Unknown

160 JANUS Saucer

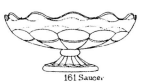

161 JANUS Saucer

**162 MILWAUKEE STANDARD
Beer Mug, 36 oz.
HONEYCOMB Pattern**

**163 RIPPLE
Covered Butter**

164 unknown

223

165 DELTA
Molasses Can

166 TEXAS
Molasses Can

167 VENUS
Molasses Can

168 CENTRAL
Molasses Can

169 Molasses Can

170 Wine Bottle

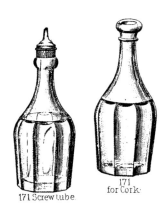

171 Bitter Bottles
Screw Tube & For Cork

172 Bitter Bottles
Screw Tube & For Cork

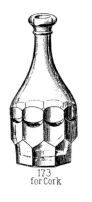

173 JANUS Pattern
Bitter Bottles
For Cork & Screw Tube

174 ROSE Pattern
Bitter Bottles
Screw Tube & Cork Tube

175 JANUS Pattern
Decanter

176 HONEYCOMB
Decanter

177 DIAMOND
Individual

178 BALTIMORE
Individual

179 SQUARE
Individual

180 OCTAGON
Individual

181 OAK LEAF
Oval

182 Oval

183 FLORENCE
Oval

184 CINCINNATI
Oval

185 SPLIT
Oval

186 BUFFALO
Oval

187 DOBSON
Oval

188 JANUS
Footed

189 CURTAIN
Footed

190 FROSTED
Footed

191 OAK LEAF
Footed

192 ROSE
Footed

193 ARCH

194 BALTIMORE
Master

195 OCTAGON FT'D
Master

196 ALBANY

197 DIAMOND
Master

177-197 SALTS

198 BRILLIANT
Stand Lamp

199 WEST
Stand Lamp

200 BAND
Stand Lamp

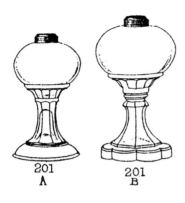

201 OHIO
Stand Lamp
NOTE: Different Bases

202 DOUBLE DIAMOND
Stand Lamp

203 CENTRAL
Stand Lamp

204 STAR
Stand Lamp

205 DIAMOND
Stand Lamp

206 PANEL
Stand Lamp

207 Hollow Stem
Stand Lamp

208-217 Fonts

208 TROY

209 HURON

210 RICK-RACK

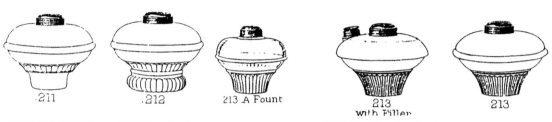

211 BASKET

212 Footed Basket

213 Baltic Basket

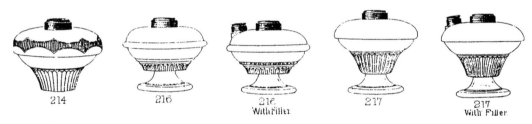

214 RICK-RACK Band

216 Footed

217 Footed

215 Unknown

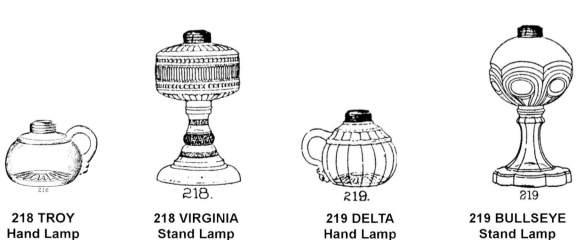

218 TROY
Hand Lamp

218 VIRGINIA
Stand Lamp

219 DELTA
Hand Lamp

219 BULLSEYE
Stand Lamp

NOTE: Two different patterns and lamps of Numbers 218 and 219

220 BULLSEYE
Stand Lamp,
Plain & Cut

220 PANEL
Hand Lamp

221 TROY
Hand Lamp

221 Stand Lamp

**NOTE: Two different patterns and lamps
of Numbers 220 and 221**

222 TROY
Hand Lamp

223, 224, 225
Hand Lamps

226, 227 Ales

228, 229 HONEYCOMB
Pattern Ales

230-232 Tumblers

233 Goblet

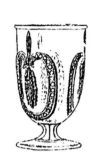

234 WHEAT IN SHIELD Pattern

235-239 Tumblers

**240, 241 WHEAT IN SHIELD
Hand Lamps**

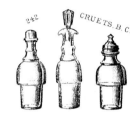

242 Cruets

243, 244 Tumblers

**245-247 WHEAT IN SHIELD
Footed Hand Lamps**

**248-250 OHIO
Footed Hand Lamps**

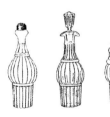

251 Cruets

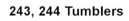

Numbers 252-264 Tumblers

Numbers 265-269 Beer Mugs

270 RUBICON
Beer Mug 69 oz

Numbers 271-274 unknown

275 Champ   **276 Sham Claret**   **277 Sham Claret**   **278 Salt**   **279 Stemware**   **280 MOUNTAIN LAUREL Goblet**

281 Tumbler   **282 Champ**   **283 Sham Claret**   **284 HUBER Wine**   **285 Sham Wine**

286 Beer Mug   **287 Cordial**   **288 Sham Cordial**   **289 Beer Mug & Sham**   **290 Stemware**   **291 Stemware**

292 Cordial   **293 Cordial**   **294 Sham Cordial**   **295 Ale**   **296 Ale**   **297 Tumbler**   **299 Tumbler**

298 Unknown

300 Night Lamp

NOTE: Two Number 300

300 Tumbler

301 Master Salt

302 Ind. Salt

303, 304 Tumblers

305 Cocktail

306 Unknown

307 Cocktail

308 Claret

309 Stemware and Celery

310 Stemware

NOTE: Two Number 310

310 Night Lamp

NOTE: Two Number 310

311 MOUNTAIN LAUREL Stand Lamp

312 Font

313 Champ 314 Champ 315 Champ

316 Champ, Plain & Eng.

317 Champ

318 Champ, Plain & Eng.

319 Goblet 320 Goblet

321 Salt

322 Ale & Cut Stem Ale

323 Stemware   **324 Stemware**   **325 Stemware**   **326 Goblet**   **327 Goblet**

328 Cocktail, Eng. & Plain

332 Unknown

333 Tumbler

329 Cocktail   **330 Champ., Plain & Eng.**   **331 Champ., Plain & Eng.**   **334 Unknown**

335-3 Toy.

336-4½ Small Pony.

337- 6½ large Pony

338-8½ Med.Pat.

339-9½ Pat.

Numbers 335-339 Beer Mugs

340 Claret. Pat.

340 Claret. Cut Stem.

**340 Claret &
Cut Stem Claret**

341 Unknown

242-4 Pony Pat.

342 Pony Ale

343 Egg Cup. Pat

343-10 Beer.

**343 Egg Cup, Ales
& Weiss Beers**

344, 345 Unknown

346;5.

346 Block Handle

**346 Beer Mug
Note:Different Handles**

347 Wine. Pat

347 Wine

348 Champ. 5 oz.

348 Champ

349 Goblet Pat'd

349 Champ

349 Wine

349 Stemware

8 in 350 Butter Salver

**350 WARE
Butter Salver Shown**

351 Wine Pat 3 oz

351 Champ. 5½ oz.

351 Goblet 10½ oz.

351 Stemware

352-10 oz Beer Goblet

352 Beer Goblet

353 Tumbler

354-10

354 Beer Mug

233

355 Jelly Saucers

356 Weiss Beer

357 Unknown

358 Bitter Bottle

359 Sherries, Plain, Medium & Full Cut

360 Bitter Bottle

361 Ales

362 Ales

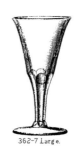

363 Tumbler   364 Tumbler

365 Stemware

366, 367 Goblets

368 Weiss Beers   369 Weiss Beer

370 WARE (LOOP) Pattern

371 Wine

372 Wine

373 Cocktail

Numbers 374-383 Tumblers

384 Ale

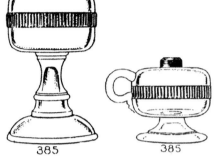

**385 Central Rib
Stand & Hand Lamps**

Numbers 386-388 Tumblers

389 Ales

**390 LOOP Pattern
Bowls
NOTE: Same Bowls
as 370 only Covered**

391 Ale

392 Ale

393 Cruets

394 Cruets

395 Ale

397 Ale

**396 Ale -
No Illustration**

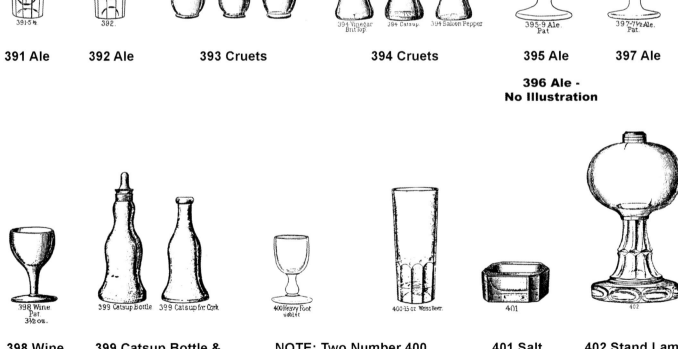

398 Wine

**399 Catsup Bottle &
Catsup for Cork**

**NOTE: Two Number 400
400 Heavy Foot Goblet   400 Weiss Beer**

401 Salt

402 Stand Lamp

403-405 Beer Mugs   406 Beer Mugs   407 Molasses Can 408 Tumbler   409 Cocktail

410 Tumbler   411 Goblet   412, 413 Tumblers   414 Ale   415 Ale   416 Tumbler

417 Catsup   418-421 Tumblers   422 Cocktail

423 Unknown

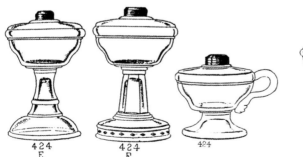 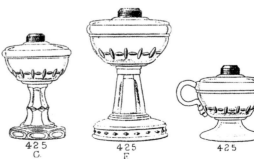 

424 Stand & Hand Lamps
Plain Base & Diamond Base

425 Stand & Hand Lamps

426 Font
With & Without Filler

427 Beer Mug   428, 429 Tumblers   430 Butter Plate   431 Ale   432 Ales

433 Tumbler   434 Ale   435 Egg   436 Tumbler   437 Pickle Jar, Plain & Eng.

438 PRISM & DIAMOND BAND Pattern

439 SCALLOPED DIAMOND POINT
or Panel with Diamond Point
Pattern

440 PATTERN
Octagon Bowls, Cheese Plates & Cov'd Cheese Plates

441-9½.

442-6

443-9

444-9

445-8½.

446-8

441 Beer Mug
E PLURIBUS UNUM   **442 Beer Mug**   **443 Beer Mug**   **444 Beer Mug**
CENTENNIAL   **445 Beer Mug**   **446 Beer Mug**

447-8½.

448-9

449 Custard.

450 Cordial.
1¼ oz.
450 Sham Cordial.
1 oz.

452 Goblet.
9oz.

453 Goblet.

447 Beer Mug   **448 Beer Mug**   **449 Custard**   **450 Cordial &**   **451 Pepper**   **452 Goblet**   **453 Stemware**
                                                   Sham Cordial   **(Partial**
                                                                      Illustration)

454 Champ.
6½ oz.

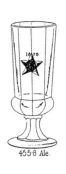
455-8 Ale.

456-14 Light   456-10½ Sham

457-14 Light   457-10½ Sham

458 Hollow Stem
Champ.
4½ oz.

459-9.

454 Stemware   **455 CENTENNIAL**   **456 Weiss Beer**   **457 Weiss Beer**   **458 Hollow**   **459 Ale**
                  ALE   **& Sham**   **& Sham**   **Stem Champ**

460.

461 Ice Cream.

462

463
1 oz.
464 Sherry
1½ oz.

465
Hollow Stem Champ.
4½ oz.

466 Sherry
1 oz.

460 Tumbler   **461 Ice Cream**   **462 Molasses Can**   **463, 464 Sherry**   **465 Champ**   **466 Sherry**

467 Stand & Hand Lamps
Plain Font or Roughed & Cut
Both with Plain Base
or Cup Foot

468 Stand & Hand Lamps
ROPE BAND Pattern
Plain Base or Cup Foot

469 Stand & Hand Lamps
OESTERLING Pattern
Plain Base or Cup Foot

470 Stand Lamp
BULLSEYE
VARIANT Pattern

471, 472 Tumblers

473 Butter & Cover
With & Without
Handles

474 Butter &
Cover

475, 476 Blown
Tumblers,
Plain & Etched

477
Tumbler

478 Ales
& Beer

479 Beer Mugs

480 Ale

481 Weiss Beer
No Handle, Handled
& Handled & Cupped

482 Tumbler
HUBER
Pattern

483
Cocktail

484
Champaign

485
Tumbler

486 Stand & Hand Lamps

487 Stand & Hand Lamps

488 Stand & Hand Lamps

489 Tumbler   490 Ale   491 Stemware   494 Sherry   495 Beer Mugs   496 Beer Mugs

492, 493 Individual Butters (No illustration available)

497 Beer Mug   498 Beer Mugs   499 PILSNER Beer   500-504 Tumblers

505-509 Tumblers   510 Goblet   511, 512 Goblets 513 Tumbler 514 Hot   515 Punch
HONEYCOMB   Whiskey   Tumbler
Pattern

516 Ale & Square   517 Cruets   518 Pitchers, Plain & Eng.   519 Ale
Whiskey

240

521 Beer Mugs   **522 Tumblers**   **523 Weiss Beer Mugs, With & Without Handles**

Nº 520 PATTERN.

520 CENTRAL LOOP PATTERN

524 Cocktail   **525 Cocktail**   **526 Beer Mug**   **527 Champ.**

528 Beer Mugs   **529 Beer Mugs**   **530 Ale**   **531 Champ.**   **532 Ales**

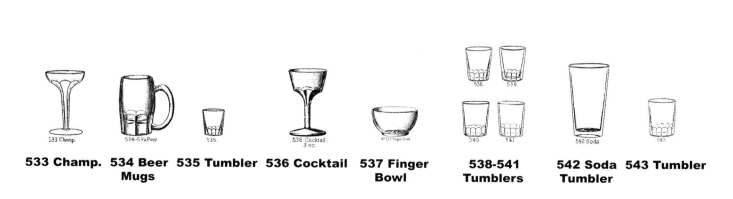

533 Champ. **534 Beer Mugs** **535 Tumbler** **536 Cocktail** **537 Finger Bowl** **538-541 Tumblers** **542 Soda Tumbler** **543 Tumbler**

No. 544,10 in. Salver.

544 Solid Stem Salvers

545 Caster   545 Vinegar   545 Pepper

545 Caster Set, Vinegar & Pepper

546 Butter & Cov.   No 546 B. Cream.

546 OPTIC DIAMOND BAND PATTERN

547-10 Sham.

547 Ales

548-10. Sham.

548 Ales

549 Plate   549 Shoppen A

549 Pattern, Plate & Shoppen

550-16 Mug

550 Beer Mug

551-17½ Mug

551 Beer Mugs

552-15

552 Weiss Beer

553 Sham 15 oz

553 Champ 4 oz.

553 Weiss Beer & Champ.

554

554 Tumbler

No 555 Sugar.   No 555 Cream.   No 555 Butter & Cov.   No 555 Spoon

555 NAIL CITY PATTERN

No 556 9 in Bowl & Cov.

556 PATTERN

557 Cocktail   558 Cocktail   559 PANEL
FOOTED BOWLS

560 URN PATTERN

561 PATTERN

562 Cocktail   563 Stemware   564, 565 Tumblers

566 Beer
Goblet

567 Stemware

568-570 Cocktails

571 Beer Mug

572 Ind. & Table
Salts

573 Wine

574 Champ.

575 Ale   576 Ale

577 Stemware   578 Tumbler

579 HAND
SALT

243

580 Stand & Hand Lamps **581 Stand & Hand Lamps** **582 THUMBPRINT BAND Stand & Hand Lamps**

583 Hot Whiskey   **584 SPINDLE PATTERN**

585 LEAFLETS PATTERN   **586 Ales**

587 Beer Mugs **588, 589 Tumblers** **590 Ales** **591 Egg** **592 Ale** **593 Ale**

594 Beer Mugs   595 Cocktails   596 Tumbler 597 Ind. Salt 598 Tumbler 599 Stemware

600 Beer Mug   601 Stand & Hand Lamps   602 Stand & Hand Lamps   603 Stand Lamp

604 Beer Mug   605 Hot Whiskey

610 THUMBPRINT BAND PATTERN

606, 607 Tumblers   608 Pickle &   609 Hot
Cracker Jar   Whiskey

611 Beer Mug   612 Beer Mugs   613 Stemware   614 Tumbler   615 Cocktail,   617, 618 Tumblers
Flared or Straight

616 Tumbler   619 Ale-
No Illlustration No Illlustration

620 Cocktail,   621 Stemware   622 Ales   623 Tumbler   624 Ale   625 Tumbler   626 Egg Cup
Flared or Straight

627 Stand   628 Stand   629 Stand   630 Stand   631 Stand   632   633 Ale &
Lamps   Lamps   Lamps   Lamps   Lamps   Schoppen   Bitter Bottle

634, 635 Schoppen   636 Cordial   637 Cordial   638 Wine   639-641 Tumblers   642 Plate

643 Cordial   644 Stemware   645 Stemware   647 Cocktail,   648 Cocktail,   649 Ales
Straight & Flared   Straight & Flared
646 Unknown

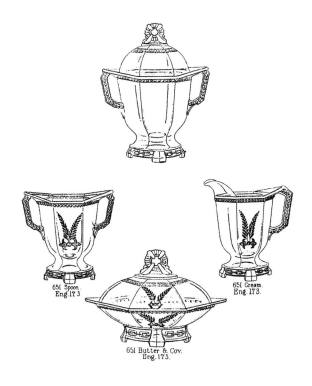

650 DOT AND DASH PATTERN

651 BALL AND CHAIN PATTERN

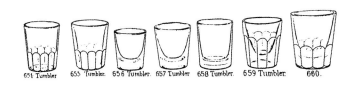

652 Wine   **653 Beer Mugs**   **654-660 Tumblers**

661 Beer Mug
NOTE: 32 oz.

662 Stemware

663 Straw Jar

664 Stemware

665 Bar Tumbler

666 Beer Mug Horseshoe Base

667 Cocktails

668 Bar Tumbler

669 Sherry

670 Ale

671 Bar Tumblers

672 Beer Mug Horseshoe Band

673-675 Bar Tumblers

676 Cocktail

677-679 Tumblers

680 Cocktail

681 Egg

682 Ale

683 Stand Lamps

684 Stand Lamps

685 Stand Lamps

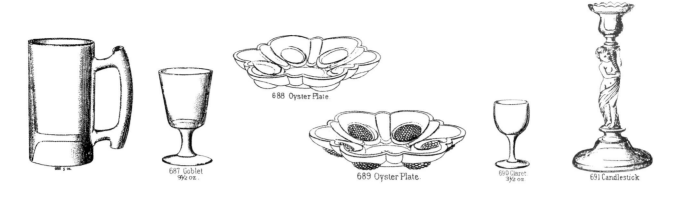

686 Beer Mugs   **687 Stemware**   **688, 689 Oyster Plates**   **690 Claret 691 Candlestick**

692 Unknown

693 Claret   **694 Whiskey, With or Without Handle**   **696-698 Tumblers**   **699 Claret**   **700 RECUMBENT HORSE Ink Stand**

695 Unknown

701 Cocktail   **702 RABBIT MUG**

705 SIMPLICITY PATTERN

703, 704 Tumblers

706 Cocktail

707 Hen on Nest Cov'd Egg Dish

708, 709 Tumblers

710 Cocktail

711 Cocktail

712-714 Tumblers

715 Ale

716 Ale

718 Blown Beer

719 Tumbler

717 Unknown

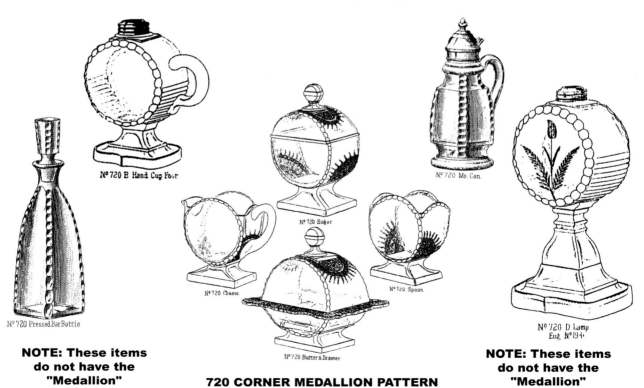

NOTE: These items do not have the "Medallion"

720 CORNER MEDALLION PATTERN

NOTE: These items do not have the "Medallion"

250

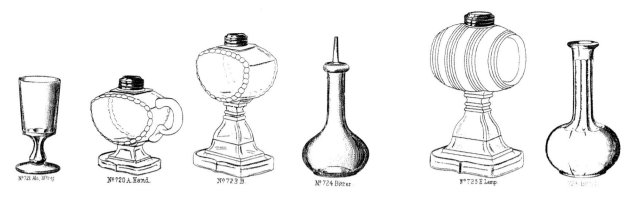

721 Ale　　**723 Hand & Stand Lamps**　　**724 Bitter Bottle**　　**725 BARREL Stand Lamp & Bitter Bottle**
NOTE: Two Number 725

722 SWIRL PATTERN Tumbler: see page with 772 SWIRL PATTERN items

726 Tumbler　　**727 DUCK DISH**　　**728 JUMBO ELEPHANT MUG**　　**729 Ales**

731 PILGRIM MOL. CAN

730 PANEL RIBBED SHELL PATTERN　　**732 OWL PICKLE**

733 Beer Mugs   734 Cordial   735 Stemware   736 Cocktail   737 Champ   738, 739 Tumblers

No 740 Water Set

740 STRAWBERRY DIAMOND PATTERN

741 Ale   742 Ales   743 Ale

744 Tumbler   745 RING STEM   746 Tumbler
Stemware

No 747 Fish

747 FISH DISH

No 748 LOG CABIN PATTERN.

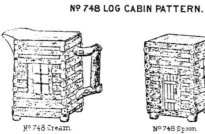

No 748 Cream.   No 748 Spoon.   No 748 Sugar & Cov.   No 748 Butter & Cov

748 LOG CABIN PATTERN

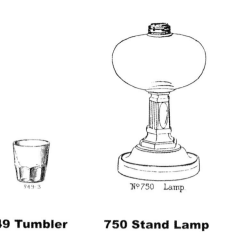

749 Tumbler　　**750 Stand Lamp**　　**752 Wine**　　　　**753 LEAF PICKLE**

751 Unknown

754, 755 Tumblers　　**756 Ales**　　**757 Cordial**　　**758 OVAL PHEASANT DISH**

759 Unknown

760 Tea Nappy　**761 Cocktail**　**762 Tumbler**　　**763 LEAF COMPORT**　　**764 FLOWER Oval Bowl**

765 Goblet　　**766 Tumbler**　　**767 Handled Tumbler**　　**768 Cream Pitcher**

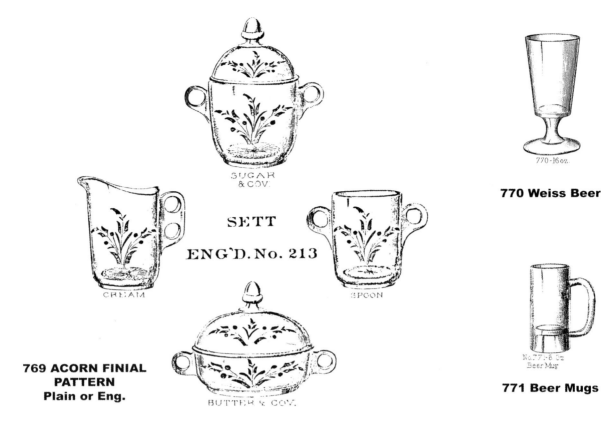

SETT

ENG'D. No. 213

SUGAR & COV.

CREAM

SPOON

BUTTER & COV.

769 ACORN FINIAL PATTERN
Plain or Eng.

770-16 oz.

770 Weiss Beer

No.771-8 Oz
Beer Mug

771 Beer Mugs

772 A.

772-9½

722 Sm. 7½

NOTE:
Tumbler
No. 722

No.772-13 Oz

772 SWIRL PATTERN

No.772.Bitter Bottle & Cork

No.772-Goblet

No.773-
Med Ale
9 oz.

773 Ales
SWIRL
PATTERN

No.774 Med Ale
5½ oz.

774 Ales
SWIRL
PATTERN

775 PRESSED DIAMOND PATTERN

776, 777 Tumblers & Lipped Tumbler   **778 Shaker Salt**   **779 Weiss Beer**   **780 Pressed Diamond & Panel Nappies**   **781 Goblet**

782 DAISY & BUTTON PATTERN

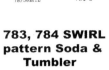

**783, 784 SWIRL
pattern Soda &
Tumbler**   **785 Ale**   **786 NEW PARAGON
Ink Stand**   **787 Weiss Beer**   **788 Ale**   **789 Ale**

790 HIVE Stand & Hand Lamps   **791 Stand & Hand Lamps**   **792 COIN BLANK
Stand & Hand Lamps**

793 Spice Caster   **794 PLAIN ROPE PATTERN**

**795 RIBBED ROPE
PATTERN**

256

796 ROPE AND THUMBPRINT PATTERN

**797 Stemware
Goblet & Hot Whiskey**

798 Unknown

**799 ALL OVER DIAMOND
PATTERN**

800 LEAF AND RIB PATTERN

801, 802 Beer Mugs

**803 Goblet
No Illustration**

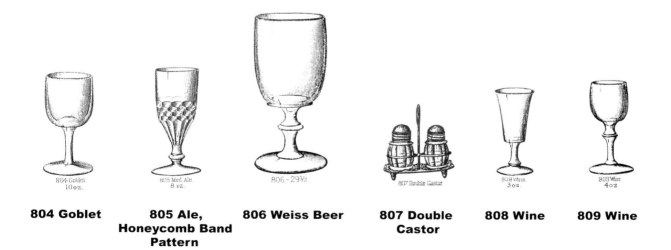

804 Goblet

**805 Ale,
Honeycomb Band
Pattern**

806 Weiss Beer

**807 Double
Castor**

808 Wine

809 Wine

810 Sugar & Cov
Eng .19

810 Cream

810 Butter & Cov.

810 Spoon
Eng 219

810 B Eng 219

810 C

810 TUDOR PATTERN

811 B

810 C

811 Stand & Hand Lamps

812 ~ 8

812 Tumbler

813 Pony Ale
7½ oz

813 Pony Ale

814-18 oz Beer Mug

814 Beer Mug

815 Unknown

816-8½ oz

816 Ales

817 Mol. Can

817 Mol. Can

818 Unknown

819 Oval Crystal Etched & Colors

819 Swan Dish

821 B

821 B

821 Shade

821 DEWDROP PATTERN

820 Goblet
Eng 205
9½ oz.

820 Goblet
9½ oz.

820 Goblets

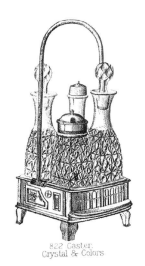

822 Salt
Crystal and Colors

823 Pickle
Crystal and Colors

824 Cream

822 Caster,
Crystal & Colors

822 STOVE PATTERN
Caster & Salt

823 HALF BOTTLE PICKLE

824 FISH CREAM PITCHER

825 Hot Whiskey
4½ oz.

826,

827,

Butter & Cov.

Cream
Eng'd 219

Spoon
Eng'd 219

825 Hot Whiskey

826, 827 Ink Stands

828 Unknown

829 OESTERLING PATTERN

830-8

830 Shober

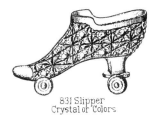

831 Slipper
Crystal or Colors

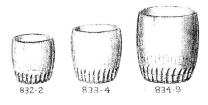

832-2   833-4   834-9

830 FLOWER DAISY & BUTTON PATTERN

831 SLIPPER ROLLER SKATE

832-834 Tumblers

835 Water Bottle.

835~9½

836 Lamp
Crystal, Etched & Colors.

837 Wine
4 oz.

835 DAISY & BUTTON PATTERN
Water Bottle & Tumbler

836 FAIRY LAMP

837 Wine

838 BARREL PATTERN

839 Water Bottle

840 MATCH SLIPPER

841 TRAIN ENGINE CLOCK

842 Beer Mugs

843 BLOCK PATTERN Tumbler

844 Beer Mugs

845 Goblet

846 Stemware

847, 848 Custards

849 Stemware, Straight & Flared

850 Unknown

851 Syrup

852 BRICK PATTERN Bottle

853 Tumbler

854 Bottle

855 BLOCK PATTERN Bottle

**856 ACORN
Stand Lamps**

**857 Stand & Hand Lamps
(Clear Panels & Ribs)**

**858 DEWDROP AND PANEL
Stand & Hand Lamps**

**859 HIGH TOP
ROLLER SKATE**

**860 DOG SALT
BLOCK PATTERN**

**861 OPEN PLAID
PATTERN Tumbler**

**862-864
Tumblers**

**865 HORSE PULLING
BARREL Match Box**

**866 OWL
Match Box**

867 Unknown

868 Double Caster

869 Fan Cut Glass Nappy

**870 BRICK WINDOW OR
PICTURE WINDOW PATTERN**

871 LANTERN
Salt or Pepper

871 Salt or Pepper

872 Mol. Can

873, 874 Unknown

872 Mo. Can

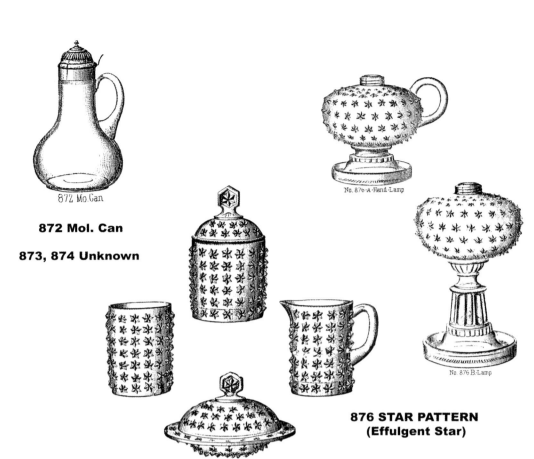

No. 876-A-Hand-Lamp

No. 876-B-Lamp

875 Cocktails

2750 Cocktail Str - 3½ oz

876 STAR PATTERN
(Effulgent Star)

Nº 877 SET.

877 FLUTE BAND PATTERN
(Ribbed Flute Band)

1P 878 - 13 oz Weiss Beer

878 Weiss Beer

879 - 30 oz Bottle
and
979 - 25 oz Bottle

879 Bottle
30 & 25 oz

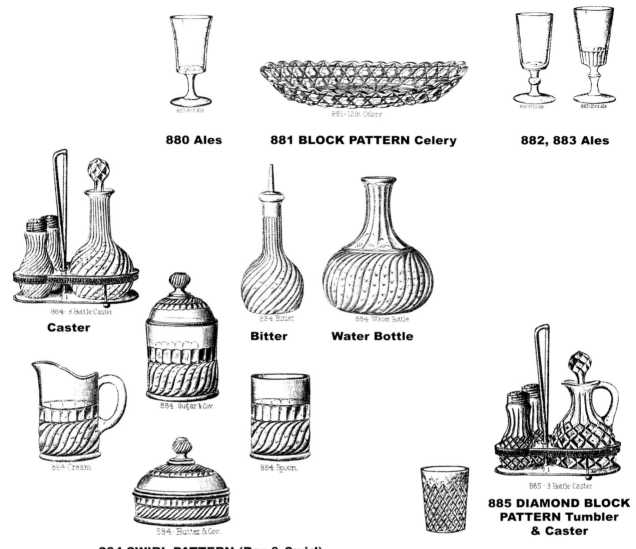

880 Ales　　**881 BLOCK PATTERN Celery**　　**882, 883 Ales**

Caster

Bitter　　**Water Bottle**

884 SWIRL PATTERN (Bar & Swirl)

885 DIAMOND BLOCK PATTERN Tumbler & Caster

886 Stemware　　**887 Weiss Beer NOTE: 36 oz**　　**888 PARAGON Ink Stand**　　**889 Ink Stand**　　**890 Footed Ink Stand**　　**892 Drum Caster**

891 Beer Mug

893 BLOCK PATTERN

894 REVOLVING CASTER

895 VERTICLE THUMBPRINT NOTCHED RIBS & PLAIN PANEL PATTERN

896 Double Salt

897 Tumbler

898, 899 Weiss Beers

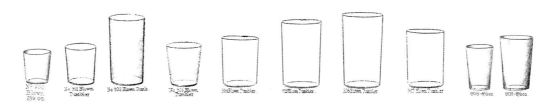

900-909 Blown Tumblers

910 Tumbler

911-916 Blown Tumblers

917-920 Tumblers

921-927 Blown Tumblers

**928 Blown Tumbler
with Small Twist**

929,930 Blown Tumblers

**931 Blown Tumbler
932-948 Unknown**

949 Finger Bowl & Pickle Jar

950 WHIRLPOOL PATTERN

| **Stand & Hand Lamps** | **Square Cologne** | **Inkstands** | **Catsup** |

951 Oil Bottle, Plain or Eng.

953 Tumbler

955 BALL & RIB Cologne

952 Weiss Beer

954 Tumbler, Cologne

**956 Tumbler
957, 958 Unknown**

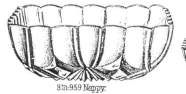

959 Nappy

960 Nappy

**961-992
See Text**

993 Cov'd Dish.

993 Covered Dish

994 Unknown

995 Lead Blown Finger Bowl

995 Finger Bowl Plate

**995 Lead Blown Finger Bowl
& Finger Bowl Plate**

996-998 Unknown

**999 THUMBPRINT PANEL
& SWIRLED RIBS PATTERN**

**1000-1005 Tumblers
1006-1007 Ales
1008-1011 Tumblers
1012 Unknown
1013 Nappy
1014-1015 Unknown**

1016 Custard.

1016 Custard Cup & Punch Bowl

1017 Unknown

1018-8 in Nappy

1018 Nappy

1019 Spice Tray-8 in.

1019 Spice Tray

1020 Egg

**1021 Unknown
1022 Tumbler
1023-1024 Unknown
1025 Custard Cup**

1026-D. No. 2 Collar.

Hand

**1026 Stand & Hand
Lamps**

1027-D. No. 2 Collar.

1027-B. Hand.

Hand

1027 Stand & Hand Lamps

1028 Spice Tray

1028 Spice Tray

**1029-1031 Unknown
1032 Tumbler**

1033 Beer Mugs

**1034-1044 Unknown
1045 Stemware
1046-1060 Unknown
1061 Stemware**

Central Glass Company
1863-1893
Patterns Missing Catalog Numbers

- **CORD AND TASSEL**
- **U.S. COIN or SILVER AGE**

- **KNIGHTS OF LABOR**
  Mug and Ale
- **COLUMBIAN COIN**

- **PUNTY MOLASSES CAN**
  named "TAYLOR"

**Also the patterns below and on the next pages are
illustrated in catalogs without pattern numbers:**

GRANT Bitter & Bar Bottle

**LIGHT WREATH
Goblet**

LIBERTY BELL Salt

Weiss Beers

OREGON Shades

VINE PATTERN Pressed Gas Shades

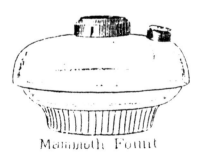

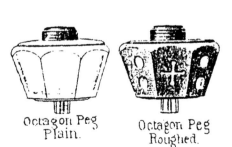

Mammoth Fount

Octagon Pegs

No. 1 & 2 Caster

BLOWN TUMBLERS without numbers

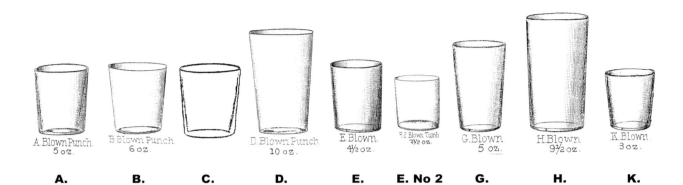

A.   **B.**   **C.**   **D.**   **E.**   **E. No 2**   **G.**   **H.**   **K.**

F Unknown   **I, J Unknown**

L.   **L. No 2**   **M.**   **N.**   **O. Punch**   **P.**   **P. Small**   **Q.**

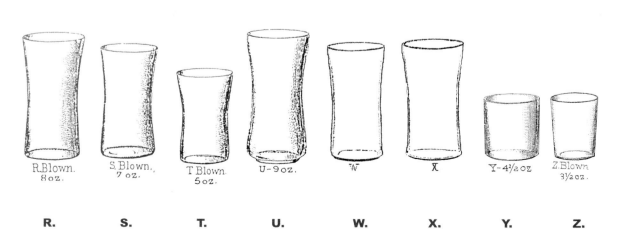

R.   **S.**   **T.**   **U.**   **W.**   **X.**   **Y.**   **Z.**

V. Unknown

INK STANDS without numbers

Tumbler Ink.
A.

Tumbler Ink, Crimpt-Top.
B.

Square Ink, Flat, Cap.
C.

Square Ink, Sponge Cup.
D.

A. Tumbler Ink

B. Tumbler Ink, Crimpt. Top

C. Square Ink, Flat Cap

D. Square Ink, Sponge Cup

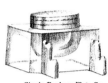

Single Bankers Flat, Cap.
E.

Single Bankers Sponge Cup.
F.

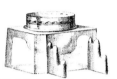

Single Bankers Flat Cap, Ground Top.
G.

Single Bankers Sponge Cup. Ground Top.
H.

E. Single Bankers Flat Cap

F. Single Bankers Sponge Cup

G. Single Bankers Flat Cap, Ground Top

H. Single Bankers Sponge Cup, Ground Top

Bankers Ink, Ground Top Flat Cap,
I

Bankers Ink, Ground Top.
J,

I. Bankers Ink, Flat Cap, Ground Top

J. Bankers Ink, Sponge Cup, Ground Top

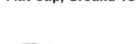

Bankers Ink, Single Pen Rack, Ground Top.
K.

Bankers Ink, Single Pen Rack, Ground Top.
L.

K. Bankers Ink, Single Pen Rack, Flat Cap, Ground Top

L. Bankers Ink, Single Pen Rack, Sponge Cup, Ground Top

Bankers Ink, Double Pen Rack, Ground Top.
M.

Bankers Ink, Double Pen Rack, Ground Top.
N.

M. Bankers Ink, Double Pen Rack, Flat Cap, Ground Top

N. Bankers Ink, Double Pen Rack, Sponge Cup, Ground Top

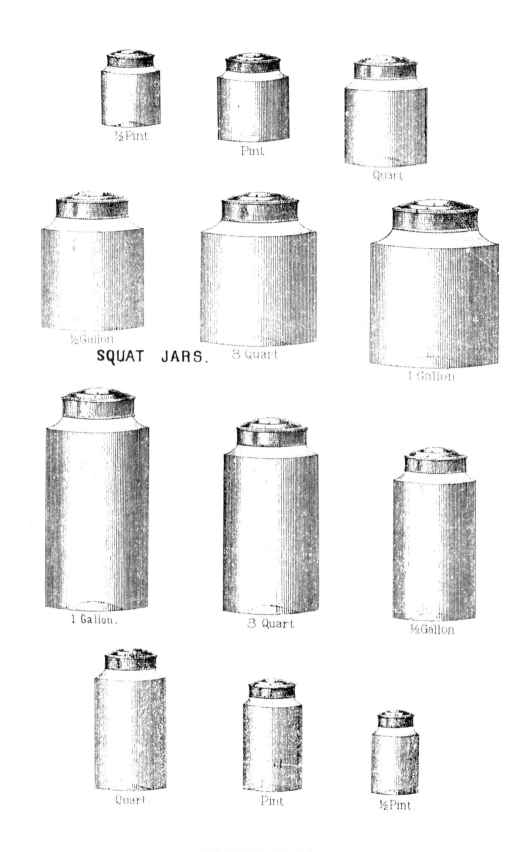

½ Pint

Pint

Quart

½ Gallon

SQUAT JARS.

3 Quart

1 Gallon

1 Gallon.

3 Quart

½ Gallon

Quart.

Pint

½ Pint.

SPECIA JARS

Endnotes

1. *Island Mould Catalog*, "Cincinnati" name from Page 19, Goblets
2. Ibid. ("Janus" name)
3. Ibid., pages 45 through 47
4. Central used "Bowl" instead of compote
5. "Royal" name from *Island Mould Catalog*
6. "Oak Leaf" name from *Island Mould Catalog*
7. Ibid, page 19
8. Ibid., Page 20
9. Central used "Mol. Can" (molasses) instead of Syrup
10. *Island Mould Catalog,* salt names from pages 15, 16 and 17
11. "Florence" pattern name from *Island Mould Catalog*, Florence set on page 71
12. "Brilliant" oil lamp name from *Island Mould Catalog* page 40
13. "West" oil lamp name from *Island Mould Catalog* page 39
14. Band Lamp from *Island Mould Catalog* page 35
15. Page 36 of *Island Mould Catalog* for Ohio Footed Lamp
16. Ibid for Central Footed Lamp
17. Ibid for Star Footed Lamp
18. Ibid for Diamond Footed Lamp
19. Page 37 of *Island Mould Catalog* for Panel Footed Lamp
20. Page 33 of *Island Mould Catalog* for Pegs
21. Page 31 of *Island Mould Catalog* for "Troy"
22. Page 37 of *Island Mould Catalog* for "Virginia"
23. Page 31 of *Island Mould Catalog* for "Delta"
24. Page 31 of *Island Mould Catalog* for "Panel"
25. Page 31 of *Island Mould Catalog* for "Troy"
26. Page 42 of *Island Mould Catalog* for Delta Cruets No. 251
27. *Oil Lamps The Kerosene Era in North America* Page 207 number 'i'
28. Ibid., same, number "l"
29. Ibid., Same, number "b" and "k"
30. *A Third Two Hundred Pattern Glass Pitchers* by Minnie Watson Kamm, page 16 & 17
31. *Two Hundred Pattern Glass Pitchers* by Minnie Watson Kamm, page 33
32. *A Third Two Hundred Pattern Glass Pitchers* by Minnie Watson Kamm, page 37, No. 48
33. *Oil Lamps II Glass Kerosene Lamps,* by Catherine M.V. Thuro, page 115, No. O
34. *A Sixth Pitcher Book* by Minnie Watson Kamm, page 2, No. 1
35. *A Third Two Hundred Pattern Glass Pitchers* by Minnie Watson Kamm, page 46, No. 61
36. *Oil Lamps The Kerosene Era in North America*, by Catherine M.V. Thuro, page 207, No. N
37. Ibid. for 628 Stand Lamp, page 207, No. M
38. Ibid., page 323, No. 17
39. *A Fifth Pitcher Book,* by Minnie Watson Kamm, page 11, No. 13
40. *A Seventh Pitcher Book*, by Minnie Watson Kamm, pages 57 and 58
41. *Inkwells Book II Identification & Values*, by Veldon Badders, page 86, plate 284
42. *Encyclopedia of Victorian Colored Pattern Glass, Book 5, U.S. Glass From A to Z*, by William Heacock and Fred Bickenheuser, page 91, plate D
43. *Yesterday's Milk Glass Today*, by Regis F. & Mary F. Ferson, pages 24 & 25, No. 79
44. *A Fourth Pitcher Book*, by Minnie Watson Kamm, page 118, No. 150
45. *Oil Lamps The Kerosene Era in North America*, by Catherine M.V. Thuro, page 323, No. 19
46. Ibid for 792 Coin Blank Hand and Stand Lamps, page 213, Fig. E
47. *The Spinning Wheel* magazine, June 1965, page 13
48. Ibid, May 1965, page 13
49. Ibid, May 1965, page 12
50. *Fairy Lamps Elegance in Candle Lighting*, by Bob and Pat Ruf, page 54, Fig. 140
51. *Oil Lamps The Kerosene Era in North America*, by Catherine M.V. Thuro, page 209, Fig. H
52. *Shoes of Glass* by Libby Yalom, page 122, Plate 49, number (599)
53. *A Fourth Pitcher Book*, by Minnie Watson Kamm, page 139, No. 186
54. *The Spinning Wheel* magazine, May 1965, page 13.
55. *Victorian Glass Specialties of the 19th Century*, by Ruth Webb Lee, sketch on page 185, plate 63 number 4, description on page 198.
56. *A Seventh Pitcher Book*, by Minnie Watson Kamm, page 83 and 84

Bibliography

Badders, Veldon. *Inkwells, Book II*. Paducah, Kentucky: Collector Books, 1998.

Batty, Bob H. *A Complete Guide to Pressed Glass*. Gretna, Louisiana: Pelican Publishing Company, Inc., 1978.

Bredehoft, Neila and Tom. *Hobbs, Brockunier & Co., Glass, Identification & Value Guide*. Paducah, Kentucky: Collector Books, 1997

Edwards, Bill, and Mike Carwile. *Standard Encyclopedia of Pressed Glass 1860-1930*. Paducah, Kentucky: Collector Books, 1999.

Eige, Eason. *A Century of Glassmaking In West Virginia. Exhibition June 8 - September 1, 1980*. Huntington, West Virginia: Published by the Huntington Galleries, 1980.

Ferson, Regis F. and Mary F. *Yesterday's Milk Glass Today*. Self Published, 1981.

Gliekman, Jay L. *Yellow-Green Vaseline! A Guide to the Magic Glass*. Marietta, Ohio: Antique Publications, 1991.

Gliekman, Jay L. and Terry Fedosky. *Yellow-Green Vaseline Revised Edition*. Marietta, Ohio: The Glass Press, Inc., 1998.

Heacock, William. *Encyclopedia of Victorian Colored Pattern Glass, Book III, Syrups, Sugar Shakers and Cruets*. Marietta, Ohio: Antique Publications, 1976.

_____. *Oil Cruets From A to Z, Book 6*. Marietta, Ohio: Antique Publications, 1981.

_____. *1000 Toothpick Holders, A Collectors Guide*. Marietta, Ohio: Antique Publications, 1977.

Heacock, William and Fred Bickenheuser. *U.S. Glass From A to Z, Book 5*. Marietta, Ohio: Antique Publications, 1978.

Heacock, William, and Patricia Johnson. *5,000 Open Salts, A Collector's Guide*. Marietta, Ohio: The Glass Press, 1995.

Hulsebus, Marjorie. *Miniature Victorian Lamps*. Atglen, Pennsylvaina: Schiffer Publishing, Ltd., 1996.

Jefferson, Josephine. *Wheeling Glass*. Columbus, Ohio: The Heer Printing Co., 1947.

Jenks, Bill, and Jerry Luna. *Early American Pattern Glass 1850-1910*. Radnor, Pennsylvania: Wallace-Homestead, 1990.

Jenks, Bill, Jerry Luna, and Darryl Reilly. *Identifying Pattern Glass Reproductions*. Radnor, Pennsylvania: Wallace-Homestead, 1993.

Kamm, Minnie Watson. *Two Hundred Pattern Glass Pitchers*. Self Published, 1952.

_____. *A Second Two Hundred Pattern Glass Pitchers*. Self Published, 1950

_____. *A Third Two Hundred Pattern Glass Pitchers*. Self Published, 1953.

_____. *A Fourth Pitcher Book*. Self Published, 1950.

_____. *A Fifth Pitcher Book*. Self Published, 1952.

_____. *A Sixth Pitcher Book*. Self Published, 1953.

_____. *A Seventh Pitcher Book*. Self Published, 1953.

_____. *An Eighth Pitcher Book*. Self Published, 1954.

Lee, Ruth Webb. *Early American Pressed Glass*. Wellesley Hills, Massachusetts: Lee Publications, 1946.

_____. *Victorian Glass, Specialties of the 19th Century, 1830's-1880's*. Rutland, Vermont: Charles E. Tuttle Company, Inc., 1985.

Lindsey, Bessie M. *American Historical Glass*. Rutland, Vermont: Charles E. Tuttle Company, Inc., 1967.

McCarin, Mollie Helen. *Pattern Glass Primer, A Pattern Guide of Early American Pattern Glass*. Leon, Iowa: Lamplighter Books, 1979.

Metz, Alice Hulett. *Early American Pattern Glass, Book I*. Self Published, 1970.

_____. *Much More Early American Pattern Glass, Book II*. Self Published, 1970.

Mordock, John B. and Walter L. Adams. *Pattern Glass Mugs*. Marietta, Ohio: The Glass Press, Inc., 1995.

Revi, Albert Christian. *American Pressed Glass and Figure Bottles*. Nashville, Tennessee/New York, NY: Thomas Nelson Inc. Publishers, 1964.

Ruf, Bob and Pat. *Fairy Lamps with Values*. Atglen, Pennsylvania: Schiffer Publishing, Ltd., 1996.

Six, Dean. *West Virginia Glass Between the World Wars*. Atglen, Pennsylvania: Schiffer Publishing, Ltd., 2002.

Smith, Frank R. and Ruth E. *Miniature Lamps*. New York, New York: Thomas Nelson and Sons, 1968.

Smith, Ruth. *Miniature Lamps II*. Atglen, Pennsylvania: Schiffer Publishing, Ltd., 1982.

Spillman, Jane Shadel. *The Knopf Collector's Guides to American Antiques, Glass Volume 1, Tableware, Bowls & Vases*. New York, New York: Alfred A. Knopf, Inc., 1982.

_____. *The Knopf Collector's Guides to American Antiques, Volume 2, Bottles, Lamps & Other Objects*. New York, New York: Alfred A. Knopf, Inc., 1983.

Thuro, Catherine M.V. *Oil Lamps, The Kerosene Era In North America*. Radnor, Pennsylvania: Wallace-Homestead, 1992.

_____. *Oil Lamps II, Glass Kerosene Lamps*. Paducah, Kentucky: Collector Books, 1992.

Timmerman, Tim. *U.S. Coin Glass, A Century of Mystery*. Self Published, 1992.

Unitt, Doris and Peter, Revised by Sean and Patty George. *American and Canadian Goblets, Volumes I & II*. Guelph, Ontario, Canada: Ampersand Printing, 1994.

Welker, John and Elizabeth. *Pressed Glass in America, Encyclopedia of the First Hundred Years, 1825-1925*. Ivyland, Pennsylvania: Antique Acres Press, 1985.

Wheeling Glass, 1829-1939, Collection of the Oglebay Institute Glass Museum. Wheeling, West Virginia: The Oglebay Institute, 1994.

Yalom, Libby. *Shoes of Glass*. Marietta, Ohio: Antique Publications, 1988.